SEEING MY SKIN

(A STORY OF WRESTLING WITH WHITENESS)

PETER JARRETT-SCHELL

CHURCH
PUBLISHING
INCORPORATED

For Rondesia, to whom 40 percent of all credit is due.

For Joshua, to whom is due the best of myself.

Church Publishing
19 East 34th Street
New York, NY 10016
www.churchpublishing.org

Cover design by Paul Soupiset
Typeset by Rose Design

Library of Congress Cataloging-in-Publication Data
Names: Jarrett-Schell, Peter, author.
Title: Seeing my skin : a story of wrestling with whiteness / Peter Jarrett-Schell.
Description: New York : Church Publishing, 2019.
Identifiers: LCCN 2019002071 (print) | LCCN 2019022050 (ebook) | ISBN
  9781640651937 (ebook) | ISBN 9781640651920 (pbk.)
Subjects: LCSH: Jarrett-Schell, Peter. | Episcopal Church—Clergy—Biography.
  | Race awareness. | Ethnic attitudes. | Whites—Race identity.
Classification: LCC BX5995.J275 (ebook) | LCC BX5995.J275 A3 2019 (print) |
  DDC 305.809/073—dc23
LC record available at https://lccn.loc.gov/2019002071

Contents

Prologue vii

Introduction xi

PART I   San Francisco. 1

PART II   New Haven 37

PART III   El Salvador. 51

PART IV   Berkeley. 73

PART V   Virginia. 101

PART VI   Maryland 131

PART VII   Ethiopia 141

PART VIII   Maryland, Again 157

PART IX   DC 181

PART X   Trayvon 1995–2012;

             Joshua Ibrahim 2013–?. 195

PART XI   An Election and Afterwards 229

Conclusion 264

Acknowledgments. 273

Prologue

I scroll through the post one last time, scanning for grammatical and spelling errors. I think I've already corrected them all, though it's hard to tell. My eyes won't quite focus right and my thumbs ache from an hour of typing on my smartphone. I confirm the edits, change the privacy settings to public, and hit "Save." The updated post appears on my feed:

 Peter Jarrett Schell with **Ronald Jarrett** and **Rondesia Jarrett Schell**
Yesterday · Edited · 🌐

While driving on the first leg of our road trip to Florida, with my wife, my son, and my brother-in-law, I noticed a white Dodge Charger in my rear view, tailgating me. After a couple minutes, I moved into the left lane to let him pass. He followed me. Then he turned on the flashing lights of the now-revealed undercover car. I pulled to the shoulder.

I've been stopped by police before (always for traffic violations that were my fault). However, several things immediately seemed unusual about this stop.

One. Two officers emerged from their car and approached ours from the passenger side, where my brother was sitting. The lead officer knocked at his window, and asked first for his license, not mine.

Two. After checking my license as well, and the registration of our rental car, and after the officer informed me he was only giving me a warning for changing lanes without signaling (he was correct), he asked me to step out of the car. While his partner stood by our car, he walked me back to their patrol car, and asked me what I had in my pockets (keys, a wallet, and my phone).

Three. He asked me to take a seat in their car, and closed the door behind me. He took his seat on the driver's side, turned, and began to ask me questions.

"How do you know the other people in that car?"

"They're my family: my wife, son, and brother-in-law."

"Where are you going?"

"To Florida on vacation. We might stop in Augusta, Georgia, to visit my wife's father."

"Where does he live in Augusta?"

"Honestly, I couldn't tell you."

"Where did you come from?"

"Washington."

"What time did you leave out?"

"Around eleven, I think."

"Why did it take you so long?"

"There was traffic all the way from Quantico to Norfolk."

"Where did you rent the car?"

"In Maryland."

"From which rental company?"

"I don't know, my brother rented it."

"Are you driving straight through to Florida?"

"No, we're stopping in Fayetteville for the night."

"Why?"

"My son is two. He needs a break."

"Is your license valid?"

"Yes."

"If I checked your vehicle, would I find anything illegal?"

"No."

"No marijuana, or cocaine?"

"No."

Four. As I answered, I noticed his partner was leaning in the rear passenger side window where my son was sitting. His hand was on his belt.

Five. After asking me these questions, he left the car and went to talk with my family. I checked the door handle to see if I could open it from the inside and get out in case . . . of something. In retrospect, this could have been a mistake. Thankfully nothing happened. It wouldn't open, anyway.

Six. After talking with Ron and Rondesia, he conferred with his partner for several minutes. The officer gestured vaguely to me and to our car.

Seven. He came back to the car. He wanted to talk again.

"Well, I'm confused. I talked to your 'wife' and her story doesn't match yours."

I could hear the quotation marks in his voice. "She just said you were going to Florida. She didn't mention her dad, or Georgia."

"We haven't decided if we're stopping on the way down, or the way back."

"She also said she was visiting her cousins in Fayetteville. You said you were just going to stop for the night."

"We are just stopping for the night. She has family there, so we're having dinner with them."

He paused.

"You seem nervous. Why are you nervous?"

"I'm nervous because you separated me from my family. I'm nervous because your partner is hovering over them. I'm not sure if you've noticed, but there have been a lot of high-profile incidents of police killing Black people in the last few months. And your partner has his hand resting on his belt near his pistol. So yes, I'm nervous."

That's what I thought. That's what I wanted to say. But the angels of discretion (or perhaps those of cowardice) kept me quiet.

"No, I'm not nervous."

"Hm."

He checked our information on the computer for several minutes in silence. Then he called in the details to double-check. Finally, he said I could go and reminded me to signal when I change lanes.

"Thank you, officer."

I walked back to the car, and waited for the police car to pull away. We compared details, analyzed, and then drove in silence until we arrived at the hotel.

We unloaded the car. I held my son. Rondesia and I hugged.

"I love you."

"I love you too."

"I was so scared for you."

"I was scared for you."

I don't remember who said which words. But my wife spoke last.

"Well," she said, "welcome to the club."

And then I realized. None of these things were unusual. Not even a little bit.

I turn the phone off and lie down. It is late. I should sleep.

The next day, our bishop calls. We tell her what happened, and she files a complaint, on our behalf. The sheriff confirms all the details of our account. He denies nothing. He states politely that everything that happened was legal and according to procedure. That is, of course, the problem. As we suffered no quantifiable damages, we have no standing for further legal action.

This club sucks.

Introduction

There is a constellation of phrases that pop up in our conversations and reading these days: "privilege," "intersectionality," "White Nationalism," "Black Lives Matter." There are several more. They provoke responses—sometimes anger, occasionally hope, often weariness.

I take part in these conversations about race; like all of us, I have opinions. But I struggle to locate the question of race in my own life. I am White, but I am not always sure what this means. Indeed, most days, I don't notice that I am White. I think this is true of many of my folk. Like them, I was unprepared when confronted with questions of race.

How do I wear my race? How does it feel? How does it show up in my life?

This book is an essay—an attempt to find the answers; to sift through the files of my memory, look for those marked "race," and record what is written there. I've divided the text into eleven parts, following the most significant transitions in my life. The first nine sections are defined geographically by where I happened to be living at the time. The last two sections are defined by major recent events in the life of our nation: the death of Trayvon Martin and the election of President Donald Trump. Both events highlighted the question of race in new ways, both for me personally and for us as a society.

Each section comprises a set of vignettes: moments from my life when the impact of race seemed evident. I have tried to tell them as clearly as possible, with little analysis or commentary. I've worked to get permission from all those mentioned to share these stories. I was grateful that, with one exception, everyone I spoke with gave their consent, though some requested to remain anonymous. In these cases, and in cases where I was unable to contact those involved, I have provided pseudonyms. The only exceptions to this practice are matters of public record, and the two vignettes involving Ms. Joana Bryar-Matons, and the Rev. Ramiro Chavez. Both were mentors to me. Both died before the completion of this book. I chose to memorialize them, if only briefly. At the close of each section, I have included a brief reflection, summarizing the themes of race from that part of my life, as they appeared to me.

As a person of faith, and a pastor, my motivation for writing this book is theological. I take it as a given that racism, and the institutions of White Supremacy, are contrary to God's will. That said, you will find neither theology nor scriptural reflection in these pages. My reasons for these omissions are twofold:

First, the theological and scriptural foundations of Christian anti-racism have been laid out by women and men far wiser than me; principally by those scholars arising from the traditions of the Black Church. If this subject interests you—and I hope it does—I refer you to the works of Delores Williams, James Cone, Kelly Brown Douglas, or one of the many luminaries who continue laboring in this vital work. Their teachings are essential to the way I frame my thinking on the subject, and, by the same token, I am certain I have nothing to add to their discourse.

Second, the matter of wrestling with Whiteness is not an endeavor for church folk alone. It is a matter of vital importance for all people who call themselves White, regardless of their faith commitments or lack thereof. Our own integrity and the well-being of our nation depend on it. I have a small contribution to make toward this endeavor, and I would like to share it as widely as I am able, not only within the walls of congregations.

I hope to make my own reflection a template for those with the will and desire to look closely at themselves.

If you are not White, I hope this book may still be of interest to you. It may provide some insight into the thoughts and perspective of one particular White man that might be helpful in navigating the spaces surrounding others of my complexion. But, in truth, I write this book especially for my people—that is to say, for White people. If you are such, I hope that the record of my experience may spark your memory and help you to sort through the archives of your own Whiteness, to arrange the contents of what you find, and to form your own picture of how race looks in your life. Whoever you may be, I hope that in reading this account you will see more, know more, and understand more than I have.

PART I
SAN FRANCISCO

1

I am six. I climb out of the car, through the window. Dad slams his hand on the roof of the car.

"Stop that!"

I hear Mom's voice reply. "He saw it on a show."

I scoff. Not on *a* show. On *my* show, the one that is starting in two minutes. I run inside, down the hall, up the stairs, and through the apartment. I stop at the refrigerator, grab an apple, and dash towards the television. I turn it on and search through the channels. I stop when I see an orange star-striped muscle car barreling through hay bales. Its horn sounds out eleven notes of an upbeat trumpet tune. Dad walks into the room, looks at me, and shouts in exasperation.

"Stop throwing apple cores behind the couch!"

I don't look back at him. "I didn't."

"I just saw you do it." He makes me stand and pulls the couch away from the wall. There is an apple core there. It looks fresh. There are several more there next to it. They look less fresh.

He points to them. "Don't lie to me."

I didn't think I had. I honestly don't remember dropping the apple core. He's frustrated. The show is still on. I turn my head to look. He turns my face toward him. I turn my eyes toward the screen. He follows my gaze. His eyes narrow.

"What are you watching?"

"*The Dukes of Hazzard.*"

He sits and watches until the ad break. He turns off the TV.

"I don't want you watching that show anymore."

"What? Why?"

He explains. It's something about history. I don't understand. He talks about a war. I don't understand. He mentions slavery and racism. I've heard these words. I have a vague sense of their meaning. They're bad. I can't see what they have to do with my show. He breathes out and looks up. I know this face. He's thinking.

He looks at me again. "They're bad drivers. They drive danger-ously. I don't want you to grow up to be a bad driver."

"Oh. Okay." I guess that makes sense.

His face shows relief and, for some reason, failure.

2

School has just let out. The other fifth graders gather at the bus stop to wait. They talk about the recent scandal: the teachers have banned War Ball. I join in their outrage. It is our main distraction during recess. The game is a variation on dodgeball. We divide the yard in half, split into two teams, and take turns hurling a single ball at one another. If you get hit you are on the bench. If you manage to catch the ball before it hits the ground, your whole team is back in the game.

I was a terrible player. I was told I threw like a girl, though clearly, not like any girl I knew personally. They all threw better than me. I threw like some girl who had no idea how to throw a ball. I was very good at dodging the ball. But I was afraid to try to catch it. This led to frequent and excruciating stalemates. My team would all get tagged out, one by one. I would be alone on the field, dodging every shot that came in, unable to tag out any of my opponents, and unable to bring my team back in the game. From the bench, they would yell "Catch it!" louder and louder each time, until the recess bell rang. Then, they would walk inside without looking at me. Towards the end of fourth grade, a friend, James, tried to teach me to catch.

"Plant your feet. Keep your head up, and your eyes open. Catch it in your stomach, like this, and put your arms around it."

The next day I tried it. The ball hit my stomach. I was not prepared for the sting of the impact. I didn't get my arms around it. It bounced away, I was out, and we lost.

James walked next to me as we entered the building again. "At least you tried."

The day after, I tried again. This time I held on. My team cheered and sprinted back onto the field. I charged the line and threw a slow, weak, and awkward shot directly into the arms of my closest opponent. He caught it and returned it with force. I was not up for the task of catching it a second time. I was out. I didn't care. After the game classmates came by and patted me on the shoulder. That was the last week before summer vacation. I started fifth grade, ready for recess to

4

be different. When they announced the ban at the opening assembly, I saw my plans for social acceptance evaporate.

We keep talking about the outrage of it. One of my classmates steps out into the street, to see if the bus is coming. He turns toward us and continues the conversation.

"It's this new place. They won't let us do anything here."

Over the summer the school moved locations, all the way across town.

Another classmate weighs in. "At least we've got the store."

He points across the street. We nod in the affirmative. There was no corner store near the old location. This is a definite improvement. Through the open door we see a candy display in front of the cash register. Suddenly my hands are full of coins and my classmates are placing orders. This is tricky. I don't have the best memory. After the last order is in, I repeat them all back. I keep repeating as I cross the street. The list is long and I am concentrating to remember it, which is why I collide with a woman just as I arrive at the store. Coins spill everywhere. I hear laughter from my classmates behind me. She stops, helps me gather the change, tells me to mind where I'm going, and continues walking. I put the coins in my pocket and enter the store.

One by one I lift items from the display, drop them onto the counter, and check them off my mental list. After I grab the last item, a pack of Apple Now & Laters, I ask for Red Vines, for me. They are in a large tub with a handwritten sign that reads: "5¢ each." Under the sign, a printed label peeks out: "Not for individual sale." I have a dime, apart from the quarter in my watch pocket. The quarter is for bus fare. I consider at length spending it and walking home, then decide against it. "Two please."

I count out the coins. After I've paid for everything, there are two quarters left over, not including the one in my watch pocket. Someone miscounted. I walk back to the bus stop to distribute the haul. My colleagues dig through the bag and find their sweets. I lift up the two quarters.

"Somebody gave me too much."

A friend peers into the now empty bag then looks up. "Those were for my M&Ms."

I review my chant again. "Snickers, M&Ms, Apple Now &
Laters . . ."

I smack my forehead. I had remembered M&Ms, but not the fact
I needed two bags.

"Sorry."

I look down the street. The bus has just turned the corner. I dash
to the store and grab another pack of M&Ms. As I pay, I see the bus
pull up to the stop. I drop the quarters on the counter and take off. I
don't wait for the cashier's reply.

"Hold up!" I yell.

My exclamation is unnecessary. One of the boys asked the driver
to wait. I get on the bus, pay my fare, and hand off the M&Ms. We all
take our seats. I can still hear my yell. I was thin and squeaky; weak. I
am angry.

"Why didn't you buy your own candy?" I ask everyone and no one
in particular.

"The owner doesn't like us."

I don't know who answered, but the answer does not satisfy. It
is only our second day here. I don't understand how the owner could
have formed an opinion about them one way or the other. And he
was perfectly nice to me. Then, a thought comes all at once: they are
Black. Our school's old neighborhood was Black. Our school's new
neighborhood is White. The store owner is White. And I am White.
That is what they are talking about.

These facts rise like a wall between them and me. I don't like this
wall, so I try to ignore it. I try to forget it. I glance around the bus at my
classmates. Do they try to ignore it? Are they even given the choice?

3

I am taking my time as I stroll back from the bathroom to Pre-Algebra. I enjoy the sneaky feeling of traveling through empty halls when the building is full. I move with the exaggerated confidence of an eighth grader soon to leave for high school. I turn a corner and see another student coming towards me. I recognize him. We have a couple of classes together. We're more than acquaintances, but less than friends. He's meandering. I imagine he's also enjoying this space between classes.

He calls out. We speak. We joke. He begins to slap-box, playfully. I am small. Awkward. Geeky. I often wonder if I am manly enough. Slap-boxing is a manly sort of thing, so I like that he thinks it's a game I would play. Surprisingly, I do pretty well. Awkwardness aside, I'm fast. But then he grabs me and wrestles.

He's still playing. But he's bigger than me, and stronger. In slap-boxing, I was holding my own. But in wrestling, I am outclassed. Badly. I try to throw him off me and fail. I try again with the same results. I feel my face flush with heat.

"Get off me, n*****!"

His body goes rigid. His arms tighten. Then he shoves me away. I turn toward him. His face is hard.

"What did you say?"

I understand the question. I know its importance. My mind goes blank. I heard the words just spoken. They were my own. But they startled me.

"Get . . . get off me. I said . . . get off me."

He looks at me. Something happens in his face. Then, quickly, it fades. He shrugs. "Whatever."

He turns and meanders on his way. But it is forced now, a caricature of a casual stroll. I wait a moment then walk to class. I tell myself I was just using words I'd heard my classmates use. That is a thing I do. I didn't mean anything by it, I remind myself. But I wonder: Was I only imitating, or was there something more?

We never speak again.

4

(Northern California)

The van jostles down a poorly paved road. Our Scoutmaster, Mr. Rose, drove up earlier in his own car to handle the paperwork. His son, the assistant Scoutmaster, drives the van. He is more lenient than his father, which explains Sir Mix-a-Lot's voice buzzing through the static of the radio. He raps something about ladies sticking out their butts, and how even White boys will shout.

The senior patrol leader, Cassius, turns. He is my age. He points to me.

"Even this guy's got to shout!"

We all laugh. As the only White boy in the troop, I'm used to it. Mostly.

The van turns into the camp entrance. There are more Scouts here than I have ever seen. We step out of the van, grab our bags, and assemble in the parking lot. Mr. Rose is waiting for us. A man with a bullhorn tells us to line up by troop. There are about twenty other troops here, maybe three hundred or four hundred Scouts. It seems they are all White.

A boy from the next troop over hisses at me. "Go line up with your troop."

Mr. Rose fixes a stare on him.

"Keep your eyes forward and mind your business." He does not raise his voice. He carries an air of authority that makes it unnecessary.

The other boy's Scoutmaster faces Mr. Rose. "I'm in charge of this troop."

"Then get your Scout in order."

They look at each other. Their faces are hard, but it passes in an instant. I know this is not my fault, but I want to apologize. I'm just not sure to whom. We all stand at attention.

The man with the bullhorn gives a mini pep rally and lays out the camp's rules. He points to a group of a dozen or so boys at one end of the parking lot. They are solo Scouts. They have no troops; they came alone. Like me, they are all White, except for one at the end. He is Asian.

8

The man with the bullhorn says each solo Scout was randomly assigned to a troop for the duration of camp. He tells us that if a Scout is assigned to our troop, we should receive and welcome him as one of our own. He calls out the assignments. The Asian boy is sent to our troop. I can't quite believe that this was random. The man with the bullhorn tells us where each troop is camping and dismisses us until dinner.

Mr. Rose greets our new addition. We grab our bags and head to the campground. Cassius makes small talk with the new guy.

"What's your name?"

"Mark."

"Cassius. I'm the senior patrol leader. Where you from?"

"Hawaii. But I live in LA now."

"Your family's Hawaiian?"

Mark shakes his head. "Japanese."

Cassius nods.

After we set up camp, Mr. Rose gathers us again. "Mess hall in fifteen minutes for dinner. Dress uniforms."

We groan. Everyone hates dress uniforms.

He repeats. "Dress uniforms."

We relent, get dressed, assemble, and head for the mess hall. As we head down the hill, we fall into a river of Scouts bound for dinner. Cassius is the first to notice it.

"I don't think dress uniform is required for dinner. No one else is wearing it."

Mr. Rose does not look at him. "We wear dress uniforms to dinner." He emphasizes the word "we." There is no further discussion.

We gather for dinner. All of the troops sit together at their own tables. After dinner we go to evening activity. It's a bunch of icebreakers, silly games and stuff. We're dismissed and go to bed.

In the morning Mr. Rose wakes us up. "Red shirts today."

We've each come with two sets of olive green shorts and three t-shirts: red, green, and yellow, each bearing the Boy Scouts' logo. We put on red. Mark doesn't have a t-shirt to match. Mr. Rose is prepared. He was a Boy Scout himself in his day.

"What size are you?"

"Medium."

He produces three shirts from his bag. Red, green, and yellow. "Wear them in rotation. Do wash each night and hang it up, so they'll be clean and dry two days later. Dress uniforms every night for dinner."

Mark nods.

We head down to breakfast. The other troops are irregular. Their shirts don't match. Most of them aren't even wearing Boy Scout t-shirts. This time I speak up.

"No one else matches."

"We do." Again, Mr. Rose emphasizes the word "we."

After breakfast, we head to the main hall to sign up for classes. I wait for my troop mates to go first, then follow their lead. I don't make new friends easily; I'm not looking to get stuck in a class with a bunch of strangers. I glance over their shoulders to see their schedules. I'm disappointed. There is one merit badge in particular I was hoping to earn this week. I don't think anyone else has signed up for it. I test the waters.

"Is anyone taking Orienteering?"

Charles shakes his head. "We all took it together last year."

I wasn't here last year. I glance across the hall to the Orienteering table, and the line of strangers in front of it. I breathe, walk across the hall, and join the line. As it happens, the first Orienteering class starts immediately after sign-up.

The instructor shouts, "Orienteering, over here!"

I join the group of strangers that gather around him. He leads us to a grove of trees, then hands out compasses and topographical maps of the camp. He walks us through the basics and sends us on our first exercise. We will be divided into groups of three. Each group will start a trail with a different marker. Each marker provides a heading and distance to the next marker. If we follow the path of markers successfully, we should arrive back at our starting point. He hands out pencils.

"Each marker has a word engraved on it. Write them down. That way we can check if you've missed any. The beginner courses all stay on the paved paths of the main camp. So there's no chance of you getting lost." He pauses. "Not today anyway."

The group laughs. I chuckle along nervously. He assigns our groups. The other two boys in my group extend their hands and offer their names. "Brad." "Thomas." We head out on the path. There's silence. Not the comfortable kind. This is why I didn't want to be with strangers. But I should try. Mom says it's best to begin with a question.

"So, what troop are you guys from?"

"Troop 14. Rah!" They say this in unison. Troop 14 is the largest and oldest troop at camp this year. I've noticed already that they always say their troop number in unison. We find the first marker, note the word "Trustworthy," and take a heading. There is more uncomfortable silence.

"You're with the Black troop, right?" The statement is simple fact. But the phrasing makes me uncomfortable.

"Troop 462. Yeah."

"So—how did that happen?"

I shrug. "I graduated from Webelos to Scouts. My mom found a troop for me."

"Wait. Where are you from?"

"San Francisco."

Brad frowns. "That's a big place. There must be other troops."

There is more silence. I hadn't really thought about it. I suppose he's right. And our troop meets halfway across the city. There are probably troops closer to my house. I try to think why Mom chose 462. I don't have an answer—not that it bothers me. Except that with another troop I wouldn't have to answer questions like this.

We find the next marker. We write down the word "Loyal." I laugh. Brad looks up from writing.

"What's funny?"

"The first word was 'Trustworthy.' And the second is 'Loyal.' They're just the words from the Scout law. So the next one will be 'Helpful.' It's kind of dumb. I mean, you could just write down the rest of the law, and head back."

Thomas raises an eyebrow and smirks. "Is that what they teach in 462?"

I know there is something behind this question. I frown and shake my head.

"No. Mr. Rose makes us do everything by the book." They glance at one another. My voice gets higher. "I wasn't saying we should cheat. Just that they made it really easy to cheat, if someone wanted to." I'm talking much too quickly.

Thomas claps a hand on my shoulder. "Relax. I was just joking. Don't take it personal."

I force myself to breathe out. "Right. Right. No, I know. I'm sorry I got worked up."

He nods and smiles. "Don't worry about it."

The third marker is a long walk away. We find it and write the word "Helpful." Brad finishes writing and puts the sheet in his pocket.

"Are you guys competing in the soccer tournament on Wednesday?"

I don't know. I hadn't heard about it before now. "Maybe."

Brad smiles. "Well, I'm guessing 462 is the troop to beat."

I don't know why he thinks this. We play baseball when we're waiting to get picked up after meetings. Some of my troop mates are pretty good. But I've never even heard any of them talk about soccer. Brad is still looking at me and smiling.

I smile back. "Thanks. I'll tell them you said so."

By the time we finish the trail, it's lunchtime. We head back to the mess hall. Brad and Thomas move toward Troop 14's table. Brad tugs my sleeve.

"Hey. Come sit with us."

I look and see my troop mates beginning to gather at a table across the hall. I look back to 14's table. I'm torn.

"I should check in with my troop."

He shrugs. "Suit yourself."

The rest of the week goes well. We meet other Scouts, learn new skills. We enter the soccer tournament and lose. Still, we have fun. Mr. Rose is strict, but he wants us to have a good time. And he's funny. Very funny. Still, he never entirely loses his edge. He checks in with us each evening and follows our progress in the merit badge classes we've taken. On two occasions one of my troop mates says he's keeping up with the rest of the class. Both times, Mr. Rose replies, "Not good enough. You have to be better." This confuses me, because on the second night he asked me how Orienteering went. I told him the other Scouts seemed more experienced, but I thought I could keep up. He simply answered, "Good."

After the first day, troops begin to mix tables at the dining hall. Guests show up, now and then, at our table. But the members of our troop always sit together. For me, it is a matter of shyness: I'm not comfortable around new folk. I know this is not true for the others. They are all more outgoing than I am. But they stay together anyway. Even Mark, which is odd. We're as much strangers to him as anyone here, but he still sticks close. One morning I go to get seconds on cereal. Bowl in hand, I turn back to the table, and see it: a cafeteria full of four hundred White children. One table with ten Black children and a Japanese kid. I wonder, again, if I should take up Brad's offer and visit 14 at their table.

The last night, after dinner, the camp staff organizes a series of obstacle challenges. We will compete as troops. Mr. Rose gathers us together. He's smiling. "Have fun tonight, gentlemen." He often calls us gentlemen. His faces flashes, not stern, just serious. "But win."

I recognize the face he makes. It's a face I make sometimes. He has something to prove. And we do win. In fact, we're winning by quite a lot. Halfway through the competition he calls us back into a huddle.

"Alright, I still want you to win. But I need you to pull back a bit." This tone of his voice is odd. Once, he took us to a shooting range. He used the same tone as he went over firearm safety. It occurs to me that he's offering a warning. He's not afraid, just cautious. I wonder what he's concerned about. The other Scouts nod. We pull back a bit. We lose a few events and win the competition by a narrow margin.

The camp director announces the rankings. When they announce first prize, Cassius stands up to take the stage. Mr. Rose lays a hand on his shoulder.

"Shake his hand, take the certificate, and smile. No gloating." He nods and takes the stage. Mr. Rose turns to us.

"Clap. No cheering. And no celebrating until we get back to camp." We clap. The camp director leads everyone in the camp song. Some of the other Scouts congratulate us. We thank them. Politely. We're dismissed. We go back to our camp. We make a fire and celebrate. Mr. Rose bakes a pineapple upside-down cake in a Dutch oven by the heat of the embers. He's done this before. It's amazing. The campground grows quiet as we eat. He takes the opportunity to speak.

"Gentlemen, you did well. You are remarkable. Do not forget it."

I frown. I like Mr. Rose, but this is cheesy. I look around, expecting someone to crack a joke. No one does. They only nod. This moment means something more to them than it does to me.

5

It is my first day of high school. I find my locker and fit the padlock to it. Another freshman finds his way to the locker next to mine.

I turn and see his face. "Hi, Tim."

His smile falls. "My name is Travis."

I feel my face flush. "Oh, I'm sorry. There's this guy, Tim—he looks just like you."

I hear my own words and wince. I am lying and I know it. They look nothing alike. But they are both Asian.

Travis doesn't respond. He fits a padlock on his locker, shakes his head, and walks away.

6

I'm sitting in Spanish 101. It's almost three o'clock. Finally, Joana, the teacher, dismisses class. We collect our things and stand.

"Espérate." Joana points to me and then to the floor. I gather I should stay. The others file out. She crosses her arms. "Hay que hablar."

God, I hate that. This is Intro Spanish. We're most of the way through the semester, but still, there's no way we can carry on a conversation. She waits for the last student to leave and shut the door.

"I've spoken to your other teachers."

I thank God, not for her speaking with other teachers but for her speaking to me in English. And then I wonder why she is talking to my other teachers. I shift my feet.

"They tell me you're coasting through."

"I don't know what you mean."

"They say you don't work, but you manage to do well on the tests."

This is true. In eighth grade I noticed that I tested well. It's more of a knack than anything else. With finals and midterms weighted so heavily I can get a B with very little effort.

She raises an index finger.

"If I don't see you doing the work every day, I will fail you."

"That's not fair. You gave us the grading standards." I start to dig through my backpack: I have it in writing somewhere. She stops me.

"My class. My castle. I am queen here."

Her tone makes it clear there is no point arguing. I don't reply. I shoulder my bag and walk out. She speaks to my back.

"Don't test me."

I walk downstairs to the front entrance. Students are flooding out of the school. The director is in his office, packing up for the day. I knock on the door. He motions me in and welcomes me by name. He knows everyone's name.

"What's up?"

I explain the situation. He looks at me blankly.

15

"Her class, her castle." He pauses. "She is queen." His emphasis falls on the word "is." I guess this has come up before. I shuffle out, grumbling under my breath, and walk up the street to the bus stop. A classmate is there already waiting. She sees me grumbling.

"You okay?"

I explain the situation and how it isn't fair. She shakes her head and rolls her eyes.

"White boys."

I don't see what that has to do with anything.

7

It's Christmas vacation. Family and friends have gathered in our living room to chat after dinner. I sip hot chocolate. I set it down and listen. A woman speaks to the whole gathering, a family friend. Like most of our family friends, she is White.

"It's weird though. It's like there's this idea of connection. But it's like an imagined connection. There's no real sense of what it means. Like, my English teacher visited there. She said she was talking to these two women, and she told them, 'I'm African, too.' And then they asked her, 'What tribe are you from?' She didn't know. So they told her, 'You're not African, you're American.'"

It is an odd conversation to have after Christmas dinner and yet, it feels important. Then, for half a second, I wonder why. There are no Africans, American or otherwise, in this room. Why does this conversation matter to us? The thought fades, and I join in as we go on talking about things that have nothing to do with us.

8

(Italy)

There's a problem with the train. I don't know exactly what. We've stopped in a small Italian town I've never heard of. There are several trains held at the station. Men in uniforms direct confused crowds here and there. We do our best to follow their gestures. We don't speak the language. I am nervous. This is my first time traveling without my parents. My sister seems to know what she's doing. This comforts me. An older man pops his head out from the windows of one of the trains.

"Where are you going?"

My sister shouts out our destination. He waves us closer.

"This is your train! Hurry up."

We rush to board in time. As we enter the main corridor of the train, the man's face pops out from a berth.

"We've got seats, come on!"

He beckons us forward with one hand and disappears back into the berth. I look to my sister for confirmation. Strangers have tried to hustle us before. She looks to the berths nearby, but there are hardly any seats on the train. She heaves her bag onto her shoulder and turns into the berth. He's seated again when we enter.

"Glad you made it."

We stow our bags in the overhead, sit down, and look at our berth-mates. The man looks to be in his seventies. He wears red shorts that stop above his mid-thigh and tube socks that reach almost to his knees. His legs are very, very pale; his face and arms only slightly less so. A green foam visor and sunglasses with neon rims complete the look. He isn't looking at us. His attention is on his companion. She might be in her early forties. She is quite beautiful and dressed very fashionably, while still looking casual. I assume she is Filipina.

They're fussing at each other. She has a diverse collection of pills in her hand. She wants him to take them. He thinks it can wait.

They go back and forth, smiling and laughing at the exchange. She wins out. He accepts the pills from her hand. She produces a thermos and a single-serving bottle of vodka. She pours a cup of water into the thermos' lid, adds the contents of the bottle, then hands it to the man. He turns and answers our unspoken question.

"Doctor says it's good for me to have one drink a day."

She interrupts. "If you cut it with water."

He nods. "Yes, if I cut it with water." He tosses the handful back and washes them down. When he finishes, she looks at us.

"So. Tell us about yourselves."

My sister takes the lead, telling the broad picture of our trip, while avoiding most specifics. She's savvy. We banter for an hour about the sights we've seen and what we're looking forward to. Then, my sister asks the question we're both wondering.

"So, how did you two meet?"

"Well," the woman says, and they both lean back into their seats. This is a performance they've given before. They enjoy it. She tilts her head in his direction. "You go first, honey."

"So a few years ago I was about to retire. Ever since my first wife died, I had been working really hard to fill the time. But then I was getting ready to stop, and I didn't know what to do with myself. I was talking to this buddy of mine, and I said, 'So what am I supposed to do now, play golf all day? I hate golf.' He said, 'You need to get back out there. Start dating again.' But I wasn't into all that: the back-and-forth, and the games. I was at a point in my life where I just wanted a sweet, pretty lady that I can see the world with. So he said, 'What you need is a mail order bride.'"

My fingers dig into my knee. I hope he doesn't notice.

"So I got this catalog." He turns to her. "Wait, what was it called?"

"Pearls of the Orient."

My jaw tightens, and I glance at my sister. She is looking straight forward. He doesn't seem to notice.

"Pearls of the Orient, right. It had page after page of these beautiful women. And there was, like, a little blurb about each one and their addresses. And so I picked about ten or twenty that I liked and . . ."

"Wait, wait, wait. This is my part."

"Okay, you go ahead."

She smiles. "Okay, so I was working as a teacher in Manila. And I knew I had to get the hell out of there, but we didn't have any money for it." Her smile doesn't quite fade, but there is a kind of seriousness in her eyes. It passes quickly.

"I told my sister, and she said, 'What you need to do is get yourself a rich man. But a rich man who wants to travel. He doesn't have to be perfect. But make sure he's nice.'"

He taps his sternum in self-acknowledgment. She sees the gesture and smirks.

"She got me in touch with this agency, and I gave them my picture, and my address."

"Can I go now?"

"Yes."

"Right, so I picked out ten or twenty that I liked and wrote them. It was the same letter every time, but with a different girl's name."

She points to herself. "And I started getting letters. His was the third one. The first guy was ugly. Just too ugly. And the second guy was really slimy. It was a gross letter. But this one"—she points to him without looking—"seemed nice. So I wrote him back."

"Yep. And then I got a bunch of responses. All the women I wrote to wrote me back."

"Most, not all."

"Okay fine, most. They all wrote these letters about how they were looking for true love, and a man of refinement, and blah, blah, blah. But this woman," he cocks his thumb at her, "says, 'I'm looking for a rich man who wants to travel. But he has to be nice.' And it cracked me up. So she was the only one that got a second letter."

"We wrote back and forth for a while."

"About six months."

She shakes her head.

"Okay, four."

She shakes her head.

"Maybe it was three."

She nods and laughs.

"Anyway, I was traveling to Manila. I had some loose ends to tie up for my business. And I wrote her and said, 'So, I'm going to be in town. Let's meet, and if we like each other, we can get married.'"

"And we did."

"I retired a month later, and we've been traveling ever since."

She pats his knee. "We go home sometimes."

"Yeah, sometimes. We've got a place in Florida. And we get back now and then to see the kids."

There is a question I have to ask. And I am sixteen. It is permissible to be somewhat tactless. "Whose children?"

She points to him. "His. They didn't like me at first. Because I'm younger than them."

"But she won them over. She's a charmer. You can't not like her."

This seems to be true.

She pats his knee again. "Oh, here we are!"

We've arrived at our destination. They suggest we share a cab. They're staying at a high-end place, well out of our price range. They ask where we're staying. We give them the name of a budget hotel on the other side of town. The cab stops at their place first. As they get out, he pays the driver then hands my sister a wad of bills. She looks puzzled.

"That's your fare, plus tip."

We thank them and continue on our way. Our hotel is fine: modest, small, but clean. We drop our bags and start to talk about dinner. There aren't many restaurants in this neighborhood. The phone rings. It's the woman from the train. She remembered the name of our hotel and looked us up.

"We're taking you out to dinner." She gives us the name of a restaurant and tells us to take a cab. They'll pay for it when we get there.

We meet up with them and eat. Dinner is good. The tomatoes in the salad are so sweet that they ask the chef to slice up a plate, of just tomatoes, for dessert. I remember laughing. There is a kind of lightness that follows them. After dinner, he writes their address down on a napkin.

"If you're ever in Florida come see us."

She chimes in. "I know people say that all the time but we really mean it."

We say our goodbyes. They're going to the opera. It's still light out so we decide to walk back to the hotel. My sister speaks first.

"They seemed happy, didn't they?"

"Yeah. They seem that way."

She pauses. "Do you think he's using her?"

I shrug. "I don't know. Maybe she's using him?"

"I mean, I guess, as long as they're both honest about what they're getting out of it."

"Yeah. Maybe." I still don't know what to think about it. The next day, I look for the napkin with their address, but I've lost it.

9

The partygoers have gone home. I put the last bottles into a trash bag. We'll drop the bag in a public trash can at the corner. His mom won't be home until morning. I think we will get away clean. I check my watch. It's 2 a.m. I cringe. I've got exams tomorrow. He invites me to crash in his living room.

"It's late. And you don't have a ride."

"I'll be fine."

He cocks his head. "If you say so."

I walk down the street to the bus stop. I don't wait long. The bus arrives and carries me just south of downtown—an area called the Tenderloin. I get off and walk a block to a second bus line that will take me home. There are a lot of people out, which surprises me. I've been to this area many times before, but always in the daylight hours. This is an entirely different crowd: strange and, to my eyes, unsavory. I step over a man shooting up. I weave past a streetwalker seeking employment. I stop at the bus shelter and take one of the seats. They're designed to keep anyone from sleeping on them—three narrow plastic rectangles on hinges, too narrow to hold anyone's butt, too tall for anyone of my short stature to balance on comfortably.

I wait half an hour. No bus. The awful seat has done its damage. Both cheeks are numb. I stand and pace the length of the shelter to shake it off. Fifteen more minutes. Still no bus. A man sits down next to me and strikes up a conversation.

"You a student?"

I don't want to talk to him. But I'm polite. I nod. "You?"

He shakes his head. "No, I make movies."

My eyes widen. "Really?"

"Yeah."

"Wow. What kind of stuff?"

"Adult."

My face goes blank. "Oh. Okay."

"You ever do that?"

"No."

He smiles. "You wanna try?"

"That's okay."

"It pays good."

I'm sure it does. I shake my head. "No thanks."

The conversation ends quickly. He gets up and leaves, but not before handing me a roughly printed business card.

It's been almost an hour. I check the large printed copy of the timetable posted in the shelter. I find my line, then blink twice. I should have checked my entire route when I first left my friend's house. This line has stopped for the night. I check my watch. It's almost three thirty. The next bus won't arrive for two and a half hours. I look at the cast of characters filling the street. I don't want to stay here. It's only a couple miles to my house.

I stand up and start walking. I remind myself to stay alert and make good judgments. I try not to think about the fact that I've already failed on this front. As I head south, the crowds thin out. I feel relieved. I cross a thoroughfare. It's weird to see it empty: in fact, all the streets here are empty. Three men walking quickly on the other side of the street catch my eye. We pass each other. For a moment, I think I see one of them point at me. I'm not sure. A block later I hear the rapid shuffle of feet running behind me. I spin.

There is a hand at my mouth. Before I see the man attached to it I notice his other hand. It holds a gun. Two other men run from behind to join him. He demands my wallet. I pull it from my back pocket and hand it to him. I am relieved to remember that I have no money with me. Then I am troubled. What will he do when he realizes I have nothing to take? The lead man thumbs through the wallet.

"You got nothing on you?"

"No."

One of the pair behind him speaks. "We shoot him now."

I feel cold. The leader in the group turns in response to the suggestion. He looks annoyed and shakes his head. He continues to thumb through the wallet.

"You gotta have something."

There is a note of distress in his voice. I wonder what he's worried about. I know what I'm worried about. He pulls out my ATM card. I opened my first bank account just a few weeks ago. He hands it to me.

"Where's your nearest ATM?"

I try to think, which proves difficult. The man in the rear fidgets, which doesn't help. I force myself to focus. There's a bank along my way home.

"This way." I point.

"You walk us there. If we pass anyone, you don't say anything. You act natural. When we get there, you withdraw the maximum. Then we're done."

I nod.

"Walk."

I start to turn. The second man puts his hand on my shoulder to stop me. Something flashes in my face. I feel an impact on my cheek. There was little force behind it. Not even enough to cause pain. Still I am stunned. I've just been struck by the stock of a pistol. He's angry.

"Don't try anything. If you even walk some way I don't like, I shoot you."

His eyes dart. His movements are jittery. I see there is absolutely nothing I can do to manage his ultimatum. I'm cold again. The leader brushes the second man's hand from my shoulder and points forward. The third man says nothing.

"Walk."

I do. The bank I have in mind is maybe a mile away. I wish it were closer. I wish I could think of any place closer. Three of us walk in silence, but the second man mutters angrily under his breath. Once or twice the leader turns and tells him to be cool. We've walked about five minutes. Maybe more.

"This is bull. He's planning something." It's the second man again.

The leader puts his hand up. We stop. He looks at the second man and then back at me. He looks at me for a long time. I try hard not to respond.

"Come on. We're going this way." He points down a side street. I want to ask why. I decide that I shouldn't. We walk another five minutes. On the street ahead, I see a bar. The door is open. I can hear music from inside. A couple patrons stand outside together smoking.

The leader whispers. "Keep walking. And be cool."

As we approach the bar he speaks again. This time loud enough for everyone to hear. "Did you see the game last night?" Crap. For the first time in my life, I wish that I were a sports fan.

"Yeah." I pray he stays nonspecific. I am not quick on my feet.

"It was a good game, right?" I'm impressed with how casual he sounds.

"Yeah."

"Who's your team?"

I pause and consider options. It's fall. So . . . football? That would leave two possibilities.

"The Niners?" I didn't mean for it to sound like a question.

He furrows his brow and looks at me. "It was Raiders versus Broncos."

So close. "Oh. Raiders."

He nods. "Good."

We pass into the midst of the smokers. Here is my chance. I should stop. Or duck into the bar. But I don't. I'm not sure why. I keep walking. The conversation ends.

We continue walking. We turn north. We are just two blocks west of where we first met. He points up the street. I think we are all relieved to see the glow of an ATM logo. I can't believe I didn't think of this place when he first asked. He catches my eye and points. I walk to the ATM and insert my card. My eyes water. They won't focus. I try and fail, twice, to enter my pin. I force myself to go slow, one key at a time. Success.

"Get three hundred. That's the limit."

My stomach sinks. "I've only got two hundred something."

"Bull." It is the second man who speaks.

"I'll show you." I call up the account balance.

It's two hundred sixty-something.

The leader leans in to see. "You can still get three hundred."

"What?"

"Overdraft. You can withdraw up to fifty dollars more than what's in your account. They'll hold it as a debt and charge you interest."

"Really?"

"Yeah. You're just going to report that you were robbed anyway, right? They'll cancel it."

I actually hadn't thought that far ahead. "Oh. Okay. Thanks."

The moment is strange. He jabs me in the neck, I assume with the barrel of his gun.

"Do it."

I do. The machine whirs as it assembles the money. I try to will it to go faster. It doesn't. Finally, it finishes. I hand over the stack of bills. I wonder if they will leave.

"This way." He points back down the street we came up. I walk.

"Take your shirt off."

This is not what I expected. I hesitate. I feel a jab to my neck again. I obey.

"Kick off your shoes." This is easier said than done. I always tie my shoes tight. It takes several attempts. I almost fall in the effort.

"Now your pants." I wonder how this will end. None of the scenarios I can imagine are good. But I obey.

"Now the drawers." I do so and tense.

"And your socks." As the first sock hits the ground, I hear the sound of feet running behind me for the second time tonight. I spin.

They are sprinting away. I watch until they turn the corner. They're gone.

I walk back up the street, collect my clothes, and dress. I see a familiar object on the ground. They dropped my wallet as they ran. Again, I consider my options. I have no money. No change to make a phone call. My parents are certainly asleep. There is nothing else to do but continue on my way home.

It's about a half-hour walk. Twice along the way, I pass someone else. Both times I hold my breath until I hear their footsteps fade. I arrive at home and let myself in. I think about whether or not to wake my parents. I'm tempted to sleep it off and try to forget, but I know they wouldn't want that. I shuffle up the stairs to their room and lay my hand on my mother's shoulder.

"Hey, Mom."

She wakes. "Oh, it's you." She rubs her eyes. "I'm glad you're home safe."

"I got robbed."

"What?"

"I got robbed. At gunpoint."

She bolts up in bed. My father wakes, too. "Are you okay?"

"Yeah. I'm fine. I just—I thought I should tell you."

"Yes. Of course. Oh, sweetie." She holds me. "Okay. We should file a report."

Dad nods and heads to the phone. After he makes the call, they ask me what happened. I tell the story with as little detail as possible. When I mention stripping down, they glance at each other. My mother interrupts me for the first time.

"Did anything else happen?"

"No. I think it was just to stall me so they had time to get away."

As I finish, the doorbell rings. My father lets two officers in. I tell the story for a second time with even fewer details. Without interrupting they trade phrases as I speak, nodding to one another. "Armed robbery." "Assault—with a deadly weapon." "And kidnapping."

The list surprises me. I didn't feel assaulted. They tapped me with guns. And there was no kidnapping. We walked somewhere together. Then they left. I learn later this is all a matter of technical definitions. I was touched against my will with a gun: assault with a deadly weapon. I was taken somewhere against my will: kidnapping. I finish the story.

The first officer looks up. "What did they look like?"

I try to remember. I'm stuck. I can remember only the roles I had assigned them in my head: professional, unstable, and silent. I don't know what they looked like except, "They were Black." I try to force my memory. More details surface. "Older. Maybe in their late thirties or early forties. They all had beards. The lead guy was in a parka. A Warriors parka. The other guy had a plaid jacket with a hood. And the last one was in, like a white tracksuit. They were all big. Buff."

"Okay. We'll write it up. Somebody will be in touch in a couple days. Be sure to report it to the bank tomorrow, after our report is filed."

They leave. It's getting light. My parents get up. I go to bed. Later we call the bank. As the lead robber suggested, the bank promises to refund the full loss once they confirm the police report. The customer service rep tells me that if it happens again I can enter an incorrect PIN four times and the ATM will then eat my card. I want to tell him this is terrible advice.

Two days later a detective comes to the house. He's pulled still black-and-white photos from the ATM security camera. The resolution is surprisingly good. My face looms large in each frame. Behind me, I see the three men. All three wear unmarked sweatshirts and sweatpants in dark colors. They are clean-shaven. I would put them at their early twenties, just a few years older than me. They are lean. One frame catches the moment when the leader draws near to look at the account balance on the screen. I can see that he's just a couple inches taller than I am.

Every detail I remembered about them was false. Except one. They were Black. I remembered nothing else. I count how many times I have looked over my shoulder this last week as Black men of all ages, shapes, and types walked by. And I see all the young, lean White men who jog the streets of our neighborhood in anonymous sweats each morning. I never gave them a second thought.

I kept one detail, and only one detail of those three men—their Blackness. I learned it. It will take me a long time to unlearn it.

10

Our Spanish teacher charts out verb conjugations on the board. "The subjunctive is a little hard for native English speakers to understand."

Unlike Joana, she conducts most of her class in English. I won't lie. I prefer it.

"You use it in cases"—she stops suddenly, and her face freezes—"in cases where"—another pause. She shakes her head in two short jerks, like a dog would shake off water. She stiffens, takes a breath, and starts again. "You use the subjunctive to indicate emotion, or uncertainty. For example . . ." She blinks and pauses again. Her face pulls in. She drops her hands to her sides, and tenses. She steels herself. "Bill, please put that away."

The whole class turns to look. The two of them have been sparring for weeks now. He has been winning. Now he sits in the back, slouching with his feet up on his desk. He cleans his fingernails with a pocketknife. A big one. He looks for all the world like every bad boy from every John Hughes movie ever: baby-faced, defiant, and White.

He doesn't look up, and doesn't stop picking at his nails. "What?"

"Please put the knife away. And please put your feet down."

"Why?"

"It's not appropriate for class."

He looks left and right. "Really? I'm in the back of the class. I'm not disrupting anything." He waves the knife casually to indicate the rest of us. "They can all pay attention. I'm not bothering anyone." He goes back to picking.

Her face flushes. "Please put the knife away."

"No. You haven't given me a good reason."

She begins to tremble, very slightly. "Stop this. Please put the knife away."

He looks up. "Are you going to take it from me?"

Tears well at the corners of her eyes. She is fighting to control herself. "Please put it away."

He shakes his head. "Nope."

She shrieks and runs from the room. There is silence. Minutes pass. No one says anything. A few of us look anxiously his way from time to time. He continues to look down and clean his fingernails. Eventually the director opens the door and takes a single step inside. He looks to the back of the room.

"Come on, Bill. Let's talk."

Bill sighs, folds the pocketknife, and puts it in his pocket. He stands and walks out the door.

The director turns to us. "Use the remainder of the period to study. Then go to your next class." He leaves and closes the door behind him.

The next day, we have a substitute teacher. Bill is in class. No one says anything about it. It never occurs to me that he should be disciplined.

11

The desert is beautiful, but I wish it were less windy. Around me, my schoolmates struggle to set up camp. The entire senior class is here. I work to press a stake into the sand with the palm of my hand. The tent is flapping in the breeze. Another student is working on the far end.

"Say, Travis, are you done with the mallet?"

He looks up. "Fred."

"What?"

"You called me Travis. My name is Fred."

"Oh. I'm sorry, my mind was wandering."

He passes the mallet. I go to work on the stake. We finish, and he walks away. Travis is standing nearby. He walks back casually. I know what we will talk about.

"You called him Travis."

My shoulders fall. "Yeah."

"We've gone to school together for four years. There are exactly three Asian guys in our class. And I'm your best friend. This is not okay."

"No. It isn't." I don't apologize. I want to, but it would sound hollow—even to me.

Debriefing San Francisco

Train up a child in the way he should go: and when he is
old, he will not depart from it.

—Proverbs 22:6, KJV

I struggled to write this section of the book. When I sat to record the stories of race from my childhood, it seemed I couldn't find them. I tried to send my mind back, to see the world as I saw it then. As a child, race seemed absent to me. I knew that there was such a thing as racism. Everyone knew that. But I imagined it was a thing of the past, or of some faraway place. I knew that I was White. But this fact seemed no more important to me than the color of my hair or the brand of my favorite cereal. For the record, it was Frosted Flakes, and my parents would never buy it.

I had been writing this book for several months and had recorded dozens of memories. I still had nothing from before my eighteenth birthday. I began to think that it might be because there was nothing there. I was raised by good, socially conscious, and progressively committed parents. I attended racially diverse schools. I grew up in the great liberal stronghold of San Francisco. I wondered if race only began to complicate my life after I left the Bay Area.

And then the recollection of calling a classmate n***** came back to me suddenly. I was texting my friend Joe when it happened. He was voicing his frustrations around discussing race with White people.

"They think they're not racist as long as they don't say the n-word."

I took his point—and I also remembered that I had said the word once. This was not a repressed or a recovered memory. It was something I had consciously chosen not to think about. The day after I used the word to dehumanize my classmate—for that is what I had done—I made two promises: first, that I would never say or write that word again; second, that I would not think about that moment in the hallway again. This book marks the first time I have broken either of those promises. And, even in breaking it, I have redacted the word: "n*****." I suppose this may be a lingering kind of evasion; a way of euphemizing what I did.

After finishing my text exchange with Joe, I sat and thought about that day in the hallway of my middle school. I thought about how I had hurled that hateful word at another child. One thing was clear: at the age of twelve I knew what I was doing. I understood the meaning of the word. I understood its power and its violence. I was not confused by the difference between how my Black classmates said it among themselves and what it meant when a White person like me said it.

I used the word according to its original purpose and intent. I used it because I felt embarrassed, emasculated, less-than, and weak. I used it in an attempt to tear my classmate down and so raise myself up. All of the mental gymnastics and the back-and-forths that played out in my adolescent head afterward were only my evasions of the inevitable fact that I knew what I had done, I knew why I had done it, and I was ashamed.

So, I made a choice: I would not say it again. And I would not think about it. I thought if I put it away, it would disappear. The whole thing had seemed like an awful anomaly—a horrific bit of hatred that appeared in my mouth out of nowhere. I thought I could cast it out and send it back into nothing. That was an absurd thought. Nothing appears out of nowhere. There are no real anomalies, only things that emerge from places we do not yet understand.

I think my classmate understood. I remember his face, and the look that passed across it when I insulted him. I have seen it since. It was that peculiar mix of hurt, anger, and confirmation. I was surprised by the word I spoke. It seemed he was not. I wounded him, but I doubt it was a new wound. I doubt very much that I was the first person to demean him in order to elevate themselves. For me, the moment was an aberration. For him, I imagine, it was further confirmation of a pattern. For the sake of comfort, I would choose to ignore that moment. For the sake of safety, he probably could not.

I tried to memorize his expression, and the feeling it produced in me. I searched through my past for other moments when I had seen an expression like his, or when I had felt that same feeling. I found many, though none of them were quite as clear as that day in a middle school hallway. After all, the use of that slur is perhaps the archetype of racism in our society. But there were moments when I had felt the same sense of discomfort and confusion. There were times when I had seen the same look of pain, rage, and resignation in a face that was darker than mine. These were moments when race was in play. Sometimes I was one of the players. Sometimes I was more of a spectator. In either case, a particular feeling of bewilderment was my marker. I tried to put that feeling on the page.

After reading an early draft, my friend Jacob Slichter challenged me about these sections. They were hard to understand. "There is a difference between a portrait of confusion, and a confusing portrait," he said. So I went back and looked again. I pulled apart my bewilderment. And I saw that I was not confused by these moments. I had confused myself about them.

Even as a child, I was aware of race and I had a certain understanding of how it worked—imperfect, to be sure, but present. This is neither surprising, nor exceptional. Countless psychological studies have shown just how early children develop concepts of racial categories, which is true for both children of color and White children. But I think we learn to manage these concepts in very different ways. Children of color learn a variety of coping strategies to survive these concepts. White children learn a variety of evasion strategies to ignore them.

I remember how oddly my classmate walked away after I demeaned him. He moved with an affect of relaxation. It seemed fake. I imagine he had learned to act as if everything was fine, even when he knew it was not. Perhaps it was required of him. I chose to forget this moment. I had learned to live as if everything was fine, even to the point of believing it. This was allowed to me.

My parents taught me about racism. They taught me that it was a thing I might see while wandering in the world. They taught me that I should confront it when it showed up. I am thankful for these lessons, but they were incomplete. They treated racism as a thing strictly outside of myself. I was unprepared to consider that racism was part of the structure of my life. Indeed, I learned explicitly that race should not matter, either in my life or in my thoughts. But it did. And it does. Despite my parents' best intentions, I learned the thoughts of White Supremacy, as most children in this country do.

When the racist realities of my life and mind collided with a deep conviction that race was irrelevant, I jumped towards confusion and amnesia. It was a choice. I repeated it many times until it became a habit. And it did not end in childhood. Another friend who read the first draft of this memoir, Dr. Tee Williams, pushed me to name race more explicitly.

"You always write around it. You'll say something like, 'His skin is like mine.' And yeah, it's poetic and everything. But it's also really confusing. You need to say what you mean, and say it explicitly. Say, 'He is White,' 'I am White,' 'This guy is Black.'"

I had an immediate defensive reaction to his observation, because I knew he was right. It was absurd: I had chosen to write a book about race in my life and yet, I was still using techniques of confusion to cloud the subject. I think this whole process is common for many White people. As I have observed it, White children are generally more aware of racial dynamics than we are as White adults. Or perhaps they are just more honest about what they see. They have not yet learned the habits of evasion. The great trouble is that we learn these habits even as we grow into the racial structures that surround us, and so we become oblivious agents of racism.

Habits can be changed. It requires intention, commitment, and time. In fits and starts, with backsliding and recovery along the way, we can practice not evading. We can uncover what we hid with the confusion of childhood. We can look and see. There is something to be gained in this effort: the strength of knowing ourselves. More than that, it seems only fair that we should try. For twenty-five years I chose to forget that I had called my classmate a n*****. I suspect he never forgot it.

PART II

NEW HAVEN

1

"It's reverse discrimination."

My face scrunches as I hear the words. We walk through the large archway leading out of Old Campus, Yale's freshman quad. I see the carved gothic lettering that names this gateway. It is the name of my ancestor, a name I had written on my college application. We turn left. I've been here about two weeks, and I've mostly learned the lay of campus.

He gestures broadly, indicating nothing in particular. "Look, I'm not in favor of racism against anyone."

I nod, but I'm skeptical. I've noticed that when people profess that they aren't racist, it usually means they are about to say something racist.

He continues. "Blacks, Hispanics, Asians—as races, they are every bit the equal of White people." I nod again. "So we should compete on an even field. That's justice."

My face scrunches again. He sees it.

"Look, it's not like it's good for them. I mean, take this place. If you got into a place like this just because there was a quota, then people are always going to doubt your qualifications. They're always going to wonder if you really deserved it."

I think a moment, then speak. "Yeah, I guess that's true. It's just, well, historically they faced hardships that we didn't."

"Of course they did, but that's in the past. We can't let ourselves get stuck in the past. How else can we move forward?"

His rhetoric is fast and sharp. His reasoning is better than mine. There's something I'm missing. I feel like there's something I could say that might convince him. I just can't think of it.

"I want to be studying with the best of the best. I don't care who that is. Iron sharpens iron, you know? That's good for me. And it's good for them too. I had to compete against the best to get in. They should too."

We arrive at the science building, his stop. I still have a ways to go. I look up to see another ancestor's name carved, another name on my application. Pieces click. My White ancestors got me in here. I know the same is true for him. His mother is an alumna—he mentioned it before. I want to say this, but I don't. I don't because it shames me.

He sees me thinking, then checks his watch. "I gotta go. We'll talk about it more later, okay?"

"Yeah. Sure."

2

My friends step through the basement door that leads to the steam tunnels under campus. I follow them. There's no particular reason for our venture. It's just something to do on a Saturday night. It's hot down here, especially coming in from the cold outside. We strip off jackets and scarves. Frances points down a tunnel. She's done this before.

"Let's go this way. I haven't been there yet."

I am the closest to the tunnel. I walk, they follow. There are puddles on the floor. Pipes are dripping, but the air is still dry. Some sections are very bright; others almost black. We walk for about fifteen minutes. She taps my shoulder.

"Can I lead for a while?"

"Okay." I wonder if I've made a mistake. She's done this before. I haven't. "Did I do something wrong?"

"No, it's just more fun to be in the lead." I can't deny that. There is a thrill of exploration in front. It is less so in the middle of the line. She cocks her head to the side and looks up and away. "Plus, there's the whole thing of you being the boy leading, two girls following behind, even though I'm the one who's done this before. It just seems kinda . . ."

"Right. Yeah, of course. You go ahead."

The corridor is narrow. I turn sideways so she can pass. We continue on for another ten minutes. I try to imagine what we're underneath. The library? Or maybe the main dining hall. That seems about right. We come to a sharp turn. There is a large rectangular aluminum tube above us. It looks like one of those human-sized air ducts that populate action movies. The bottom end is open and about a foot above our heads.

She points up. "I'm going in."

The hangers on the duct are bolted into concrete. She is the smallest of us. I suspect it will hold her weight, but perhaps not ours. And certainly not the three of us at once. I look at her face. It seems she's made the same calculation.

"I'll try it first; you wait here. If it seems sturdy, we can go through one at a time."

We boost her up. She grabs hold and lifts herself in. I hear a metallic banging against the duct as she moves along, which makes me think of *Die Hard*. The noise of her crawling fades. We wait in silence. Minutes pass. I look down the hallway. A man is walking towards us. I catch enough of a glimpse to register the blue colors of a police uniform.

I don't know the consequences for being caught down here. I believe, technically, we are trespassing. I'm not sure if the steam tunnels are university property, or if they're held by the city. If they belong to Yale, I suspect we would face collegiate, rather than legal, penalties—a reprimand or a citation. Probably nothing severe, but I am uncertain. I have a lot of questions that I would prefer to answer in theory rather than in practice. I turn to Lynn.

"Run."

We take off and turn down the corridor. We make a few turns. Four thoughts form in rapid succession: (1) We've left Frances behind. (2) At some point she will come down from the air duct. (3) She will likely bump into the police officer alone. (4) That is not okay.

I grab Lynn's sleeve. "Wait." We stop. "We have to go back for her."

"Yeah. I know."

We turn and walk back, retracing our steps. I feel resignation in my chest. We make the last turn and I see Frances standing beneath the air duct. She's facing down the bend of the corridor, away from us. I imagine she is talking to the officer. She hears us approach and turns.

"Where did you go?" She is alone.

I look both ways. "What happened to the cop?"

"What cop?"

"There was a police officer down here."

"We saw him and we took off running."

Frances shakes her head. "I came down from the vent and there was no one."

We look to one another and all seem to have the same realization. The officer went looking for us, lost us, and is probably still nearby.

"We need to go." And we run again. Despite our haste, the way seems longer than when we came. The air down here is dry, hot and just a little acrid—bad for running. We make it back to the basement entrance and stop to catch our breath. Lynn is wheezing.

Frances puts a hand on her shoulder. "Are you okay?"

Lynn shakes her head. "Breathing's hard." She pulls an inhaler from her bag and takes a puff. "I think I need to lie down." My dorm isn't far. We help her to her feet. We leave the building as discreetly as possible. The air outside is cold and damp. I hope it will help.

As we head to the dorm we pass two more officers. They are walking past gratings on the street, pointing their flashlights down each one as they go by. We make it to the room. Lynn lies on the couch. She asks for water. I get it. Twenty minutes later she says she's feeling fine. We walk her home anyway. Frances and I head back to the dorm.

"I'm sorry we left you up there. It wasn't right."

She shakes her head. "If you had waited, the cop would have stopped you, and then he would have stopped me when I came back down, and then we all would have been caught. So, it turned out better this way."

She is like that: rational, analytical. Of course, she's right. Still, a question remains in my head. What says more about me: that I ran, or that I came back?

———

Sunday passes forgettably. On Monday, I go to meet my writing partner to work on our history project. He asks what I did over the weekend. I tell him and ask if he's been to the steam tunnels. He shakes his head.

"I can't get expelled over something dumb like that," he says with the weight of certainty.

It never occurred to me that I might be expelled. I doubt it would have gone that way. But he seems so certain, and I wonder why. I look at him. He is Black. I am White. I wonder if that might be the reason. But then I wonder if I am reading too much into it. I want to ask him, but I don't.

3

The chairman of our committee offers analysis to a packed room at Dwight Hall, Yale's social justice–community service building. He describes connections between the school contracting with companies that run sweatshops for producing collegiate wear, the delegation of teaching loads to underpaid TAs, and the use of undergrad work-study to trip up unionization of the university's service force. We share his outrage and discuss strategy for the coming year. What can we push back on? What can we accomplish? We brainstorm for half an hour. Our chair suggests we should do something to address the racialization of the undergrad workforce.

"As regards work-study, students of color are dramatically over-represented in dining hall placements. They are dramatically under-represented in library placements."

"And here," someone says from the back of the room. I don't recognize the speaker. I think she's a freshman.

"I'm sorry?"

"Students of color are dramatically under-represented here."

She is correct. We are perhaps two dozen. Hers is the only non-White face. We are silent.

The chair responds. "Yeah. That's something we'll need to work on."

We work for another half hour and the topic doesn't come up again. He adjourns the meeting. I gather my things and stand to leave. She is gone. Sometime in the last half hour, she slipped out. Once again, I want to say something, but I don't. After all, everyone here is trying to do the right thing.

4

I pack my diploma into a box and stack it along with the others. I get started on another pile of stuff. After graduation, Mom told me I could leave my things at the house while I'm out of the country. I'm doing my best to get it well organized. The last box I set down doesn't sit right. It falls to the ground. Photos scatter everywhere. I curse and kneel to gather them. I scoop them into a pile, straighten them out, and put them back in the box. The one on top catches my eye. It's familiar though I haven't seen it in a while.

There are six young Boy Scouts sitting on a picnic table laughing at a summer camp. I'm towards the middle. I notice something about the group. It is something I had known before but not thought about in some time. I remember another Scout asking me about it. I put the photos away and stack this box with the rest. I head downstairs. My mother sits at the kitchen table, sipping tea and reading the paper.

"Mom, I have kind of a random question."

She puts her tea down. "Sure."

"Did you pick my Boy Scout troop because it was all Black?"

"Oh." She seems surprised. "Yes."

"Why?"

"Well . . . we thought it would be good for you. All your friends were White."

I take a quick tally in my head. Things haven't changed. I have always had one close friend who wasn't White, but never more than one. I don't know if that is a matter of circumstance or preference. I wonder if the difference really matters.

"Are you okay?"

"Fine. I guess."

Debriefing: New Haven

Bright College years, with pleasure rife, The shortest, gladdest years of life.

—Yale Alma Mater

College was a time of fond memories, and fundamental to the formation of my character as an adult. I learned a great deal at Yale. Many of the lessons only became clear in retrospect.

During my time in New Haven, I met some of the most intelligent, hard-working people I have ever known. There were many of them. My first months on campus, I had a strong feeling that I was at the rear of the pack. It was sometime during my second semester that I began to notice that there were others among our ranks. Some were of average intelligence (or less); others were content to coast their way toward graduation. Some fit into both categories. There were many of these folks as well.

I wish I were the kind of person who finds confidence within. I admire such people. I am not one. I have always measured my worth by comparison to others. It's a bad habit. Knowing that there were a great number of mediocre students at Yale gave me comfort. I fit somewhere into the middle of the group.

My comfort was shaken at the end of my junior year. I had signed up to work graduation, setting up chairs, tents, and the like. I was essentially a stagehand. Yale's graduation tradition is peculiar. It is a two-day event. On Class Day, a notable speaker addresses the graduating class. On the following day, Commencement, graduates receive their diplomas. The university's website states, "By tradition, Yale does not have a Commencement speaker, although an exception is made when a sitting president is awarded an honorary degree, as was the case in 2001."[1]

I was present for this exception. At the time, the rumor around campus was that after Hillary Clinton had been scheduled to speak at

---

1. "Who Is the Commencement Speaker?" Yale University, accessed October 25, 2017, *http://commencement.yale.edu/faq.*

Class Day, the White House contacted Yale's administration, stating that President Bush would be available to speak at Commencement and receive an honorary doctorate. It was known that Yale's corporation had approved the president for an honorary degree without the consultation or approval of the Honorary Degrees Committee, an advisory board of faculty and alumni. A contingent of faculty took this as a snub and boycotted the proceedings.

At Commencement, I was standing at one of the gates to Old Campus when the president took the podium. He knew he was facing a tough crowd. He turned to humor to break the ice.

"Congratulations to the class of 2001. To those of you who received honors, awards, and distinctions, I say, well done. And to the C students, I say, you, too, can be president of the United States."

I laughed, in spite of myself. Most of the crowd did, but not all. One graduate caught my eye. As the crowd chortled, he crossed his arms and shook his head. His face hardened. He was Black. I kept glancing at him throughout the speech.

The president delivered another quip. "There will be some people and some moments you will never forget. Take, for example, my old classmate Dick Brodhead, the accomplished dean of this great university. I remember him as a young scholar, a bright lad, a hard worker. We both put a lot of time in at the Sterling Library, in the reading room where they have those big leather couches. We had a mutual understanding. Dick wouldn't read aloud, and I wouldn't snore."

More laughter followed. The graduate who had caught my eye buried his head in his hands. He was not alone in his anger or disdain. I suspect at least half of the crowd was incensed by the simple fact of the president's presence. But this graduate's anger seemed more focused. I watched his body, his face. I saw him tense every time the president joked around his own lackluster academic achievements. I don't know what that graduate was thinking about. But I formed a guess, and that guess shook me.

My mind wandered back through memories of all the people I had met at Yale—the remarkable, the average, the second-rate. With one exception, all my friends were White. Still, there were people of color I had known well enough that I had formed a rough judgment of their character: people I had studied alongside, or collaborated with. The list was not long—five or ten names at most. They were quite different from one another. But there was also a consistency. They were all sharp, creative, and driven. They had hang-ups and personal drama, like we all did. They partied and acted foolishly, like we all did. I watched a few sabotage themselves, like we all did. But they all brought seriousness and commitment to their work at Yale. They had a sense that this time mattered.

And here was our president, saying that he had succeeded in spite of his laughable work ethic. Here he was joking that academic accomplishment bore no correspondence with one's future. Whether he knew it or not, he was mocking them. And in that moment, there was something familiar about him. In his cavalier demeanor, in his implication that his academic effort did not matter, I saw every student I knew who was coasting their way through. Like him, and like me, they were all White. I suspect many of us had something else in common as well.

The president was a legacy student. I was a legacy student. As my friend Frances put it, I was "a super-legacy." My mother, grandfather, great-great-grandfather, and great-great-great-grandfather all attended Yale. The school's main science building, Sheffield, was named after an ancestor of mine. The most iconic entrance to campus, Phelps Gate, was named for another. I assume both were the result of significant donations.

I don't mean to oversimplify the issue. I knew many talented and hard-working White students. I knew a few legacy students who were wholly commendable. Likewise, and though I never met any, it is possible there were students of color among us who glided through on Cs.

Still, in my experience one thought shone clearly through the complexity: only a White man could take this time for granted. Only a White man could take it as a given that he was entitled to a place at one of the nation's most prestigious universities, all other considerations aside.

Some years later, I was struggling to find a position in my chosen field. I had set an appointment with an employment agency. During intake, the interviewer glanced over my resume.

"Wow." Her eyes widened. "Yale. Don't worry, we'll place you in no time."

She was correct. They called me later that afternoon with an offer. It happened that I had already received another job offer, which I took, but the speed of their response was telling. It's hard to deny that an Ivy League degree provides certain opportunities.

We take it as gospel that education is the path to upward mobility. It might be more accurate to state that the credentials of education form that path. It is not what I learned and accomplished during my college years that opened doors for me. It is this single line of text I can write on my resume: "Bachelor of Arts, Yale University, New Haven, CT, 2002." That is my key.

The meaning of these credentials varies greatly depending on who writes them. For many students they mean years of hard work. For most students of color they mean that and more. Among the people I know well, and excepting alumni of historically Black colleges and universities, every university graduate of color I've spoken with describes wrestling with racism throughout their college career. They were in an uphill battle. For other students, including certain former presidents, a college degree means family connections and a few years of coasting through classes between bouts of revelry. If I am honest, my own college credential means something between these two extremes.

Ultimately, the actual meaning of my degree—what it represents in terms of what I learned and the skills I gained—is irrelevant. The strength of a college credential is the same, regardless of the work required to achieve it. In fact, a degree gained with the assistance of Whiteness may overpower a more hard-earned one gained without such aid. A recent study demonstrated that White graduates of state universities receive job callbacks at rates equal to Black graduates of Harvard. And when called back, White state graduates are offered higher starting salaries.[2]

We are taught to believe that higher education is the great equalizer. The power of an advanced degree to positively affect an

2. Michael S. Gaddis, "Discrimination in the Credential Society: An Audit Study of Race and College Selectivity in the Labor Market," *Social Forces*, vol. 93, issue 4 (June 2015): 1451–1479.

individual's economic outlook is well documented. But access to higher education and the credentialing it offers is sharply divided along racial lines. Likewise, the concrete economic benefit of such a degree splits along racial lines.

Considering these facts together, we face the uncomfortable possibility that institutions of higher education are themselves drivers of racialized economic disparity at the societal level.

In 2015 Jeff Hobbs published *The Short and Tragic Life of Robert Peace*, a biography of his college roommate. Jeff, Robert, and I were in the same class at Yale. I never knew either of them, though I'm sure we crossed paths. It is a small campus. Jeff is White; Robert was Black. In the book, Jeff records how Robert grew up poor in Newark. He received a sponsorship to attend Yale, where he majored in molecular biophysics and biochemistry. He graduated with honors. After graduation he returned to Newark. He was never able to capitalize his drive, brilliance, or degree into success. In 2011 he was shot and killed in a "drug-related murder." Had the book not been published, Robert Peace's name would, most likely, have been forgotten except by family and friends (of which, to be fair, he had many).

Throughout the book, Hobbs implies that Peace was sabotaged by the tension between two worlds: a world of familial ties and struggle (represented by Newark), and another world of academic achievement and social prestige (represented by Yale). Knowing the story only through Hobbs's own account, I can't judge the accuracy of this analysis, but I do see an injustice in what he describes. To one extent or another, most students of color must choose between these worlds. They must sacrifice something of their history and their identity if they wish to access the power of their credentials, whereas White students may wield their history and their culture like a bullhorn to amplify the power of their own credentials.

One son of Yale fell into a degree and it helped him gain the most powerful office in the world. Another fought hard to graduate with honors and died in poverty and anonymity. The most immediate and obvious distinction between them is the color of their skin. I resemble the former of these two men. As I look back on those bright college years, I see two truths. First, for me, college was a time of fond memories and fundamental to the formation of my character as an adult. Second, it amplified the powers already granted to me as a White man in this nation. I must now consider the possibility that these facts depend on one another.

PART III
EL SALVADOR

1

We walk together down the unpaved street, about four or five blocks so far. I'm annoyed, and impatient. The flight down took a lot out of me and I'm wasted from struggling in Spanish all day. I was about to lie down when the Doña showed up and told me we were taking a walk. Father Ramiro, my boss, said it was important for me to get on her good side. So, I'm walking. But I just want to go to sleep. She points at a stop sign and then gestures to the expanse of street before us.

"Mirá, éste. No andés por allá." She speaks slowly and emphatically with gestures, so I will understand. She turns to the left. We walk for another ten minutes maybe. She points to another street sign, and then to the street beyond.

"Mirá, este. No andés por allá." Again, slow and emphatic. She turns left again. We repeat the process once more, and then walk until we reach a broad freeway. She points across it.

"Y esta es la carretera. Tené cuidado acá. ¿Comprendés?"

I think for a moment, then nod. It's a box, half a mile wide. I should stay inside it. We walk back to the church. I start to lie down again. My next-door neighbor, Antonio, arrives and introduces himself. I want him to leave, but he's charming and patient with my shattered Spanish. And I'm too tired to argue, so we talk. I try to explain the strange tour the Doña took me on, which takes several attempts. Eventually he nods.

"¿Por qué?" I hope he understands my meaning from context.

"Las maras. Hasta la policía no andan por allá."

He uses a word I don't know.

I ask. "¿Qué significa 'maras'?"

He explains. I don't get most of it. I think it's something about soccer teams. I write down the word to check in the dictionary later. He taps my hand. I look up.

"No salgás por la noche, no importa lo que sucede." He wags his index finger slowly as he talks. He sounds serious. I ask him to repeat. I think I've understood. I shouldn't go out at night. He leaves. The groundskeeper stops by. I've already met him. He drops off a newspaper on the way out. I thank him. One of the headlines has the word Antonio used: *mara*. There is another word I am unfamiliar with. I write it down as well. I retire to the shed. I close the door and lie down. Hours pass. I can't sleep. I get up and find my dictionary. I look up both words.

Mara *nf* group, gathering, criminal gang.

Homicidio *nm* murder.

I chide myself. The second one's obvious. I should have been able to figure it out. I put the dictionary away, lock the door, and lie down. I get up and brace the door with a chair. I lie down and look at the ceiling. I am twenty-two years old and, for the first time, I have a curfew. For the first time, I am not allowed to travel where I please.

A half-thought forms in my head. At home there are gangs, but I never blockaded my door. At home I read news of violent crimes, but I never blockaded my door. At home I was held up at gunpoint, specifically because I was out at night, but I never blockaded my door. And I wonder if I should go back home.

2

I collapse into my room. I have been here only one week, but it has been the most exhausting week of my life. I start to drift off. A gunshot wakes me. It's come from nearby. Next door, I think. Antonio's house. I take off running.

I've made several acquaintances already. Antonio is the only one I would consider something like a friend. I start pounding on his door. I shout his name. Seconds later the door opens. He stands there. He is calm. I stumble through telling him that I heard a gunshot and ask if he's okay.

He gets angry. He reminds me that he told me not to leave at night. No matter what. He points out that running towards a gunshot was stupid. He repeats this fact several times. Even as I brace myself against his anger, in the back of my head I congratulate myself for understanding him so well. Somewhere over the last week all my Spanish classes have begun to kick in. He asks me what I was planning to do if someone had been trying to shoot him.

I have no answer. It didn't occur to me that I might be in danger. I am embarrassed. I look down. I see that he's holding a pistol. I frame my next question carefully.

"Antonio, ¿Qué sucedió?" He follows my gaze to the gun.

"Nada." He smiles. "¿Has probado tacuazín?"

I shake my head. No, I have not tried *tacuazín*. I don't even know what it is. He walks me to the back of the property by the chicken coop. A possum lies on the ground. It is still twitching. Apparently it was trying to get to the hens. He points to it, smiles, and raises his eyebrows. I take it to be an offer. I can never tell when he's messing with me. I shake my head, say good night, and go back to bed.

In the morning he brings a plate over. He tells me it's breakfast. I don't want to appear rude. I think this is what he's banking on. I eat. It is very, very greasy. I try not to remember seeing it the night before, but the memory of it twitching on the ground is persistent. Should I worry about parasites? It's been grilled, but I'm still unsure. I feel queasy. He stares at me while I eat. I have never felt so uncomfortable at a meal before. When I finish, he takes the plate from me, and wags his finger.

"No salgás por la noche, no importa lo que suceda."

3

I walk to the freeway and make my way to the bus stop. It is my first day off in two months. I'm going into the city to see a movie. I find an open spot along the wall and settle in. The microbuses have no schedule, but they never take too long to arrive.

"Hey there." I turn to see who's speaking. It is not someone I recognize. He smiles. "You're American, right?"

"I'm from the States, yeah."

"I can always tell. You guys walk differently."

I imagine this is true. I also imagine the facts that I am extremely pale, blond, and taller than almost everyone here were also significant clues. I play dumb.

"How's that?"

"I used to live in LA."

"Oh."

"Can you help me with a dollar?"

I expected this. I am always noticed here. It is uncomfortable. About a third of the time, the conversation leads to a request for money. I've budgeted five dollars a day for it. I have individually folded bills in my front pocket. It is not a matter of charity. I just want to be left alone. I hand him a bill. He takes it.

"Thanks. Maybe I'll see you around." He walks on his way.

The bus arrives. I ride to the city. I get off. There's a pedestrian bridge to cross the street. I climb the staircase. An elderly woman passes me coming down. She looks down and spits. She calls me gringo; tells me to leave; says that this is their country. Another third of the time something like this happens. I remind myself that I only have eight months before I go home. Two hundred and thirty-four days, exactly. I am keeping track in my journal. A young man passes me on the bridge. He says nothing but stares at me the whole time. Silent stares account for the final third of people noticing me.

I come down on the other side of the bridge. Two men stand at the bottom with a battery-powered radio. It plays a new single, "Frijolero," from a band called Molotov. I had heard it before on the radio. I like its Norteño/punk sound and its commentary on American racism and neo-colonialism. I like it less when people sing it loudly while pointing at me. I avoid eye contact and keep walking. I remind myself again: two hundred and thirty-four days. They are still singing. I tell myself that I've got enough in the bank to buy a ticket home today, and that there are daily flights back. I can leave at any time. Without this fact, I know I would give up.

4

I've arrived back at the shed. The movie was forgettable, but I was grateful for the chance to turn my brain off. Now, as always, I am grateful for the chance to go to sleep. I am out within seconds of my head hitting the pillow.

There is a knock at the door. I look up at the digital clock. It's midnight. I remember Antonio's warning. I am afraid, not only of whoever might be on the other side of the door, but also of the possibility of being made to eat possum again. Since that first time, I have learned that no one here eats possum, that Antonio was just messing with me, and that he is the sort of person who would do it again, if he felt it were called for.

I resolve to ignore the sound. There is another knock and a voice commands me to wake up. It's the Doña. I relax, drag myself from bed, throw on a shirt, and open the door. She stands there smiling and asks for a cup of coffee.

I know this is a pretext. She didn't actually come over for coffee. I know this not because of the hour. Her husband tells me she drinks coffee right until she goes to bed. However, my coffee is bad and everyone in the neighborhood knows it. Given that everybody here drinks instant, this is saying something. I'm tempted to ask what she really wants, but I don't. I've learned to let her do things in her own time. It doesn't work out well for me otherwise.

I shuffle off to boil water. It doesn't take long. I pour it into a cup then get the coffee tin, the sugar bowl, and a spoon. I lay all four items before her. She pushes the tin and the spoon back in my direction and tells me to add the coffee. Now I'm sure something is up. Getting the right ratio of instant grounds to water is the part I always mess up. But I don't argue. I'm a bit scared of her. I ladle two spoonfuls of instant coffee into the cup, stir, and hand it back to her along with the spoon. She adds several spoonfuls of sugar, stirs it again, sips, then adds more sugar. We sit. Finally she speaks and says that I am smart, very smart. I never know how to handle compliments, but I'm glad she thinks I'm clever. I begin to thank her.

She cuts me off. "Pero a la vez pendejo."

I'm not sure what startles me more: the specific fact that she just called me a dumbass, or the more general fact that she cursed. She never curses. Maybe I misheard. I ask her to repeat. She sounds it out, syllable by syllable: "pen-de-jo." She waits to see how I will respond. My accent falters as I tell her I don't understand. How can you be smart and a dumbass? They're opposites.

She sets down her coffee cup then spreads her hands like she's laying something before me. She says that I think I'm a teacher. Of course I think that. Teaching is part of the job description the bishop gave me. I have it in writing somewhere. I tell her so.

She shakes her head. She tells me I'm a student, not a teacher, that this is the reason my bishop sent me. I start to object, then stop myself. She is right. I did come here to learn. That's what I told my bishop when I proposed the trip. That's why he went along with the idea. That's why he agreed to partially fund me. She takes another sip of her coffee and sets it down.

"Es verdad que sabés muchas cosas. Pero nosotros sabemos muchas más. Y hasta que aprendés a aprender, nadie querrá recibir tu enseñanza."

It takes me longer than it should to understand these words. I admit, I'm a little reluctant to decipher what she's said. It's something about how they know more than me. And that I need to learn before I can teach. I frown and look down. She points to me with an open hand. She smirks and explains that this is why I am smart, but also a dumbass. I feel a sinking in my stomach. I drift away in guilt for a moment. She raps my hand with the back of hers and pulls me back. She's heavy-handed for a woman in her seventies.

I look up. She's wagging her finger. She tells me not to worry. She assures me that we're all smart dumbasses. I suppose it's good she doesn't think I'm uniquely stupid. She swallows the remainder of her coffee and grimaces. Apparently, I still haven't figured out the right mix of instant grounds. She leaves and I go back to bed and try to fall asleep. I fail.

In the morning, Antonio stops by to say hi. I want a second opinion. I ask him if I'm a dumbass. He pinches a bit of air with his thumb and index finger, then nods with an apologetic smile.

5

I pace the length of the station. My legs are stiff. The bus trip from San Salvador to Ciudad de Guatemala was long and cramped, but worth it. I needed the break. I see Frances on the other side of the street and wave. I'm looking forward to another adventure together, though I do hope this time there will be no steam tunnels. Her companions are with her. We meet and embrace. She introduces me to Jane and John. We walk and chat. A part of me relaxes that I hadn't even noticed was tense. It's good to be with people who are like me again. That is to say, other White Americans.

They take me to the hotel. The room is tiny, but the shower has a heater. It is the first warm shower I have taken in four months. The experience is better than all the sex I have had in my life thus far. I finish and get dressed. We go out for a late lunch where we discuss plans for the week. There are Mayan ruins in the northeast. We can catch a plane, but we will need to see a travel agent today. They've found one already. We go together. Jane's Spanish is better than mine. She negotiates. The travel agent gets to a price we can live with. She picks up a phone and calls in the details. She takes out a piece of letterhead and a pen. I peek at what she is writing. At the top, I see the name of an airline, a time, and our destination.

The note continues: "4 boletos. Todos americanos. 2 rubios, 1 rubia, 1 pelinegra." There are no names, just the fact that we have four tickets, that we are from the States, and the color of our hair. At the bottom are her signature and the date. She hands the note to Jane and admonishes us not to be late. We pay and she waves us out.

I am confused. "Did we just get hustled?"

"I'm not sure."

We head back to the hotel, get dinner, go to sleep. The next morning, we catch a cab to the airport, very early. I feel uncertain. The airport is a single runway lined by several corrugated steel hangars. A bank of fog has rolled in. We walk to the small cinder block building labeled "Terminal." A man stands behind the counter. We show him

60

the note. He looks it over, looks at us, nods, and hands it back. He tells us that the flight is delayed, on account of the fog. This is not a problem. We're in no hurry. We look around. The room is packed. There is nowhere to sit. We find a spot of wall near the door and lean.

An hour passes. A bell rings outside. I imagine it may be a notification about the flight. I go outside to check. A man pushes a cart. He's selling green mangos with hot sauce. We haven't had breakfast. I buy four bags for the group. We eat. I learn that eating spicy, underripe mangos on an empty stomach is unwise.

Another hour passes. The fog lifts. A more official-sounding bell rings. We walk outside. A scuffed-looking steel prop plane waits on the tarmac. Jane sees it and stops.

"I know this model." She knows airplanes. It's something to do with her father's profession. She mentioned it at dinner last night, but I don't remember exactly what he does. "It was taken out of service in the U.S. in the fifties."

It looks very fifties. We walk out to the plane. The cargo bay is open and a man stands inside. He motions for us to hand him our bags. We board the plane. The interior is faded. We take our seats. I look to the rear of the plane. Mounted against the bulkhead in three glass cases are the safety devices: a fire extinguisher, an ax, and a Bible. Two flight attendants board carrying our in-flight breakfast: shortbread still steaming from the oven, fresh-squeezed orange juice, and coffee. We eat again.

The plane makes a slow turn at the end of the runway. Everything rattles as the engine fires up. We accelerate. I am a little scared, but I smile. This is sort of an adventure. I will have to tell someone this story, if we don't die. I glance across the aisle at the flight attendant. She has strapped herself into a bucket seat. The look on her face is close to boredom, but not quite. I know that face. I've made it. It is the face of a daily grind. I frown. For me, the underdevelopment of this place is exciting and strange: the outdated plane, the hand-scribbled note, the seeming improvisation of it all. For her, it is just life.

6

I've made it eight months without getting sick. I suppose it was too much to hope that I would get through the year without illness; last night was bad. I let Father Ramiro know I would be staying in today. I've spent the morning lying on my back, counting the cracks in the ceiling. There's a knock at the door and Santiago steps into the shed. He's Father Ramiro's assistant and also the go-to guy for medical advice. He looks me over and tells me I look ugly. I've learned just enough not to take this personally. Besides, I saw the sight in the mirror this morning and I know what I look like. He asks me what happened.

"Estuve toda la noche . . ." I realize I don't know the word for vomiting. I mime it instead.

He guesses. "¿Vomitando?"

Of course. I nod. He looks concerned. "¿Tenés diarrea también?" Diarrhea. That one I know. I nod again. He asks me how many times. I try to count. It all sort of blurred together after four. "Más que diez."

He frowns in a decisive way. I gather he's about to offer a diagnosis. "Tenés cólera."

I'm quite certain I heard that wrong. "¿Cómo?"

He repeats, "Cólera," then explains that it's a disease of the stomach.

I ask him if I should go to the hospital, which would be tricky. Medical professionals are on strike throughout the whole country. He looks up and away a moment.

"A ver."

I don't like this response. I was under the impression that cholera was not a wait-and-see kind of thing. He takes my hand, presses on my nails, and looks at them. He tells me to wait here and to drink as much water as I can. He says he'll be back soon. He gets up to leave. As he goes, he tells me not to worry.

I reflect on the absurdity of telling someone they have cholera and then advising them not to worry. I almost laugh. My stomach spasms painfully in response. Laughing is not good. Maybe he's right not to worry. I've probably misunderstood something.

Maybe it's a false cognate. I dig out the book, and scan until I find the word.

Cólera *nf* cholera.

"Huh." Per instructions, I pour myself a glass of water and drink. It does not sit well. When he returns, I'm back in the bathroom. He bangs on the door and asks me where it's coming out. Under ordinary circumstances, I would consider that a forward question. In my current context, I think it's clinical. I respond with the same frankness: both ends. I finish and come out. He's carrying a large pot, a ladle, and a grocery bag. He tells me to sit. He washes his hands, fills the pot with water, then sets it on the stove to boil. He adds salt, sugar, and the juice of several limes. The pot comes to a boil. He stirs it for a few minutes, then turns off the heat.

He points to the ground and gives more instructions. I'm to stay here, and rest. This will be easy. I don't think I'm capable of anything but resting right now. He points to the pot. I am to drink one glass every half hour. I nod.

His voice goes stern. He reminds me to stay in the shed, and to wash my hands—a lot. My shed sits on the same lot as the church's parochial school, and we've got to keep the kids safe. I had actually sorted that one out. Mom's a nurse. I learned the importance of handwashing as a matter of religious conviction. He points to the grocery bag and extends his hand. "Tres colones."

I had gotten pretty good at converting currencies, but my brain seems to have stopped. I ask him to give me the total in dollars. He looks annoyed. Most Salvadorans I've met are unhappy about the dollarization. People still quote prices in colones, even though colones don't exist anymore. At this particular moment, I find the practice more obtuse than admirable. Plus arguing over colones seems a bit too on the nose right now. He sees my frustration and concedes: thirty-seven cents. I rummage up a dollar and move to hand it to him. He hesitates and looks down at my fingers. He asks if I washed my hands. In fact, I scrubbed them raw. He takes the dollar from me and stuffs it in his shirt pocket.

He tells me he'll hold on to the rest, for the next batch. He gets up to leave. I can't hold my tongue anymore. I ask him if cholera is serious. He tells me not to worry. But I am worried. Santiago is smart, and a trained paramedic, but he hasn't been to med school. I wait a moment, then say what's on my mind. I remind him that he isn't a doctor. He smirks and reminds me that I'm not one either.

———

It's been two days. I get up from bed and choke down another glass. This is the fifth vat he's made me. He still doesn't seem concerned, though I did notice he hung a sign reading "prohibido" on the door of my shed. Father Ramiro has come to see me—in his role as supervisor, rather than that of final dispatcher. That's what I hope anyway. But maybe not. I am sore in places I did not know I had muscles. Last night, I stood up from the toilet, reflexively looked back, and saw clear water below me. The knowledge that I am squeaky clean inside and out was not comforting. And I feel bad about how much of his time I'm taking. I tell Ramiro this last thought.

He frowns. "¿Quién, Santiago?"

I nod. He shakes his head. He reminds me that Santiago is a paramedic and he loves this kind of thing. It makes him feel like a hero. At least I'm contributing to his ego. I feel it coming again. I excuse myself. He stands up to leave. I am grateful that he doesn't make me explain.

———

Another two days have gone by. I'm sitting up now. Santiago knocks on the door. I open it. Before greeting me he looks in the vat. It is mostly full. He makes a disappointed face. He asks me when I drank my last glass. I'm not entirely sure. Time is more flexible than it was a week ago, and not in a good way. I guess—maybe three o'clock. He checks his watch and shakes his head. Apparently, that was two hours ago. He tells me to have another. I sigh and shake my head.

"No puedo," which is true. I can't drink any more. I feel bloated to the point of bursting and the sweet, salty, sour trifecta has become intolerable. My throat refuses to swallow. He crosses his arms. I explain that I'm getting better, which is also true. Things have slowed down. They have not, however, stopped. He takes the ladle and pours another glass.

"For real?" Exasperation is hard to accomplish in a foreign tongue.

He pushes the glass across the table toward me. I hate this place. And again, a half-thought forms. At home I have been sick many times to the point of vomiting. And it never made me hate that place.

7

I take a seat at the back of the restaurant. The waitress brings me my breakfast: rice and beans, one egg, sunny-side up, a fried plantain, and coffee. My stomach is right again, finally. I'm eager for proper food. She smiles at me. She is new. I haven't met her before.

She asks my name. I offer it and request hers in exchange. She answers. She tells me how handsome I am. This is strange, in part because two days ago I was still in the throes of projectile diarrhea. I don't really feel up for flirting. But it's more than that. Before coming here, no one ever flirted with me. Now it happens with some regularity. It makes me uncomfortable. Mercifully, I have learned the script of it. It is, at least, a predictable discomfort. In a moment, she will tell me she likes my eyes.

"Qué lindo los ojos." They're blue—a quite unremarkable blue. We chat a few minutes. She makes me laugh. And it's an honest laugh. Then she has to leave. She has tables to wait. She waves by fluttering her fingers. "Nos vemos."

The statement is a standard goodbye, the equivalent of "See you later." But I realize that I am looking forward to seeing her again, so I respond in kind. "Nos vemos." She smiles, adds that she hopes it's soon, and walks away. I frown. I wish she hadn't added that. I eat breakfast here every day. Of course I will see her tomorrow. And now, I expect to feel awkward.

Shyness aside, in other circumstances I would be interested. She is funny and good-looking. She seems smart, at least as much as one can tell from a two-minute conversation, but I don't know what she sees when she looks at me. And I don't know if it has anything to do with me.

I pay and get up to leave. I pass one of my students. He's having breakfast with his mother. She asks if I can walk him to school because she needs to get to work. I nod. We walk. I gather he heard my earlier exchange. He looks at me and tells me he wishes he had eyes like mine. I shake my head and tell him they're weak. He looks at me quizzically. I explain that the sun damages blue eyes. He looks at me again, skeptically. He's not dumb. What I said is true, as far as I understand the science of it: blue eyes are less resistant to ultraviolet radiation. But I've never actually worried about it, and I think he can tell. We arrive at the school and the day begins.

I teach English in the morning and religion after lunch. I tell the children the story of Jesus and Zacchaeus. I ask them what the story means. They shout out: that Jesus notices people who get ignored; that we have to stop doing bad things, and start doing better. It's a solid summary. I hand out paper and crayons. I ask them to draw a picture of the story. As they finish, they bring their work up to show me. The pictures are all different, but common themes emerge: several brown figures in a crowd; a single, small brown figure sitting in or, more often, standing directly on top of a tree; and in the center, or sometimes off to one side, there is a single tall, pink figure, with yellow hair, blue eyes, and a halo.

I don't have to ask, and I don't know what to say, but I know I don't belong here.

8

The line at the border crossing inches forward. I glance at my watch. *I'm not nervous. Don't be nervous.* The man ahead of me finishes. Without looking, the officer motions me to the window. I approach and hand him my passport. He flips through the pages, still without looking at me. He asks me how long I'll be in the country. I tell him ten weeks.

In fact, I'll be in the country another four months (one hundred and fourteen days exactly, I remind myself); however, the tourist card allows a maximum stay of three months. Any longer and I would have to apply for a visa, which I probably wouldn't get.

He turns to the last page of my passport and scans the stamps there. This is the third time I've made this trip. As I did the first time, I took the morning bus up and stopped for lunch in Ciudad de Guatemala, before catching the evening bus back to purchase a new tourist card. The legality of the practice is questionable, but folks assure me it's common enough. He runs his index finger across the handwritten dates on my previous tourist card stamps, one at a time. His eyes narrow.

I start making plans. If he refuses to sell me the tourist card, I will have to return to Ciudad de Guatemala. There's a bus stop here at the border. I have enough cash on me for the trip, plus one, maybe two nights at a cheap hotel. I kick myself for not being better prepared. I'll have to call the bishop. I know he has friends in Guatemala. Maybe he can help resolve the visa thing. I tell myself it won't be a disaster, but I know that it will be a pain. A big one. The officer raps the page with the tips of his fingers and tells me it's no good. I hold my breath. He points to the northbound bus stop. He tells me I have to go back to Ciudad de Guatemala. Then he looks up at me for the first time and stops. He squints at me and declares that the tourist card costs fifteen dollars.

He's wrong. The tourist card is ten bucks. I tell him so, as politely as I can.

"Vale quince," he repeats. I can be slow. I pause while the pieces connect.

"Ah, sí. Tiene razón. Disculpe." I pull fifteen dollars from my wallet. He stamps my passport, signs it, dates it, and waves me along. Our bus driver motions me over to wait while the other passengers finish their transactions. I sit.

I see the next man in line. His mother is Guatemalan, his father Salvadoran. He's here visiting family. It's a finding-your-roots kind of thing, I guess. I know these things because he told me. We sat together on the first leg of the trip. We were both born in California, and we are the same age. Through half an hour of talking, we were unable to find any other common ground. Conversation fizzled and we spent the last forty-five minutes in awkward silence.

He approaches the officer and hands over his passport. The officer looks at the cover, then up to his face. He lays the passport back down on the counter. Again, he points to the northbound bus stop. He declares my compatriot must go back to Ciudad de Guatemala and get a visa. My seatmate shakes his head. He's only staying two weeks, he says. He pulls a ten-dollar bill from his pocket and holds it out. The officer crosses his arms.

The young man's eyes narrow. "Quiero hablar con el encargado de acá." I feel a flash of kinship. Somehow, asking for a supervisor strikes me as a very American move. The officer shakes his head. He declares that he is alone at the station. He is the supervisor. My countryman's face hardens, then softens. He puts his hand to his chin. He apologizes, declares that he was hoping to solve the problem here, and asks, casually, if there is some sort of fine he can pay instead. He does this smoothly. I'm impressed. If the officer hadn't created an opening, I would have had no idea how to initiate a bribe. Unfortunately, the officer's arms remain crossed. He points with his lips to the far side of the border crossing, where the buses leave going north.

Our bus driver sees the proceedings and strolls over. He leans in close and speaks in the officer's ear. I can't hear what's said. A moment later, he puts his hand in his pocket, and takes out a bill. It's a twenty. He folds it in the palm of his hand, and then lays his hand on the counter in front of the officer. Palm down. The officer takes the young man's passport, stamps it, signs it, and hands it back. The bus driver walks the American back toward the bus and whispers in his ear. The younger man frowns, takes out his wallet, and hands over a twenty. He rolls his eyes, then joins our group. I lean toward him. "That was weird." He doesn't answer. I clarify. "I mean that he gave you so much more of a hard time than me." He still doesn't respond. "I mean, because, you know, I'm White, and you've actually got family here." Without looking, he shakes his head and half-waves in my direction. Like he is shooing a fly away.

I gather we will not be sitting together for the second leg of the trip.

Debriefing El Salvador

We travel to lose ourselves.

—Pico Iyer, *Why We Travel*

I don't quite remember why I went to El Salvador. My Spanish was poor. The church I worked with had no established program, or precedent, for receiving foreign volunteers. There were no Americans or English-speakers in the town where I would live. I would not be paid. I had to raise the money for the trip, something I had no experience doing. In retrospect, the whole endeavor was poorly planned. I'd like to say that my choice was a matter of youthful bravado. It wasn't. I simply didn't think it would be difficult. It sounded simple: go, work with a Salvadoran priest, learn life lessons, come home.

About a week before I left, in a weak nod toward preparation, I read a blog entry about cross-cultural immersion. The author stated that before culture shock sets in, most people experience a honeymoon period. Mine lasted four hours. From the evening after I arrived until I left a year later, I was unbalanced, uncertain, and uncomfortable. It wasn't all bad, but it was all difficult. There were many adjustments to make to culture, to language, to climate, and to the standard of living. I handled most of these poorly. Circumstances and events that I would have taken as mere inconveniences at home became, in El Salvador, proof that there was something confounding about that land. In fact, the problem wasn't that El Salvador didn't make sense; but rather that I didn't make sense there.

I had become, for the first time in my life, a minority. El Salvador is less racially diverse than other parts of Central America. It was clear I didn't belong. I received stares everywhere I went. Strangers, acquaintances, and even friends were more likely to call me "gringo" than my name. Sometimes it was said with affection. Occasionally, the word was hurled with disdain. Usually, it was given as a statement of fact. It was the simplest way to distinguish me from others.

Most people had a visible response to me before we spoke—discomfort, curiosity, admiration, or contempt. Sometimes these responses were quite explicit. More often, an expression would flash across their face, and they would then spend the rest of the conversation trying to act natural. The effect was so consistent that when people didn't respond to me this way, I became nervous. I wondered what they were thinking about me.

Not all the attention was overtly negative. Women flirted with me. People assumed I was well educated. On the bus, strangers asked me to tell them about my home. But even these flashes of interest and attraction were uncomfortable. It seemed they had little to do with me specifically. I assumed they came up because I was a White man.

As a deep introvert, my greatest discomfort was that I was never anonymous, and I was never really allowed to be myself. I was that White guy over there: visible and obvious. I don't mean to cast aspersions. Most Salvadorans treated me with distant courtesy and respect. Though tough and frank, my neighbors were also warm and welcoming. But through it all I was exotic, and an outsider.

This experience shaped my understanding of race. It still does. At the time, however, I overestimated its importance. Somewhere around my sixth month in the country, I was waiting at a bus stop when a woman walked past and spat on the ground as she said "gringo." It was the fourth time that had happened to me. For cultural reasons I do not entirely understand, all four incidents involved older women.

A thought popped into my head as our bus arrived. In El Salvador, the major routes were serviced by brightly painted school buses. So, in that strange way memories weave together, the thought is forever linked to an image of a rainbow-painted school bus emblazoned with a flaming "79" on its side: "This must be what it's like for Black people in America."

It was a revelatory insight, and it was both crucial and false. Crucial because it is the closest I have come to knowing that experience in its truth. False because I had chosen my situation and that choice gave me a sense of purpose through it all. False because the prejudice that came my way elevated me as often as it demeaned. False because this was new for me, not an established fact. False because it was temporary, and I would soon return to my life. False because in all these ways what I experienced was quite unlike what Black people experience in America.

This is an important tension for White people trying to understand our country. We can, and should, strain with all our imagination and experience across that divide of race, to glimpse what it looks like on the other side. And yet, we must acknowledge that for all our reaching we are still separated by an ocean. We can only glimpse, only imagine. We can never see. It is unsatisfying, like walking out onto a half-built bridge. But it matters and it must be done because imagination is the foundation of empathy: that act of picturing what the world looks like from another's perspective. Empathy, in turn, is the foundation of action and change.

We can, should, and must educate our imaginations. Our most important textbooks are firsthand accounts and reflections by people of color. The second is our own, fleeting, limited experience of alienation and marginalization, come where it may. We weave these sources together to form an incomplete picture of the shores on the other side of the racial divide. This is necessary. If we do not stretch to try to understand our neighbors' lives, we will never feel the aching that leads to action. But we must always keep in mind that our imaginations are only that: imaginations, passing shadows of the truth. When we forget, we entertain a dangerous illusion, to the detriment of all.

PART IV
Berkeley

1

My seminary classmates and I sit together in the pews. I look up. The school's chapel has hardwood beams. It's been a year since I've worshiped under anything but a corrugated steel roof. It's nice to be back in the States. A very short and very beautiful woman is preparing the chapel for evening prayers. She wears her hair natural and dyed red. I've noticed her before. Her name is Rondesia. She refuses any nickname. She's an upperclassman. She is also one of two other people here in their twenties; the average age of the student body is north of fifty. I am the youngest.

After setting the scripture readings, she walks over to me and taps my hand to get my attention. Even in the dim light of the chapel, the contrast between her black skin and mine is stark. She points to the opposite pew.

"The kiddie section is over there." She laughs and smiles. I do the same, then hold my breath for a moment. I think I manage to conceal this last fact.

2

Counselor Troi senses great hostility and tells the captain.

"Useless!" Rondesia's sudden exclamation startles me. I look over and purse my lips. She sees my confusion and gestures towards the television screen. "Of course they're hostile. They've locked weapons on the *Enterprise*." She shakes her head. "Useless."

I smile. I like being here with her. Someone clears their throat. Barbara is standing in the door of the guest house common room. She is a friend, and it happens that she is also my boss. I remember that I am on the clock and I am supposed to be cleaning guest rooms. I jump up from the couch and point at Rondesia.

"It was her idea!"

Rondesia crosses her arms, shakes her head, and frowns. "I am never robbing a bank with you."

I must admit, I am sad to be dropped from her list of theoretical co-conspirators. Then it occurs to me that to be dropped means I made it onto the list in the first place, which leaves a warm feeling.

3

We sit with friends in the dining hall. Jason frowns as he speaks.

"It was a total Disney-pandering-box-office-blockbuster-extravaganza . . ." He pauses for dramatic effect, and then smiles. "I loved it anyway. Picture Johnny Depp prancing across the big screen for two hours like a giant queen."

I look to Rondesia. "Have you seen it?"

"No."

"Me neither," Ken chimes in.

I do not look at him. "Do you want to?"

Her eyebrows crinkle. "See the movie?"

I nod.

She smiles. "Yeah. When?"

"Are you doing anything tonight?"

"No."

Ken chimes in again. "Me neither."

She does not look at him. This is promising.

"Great. I'll . . . I'll check the paper, and give you a call."

"Cool." She smiles again.

That evening, I walk down the hall toward her door. I'm not entirely sure what's going on. We've become close and I am interested. I can't tell if she is. This is either a date or a get-together between friends. Dressing was complicated.

Once, we were driving together on an errand. She stopped at an intersection as two young people entered the crosswalk. It was clear they were walking together. The woman wore a black cocktail dress and heels; the man, faded jeans and a forgettable t-shirt. Her hair was done. His was not. From the driver's seat Rondesia pointed at the man, and laughed. I didn't know why. She saw my confusion.

"He doesn't know he's on a date. If he had just put in a little effort," she pulled her thumb and index together to show how little, "it could've been something. Now she's just mad at him."

I looked again. Yes. It was definitely the walk of an angry woman.

I remembered that moment as I considered my limited wardrobe options earlier in the day. I chose something neat, but casual. Close enough to the realm of date to be admissible, but far enough for plausible deniability. I knock on her door and wait. I'm hoping her outfit is not so far into the territory of either date or casual as to make my choice seem clueless, but still clear enough to tell me where we stand.

The door opens. She is stunning. She always is. And she is dressed . . . neat, but casual. She is not wearing makeup, which is normal for her. But many people who don't ordinarily wear makeup will do so for special occasions. So the lack of makeup could be evidence of friendly get-together. Except I did tell her I prefer women who don't wear makeup. Not that it wasn't true. I do prefer women who don't wear makeup. But I have inadvertently blocked out a potential avenue toward clarity.

"What?" Her question jogs me from my analysis.

I realize I've been staring. I shake my head. "Nothing. Just got lost for a second." I think I see the hint of a smile flash at the corner of her eyes. "You ready?"

"Yep."

"Let's go."

We walk down the hill. We talk. I think this is the longest we've ever been together, just the two of us. We stop for dinner at an Indian restaurant. She requests a booth, and I wonder if that is significant. I decide that it means nothing. Everyone prefers the booth.

I notice she doesn't order anything with garlic or onions, which is not easy at an Indian place. I do the same. I wonder if this is meaningful. Maybe. The conversation is smooth and easy. I feel like myself around her—or, at least as much as I ever feel like myself around anyone. We finish our meal and the waiter brings the tab.

"Let me get it," I said.

"Sure, I'll get the next one." Pros: an implicit assumption of a next one; cons: reciprocity. That is more typically the stuff of friendships. Except, she's a self-avowed womanist. So, maybe not?

We walk to the theater and purchase tickets. Two young White men stroll through the lobby carrying golf putters that they swing in wide circles, like Astaire in a cane-and-top-hat number. They walk with an exaggerated bravado. I have the immediate assumption they are both Tarantino fans. She changes course, slightly, which I notice but it takes me a moment to recognize its purpose. She is maintaining distance from the men and keeping them in her sight at the same time. She is not afraid, but definitely alert.

When I am confident we are out of earshot, I gesture toward them and smirk.

"They're kind of ridiculous, right?"

Her face purses momentarily. "Hmm." She does not share my assessment. I wonder what she thinks. The moment passes.

The walls of the theater bear photo murals of cinema luminaries. We pass Patrick Stewart. She glances from his face to his feet and back. She makes a sound as if she has just tasted something delicious.

"Patrick Stewart?" I'm surprised.

"Oh yes." Her inflection of the word "yes" makes it two syllables and seems only halfway joking.

"Huh." I think about the implications. Pros: he is lean, sharp featured, with a prominent nose, and I am lean, sharp featured, with a prominent nose. Neither is it lost on me that we are both White. Cons: he is bald, with a British accent. I am neither. Uncertain: he is smart. Does she think I'm smart? I feel my brow furrowing. She notices my deliberation.

"Why, who's your celebrity crush?" Three names come to mind. Each could turn our interaction in a different direction. I pause and then choose one.

"Queen Latifah." Her eyes widen almost imperceptibly.

"So . . . you like full-figured women."

"I like women who look like women." My statement is true, ambiguous, and about as much of my hand as I'm prepared to show. In fact, one of the other two stars I had considered naming is also full-figured. But only Latifah is Black, and I was signaling. I wonder if my method of communication is problematic.

"Huh," she says.

We find the theater and our seats. The movie is fun. We talk about it on the way home and laugh. I ask her deeper things—what she cares about in life, what inspires her. She moves between the superficial, the profound, the personal, the political, and the absurd seamlessly. We arrive back at the dorm.

"I had fun."

"Me too."

"Well, good night then."

"Good night." We both pause and then we walk our separate ways. I get back to my room and the phone rings.

"Was there something you wanted to say to me?"

I think before I answer. "No."

Yes.

4

We're back in the dining hall. Our friend Molly takes a seat across from us and takes her first bite of lunch. Rondesia looks at me and then lifts her chin in Molly's direction. I take her cue.

"Molly, there's something we wanted to tell you."

"What?" She points between the two of us with her fork. "That you two are together?"

My face goes blank. "Oh. Yeah. That."

She laughs. "Oh good. It would have been really awkward if I was wrong." She sets her fork down and looks up. "And thank God. It has been agonizing watching the two of you dance around each other." We laugh. She smiles. "Seriously though, I'm really happy for you both."

"Thanks."

5

The rest of my class gathers at tables. Our facilitator tells us that after breakfast we will have morning prayer and then the retreat will be over. We say grace and serve ourselves from trays of eggs Benedict. They taste off somehow. I eat four helpings in spite of it. I am hungry. I excuse myself and say my goodbyes. I'm not staying for morning prayer. I have to get back to campus.

An hour into the drive my stomach gurgles. I feel nauseous. Pressure builds, slowly at first, and grows painful. Suddenly there is relief and a moment of elation. Then the smell hits. It is not only rank, but unnatural: acrid, chemical, and metallic. I heave. Thankfully, nothing comes up. The smell is everywhere. I roll down the window. I am passing between two fields that are being sprayed with organic fertilizer. In contrast with the smell of the car, it is an improvement.

I am driving my new girlfriend's car. I borrowed it for the class retreat, and she needs it this morning, so I had to leave early. I was hoping to maintain a certain level of naive idealism around one another's bodies—at least for another few months. The rankness I have brought to her vehicle could end that. There is about an hour left in the drive. The windows are all hand cranked. I pull over and let them all down. I run the air full blast, and drive.

I pull off the freeway and follow side streets that lead to the seminary. It is Sunday and still early. The streets are empty. Just ahead, a man steps into the street to cross. He is Black and tall. I brake hard to stop. I expect him to hurry across, as most jaywalkers do in these situations, but he does not. In fact, it seems he slows down a bit as he turns to look at me. He strides with confidence and a hint of swagger. He holds eye contact longer than seems polite or comfortable. I am pointedly aware of three facts: we are within a few feet of each other; we are alone; and all my car's windows are open. My fingers tighten on the steering wheel. It is true that his sudden appearance startled me, but I know it is his Blackness that frightens me. And I know it is absurd. After all, I am in a car, and he is not. As a simple matter of physics, I pose a far greater danger to him than he does to me. But still I am afraid.

He crosses past me. I force myself to wait until he is all the way across the street. I force myself to drive off slowly. I force myself to breathe calmly. I will see Rondesia soon. I don't want her to ask why I am flustered. I don't want her to know I have these kinds of thoughts and feelings. I pull into the seminary parking lot. She walks up just as I finish rolling up the last window. She has errands to run. She tilts her head my direction.

"Come with?"

"Sure." We get in the car. She sniffs and grimaces.

"You smell something?"

"No. No I do not."

6

(Virginia)

The flight to Virginia wasn't too long, but I was hoping for a chance to stretch my legs. Instead, Rondesia's mother has decided we're going out to lunch. This is my first time meeting her, and I don't want to be rude. We pile into the car. Rondesia moves to sit next to me, but her teenage brothers wedge themselves between us. There's no room left in the back seat.

"You can sit up front," DeVito says to her. We buckle up. The car starts. He turns to me. "Are you marrying our sister?"

"What? No."

"So why are you here?" I blink. There is no accusation in his tone. It's just a request for information.

"I wanted to meet you?"

"Oh. Okay," he says blankly. He thinks a moment. "What's your favorite video game?"

I head back to the guest room, thumbs numb from two hours of getting beat down at Super Smash Bros. DeVito insisted we play as soon as we got back from lunch. I'm thankful to have connected with him. I'm also ready to collapse. There is something on the bed. Two somethings actually, both bibles, each laid open. Each has a passage underlined in pencil:

> *Flee fornication, every sin that man doeth is without the body; but he that committeth fornication sinneth against his own body.*

And,

> *It is God's will that you should be sanctified: that you should avoid sexual immorality; that each of you should learn to control your own body in a way that is holy and honorable.*

"Hey." I turn toward the voice in the doorway. It's DeVito. "I just wanted to let you know, I had fun. You're alright."

"Thanks."

He sees my hand on the book, and points. "I laid out two bibles for you. I didn't know which translation you like."

"Oh. Thank you."

"You're welcome." He smiles and pats me on the shoulder.

———

She and I take a walk that evening. I'm grateful. Meeting new folks wears me out and I needed a break. I tell her about the bibles. She laughs.

"He's wondering if you just wanted to try brown sugar." It takes me a moment to decipher her comment and there is a sinking feeling in my stomach. She stops laughing and looks away. "Actually, I've wondered that, too." My stomach sinks further.

"Oh."

7

Jason's waiting at the terminal's curb. Two days ago, Rondesia and I were waiting for a cab at the exact same spot. I pull close and stop. I step out and hug him, take his bag and put it in the trunk. We get in and drive off.

"How was the flight?"

"Fine. I slept some."

"Good. How about the conference?"

"Oh my God! It was amazing. I met—" he stops suddenly. I hear him catch his breath, then breathe out. "—some good people. Made a lot of good contacts."

"Great."

He laughs. "I was hustling hard for the job openings. I'd printed off these business cards on the cheap—" He stops again. I look over. His face is scrunched, then it relaxes. "—I um, I ran out on the first day. I was jotting down my info on scraps of paper. I gave this one professor a sheet of toilet paper with my email on it."

I laugh. He laughs too, then yawns. "But, I'm wiped now."

I smile. "Well, you're in luck. Liza smoked a rack of lamb, and Molly's got the hot tub on." They're throwing a little end-of-spring-break shindig.

"Oh thank you, Jesu—" he stops again. I look at him. He looks frightened.

"Are you okay?"

"Yeah." His answer is unconvincing. His face scrunches. "You know, I think I'm just tired from the trip. Do you mind if we don't talk for a while?"

My brow furrows. "Yeah, sure."

I drive on to the party. At one point I look over. His head is bowed and I see him mouthing words. This is worrisome. I'll ask about it once he's had a chance to rest a bit.

We arrive. We get out. We enter the house. Rondesia is the first to see us. She hugs him. He looks suddenly better, relieved.

He points at me. "Sweetie, your boyfriend is the most terrifying driver I have ever ridden with. I don't believe in God, but he had me praying to Jesus." He pronounces the name with a very long *e* and two *z*'s.

She pushes her lip up and nods. "Tell me about it."

They both laugh. My stomach tightens in defense. I make myself relax. I am slowly beginning to realize that she neither requires nor even wants me to be perfect.

But I'm sure she would appreciate it if I improved my driving.

8

"So, what's it like dating a Black girl?" This is the third time I have been asked this question. The first two people were very nearly strangers. It was easy to brush them off. But this is my friend.

"Complicated. She experiences the world very differently than I do. She sees things differently; notices things I don't. I guess that's true for everyone, especially for people who aren't White, but she tells me about it; shares it with me. Some of the time, anyway. And then I have to figure out what to do with it. Then there's the cultural difference. We talk differently. We think differently. We remember very different things about our childhoods." I pause. "Actually, I mostly end up bumping into my own assumptions. A lot. Like, we'll be in a situation together, and she'll see something about how race is in play and I don't because I assume people are fair and reasonable. I get to do that, because it's safe for me, but it's not safe for her, so she doesn't get to make that assumption. Or we have a fight and I learn it's about some deep core value or perspective that I didn't even know I had. But she knew I had it, or at least suspected it, because she's had to navigate around these assumptions her whole life. I haven't. She notices things about me that I've never noticed or thought about. Sometimes it's just something that's different between us, like the phrases we use, or the fact that I don't use a washcloth in the shower. Sometimes it's"—I grimace—"sometimes it's something pretty messed up. And then, well, honestly, I usually get defensive because she saw something about me that I didn't. And maybe I didn't like what she saw. Then I get a minute to calm down and I've got to deal with it. I guess I've learned a lot more about myself than about her. And at the same time, I'm trying not to get so wrapped up in seeing myself that I can't be there for her, because I want to be there for her. There's always this gap between us. The race thing is always there. It ebbs and flows, but it's always there. Sometimes I wish it wasn't. Sometimes I wish she could just ignore it, or that I could be, I don't know, like the perfect enlightened White person." I frown. "But then, she wouldn't be her and I wouldn't be me. Or we'd be living in a fantasy and I don't want that either." I laugh. "I don't mean to be all doom and gloom. Mostly it's great. She's incredible. And smart and fun. And I love her. I've never been in love before. It's kind of amazing." I look over at him.

"Oh," He says with a blank expression.

It occurs to me that I may have answered a different question than the one he asked.

9

Our professor talks fast when she lectures. I have a compulsion to try to write down everything, so I have trouble keeping up. I need to get better at choosing what's important. She pauses and solicits questions. One student raises his hand immediately.

"Okay. I've been wondering about this for a while. So, you've got these reformers, and they're all talking about Christian liberty. And they're writing at exactly the same time that the trans-Atlantic slave trade is taking off. I mean, what's that about? It's hard to imagine it's just historical irony."

She frowns. "That's probably outside the purview of today's seminar." Q&A continues, but I'm disappointed. I assumed he had some personal stake in his question because he's Black, but it was a good question. I raise my hand. She calls on me.

"I think the question about the relationship between doctrines of liberty and the slave trade is important. I mean most of the ninety-five theses are about how the prevailing teachings of the Church are oppressive for the average Christian. And Luther seems quite aware of his current events, so he probably knows about the initiation of the slave trade. I'm not sure what the connection is there, but it seems important."

She thinks a moment. "I guess that's a good point." She checks her watch. "Okay, let's take the remainder of the class. That's about fifteen minutes. Maybe we can follow up a bit next class, if people want to." I look over at the student who initially raised his hand. His eyes flash at her, and then at me. The look lasts for just an instant and then is gone.

10

Rondesia and I walk down the street, holding hands. It's nice to have a day away from classes. We move through crowds leaving the UC Berkeley campus. Teenagers with t-shirts proclaiming a hundred different causes and a thousand different musical acts flow past us. One collides with us. His hands grasp our arms and yank them apart. He plows through the gap, and on his way. I turn to look as he walks away.

"That was weird."

"No," she says, "that's how it is."

11

We pull through the toll plaza. I know this means there are twenty minutes left. I check the clock for reference. I try not to count the seconds because it only makes the time go slower, but I can't help it. We make the drive every Sunday, which is the longest seventy minutes of my week. It's because of the conversation. Right now he's saying something about traveling.

"You've been abroad though, right?" I think about how to respond. It's tricky. A longer answer gives me a chance to control the conversation and minimizes the opportunities for weirdness—and it's always weirdness with him—but that requires me to provide more information, and I don't trust him with information. I offer him something he already knows.

"I lived in El Salvador for a year. You know that." I look out the window. We're on the causeway. Soon we'll ascend to the bridge that seems to go on forever. I feel more trapped because of it.

"You have a good time there?"

"Yeah," though that is not how I would describe it.

"Did you meet any girls?" Of course I met girls, but I know he means something else by the question.

"A few."

His grin broadens. "Yeah, you get a kind of special attention as an American abroad." This is also true, but I gather he means something different by the statement than I do. He chuckles. "There was this one girl I met when I was traveling. She picked me out of the crowd right away. Anyway, one thing led to another, and she ended up giving me this incredible massage."

"Oh." I offer the interjection reflexively, a matter of polite pretense. I kick myself for making an opening.

He looks my way and winks. "Happy ending."

I try hard not to form a mental picture. I fail. Now I must look straight forward with a stony face so as not to grimace. There is a pause. He nudges me gently with his elbow. "So, how are things going with you and Rondesia?"

Rondesia told me this would happen. "People will ask you about our sex life," she said. I told her I didn't think it would come up. "You are a White man dating a Black woman. People will ask you about our sex life," she repeated. "When they do, you will tell them nothing." I suppose it has come up before this moment, but in ways I could second-guess or dismiss. Now, context makes it clear what he is asking. I've been silent for too long. I remind myself to answer.

"Fine. Things are going fine." I force myself to keep looking forward and keep my face still. He chuckles again.

"Well, give it time." I look at the clock. Fifteen more minutes.

12

We climb the steps to the apartment. I am a little nervous. This is the first time she's come with me to a gathering of my friends. As we enter the apartment I scan the room. It is lily-White. As it turns out, I only know about ten of the people here. Four of these ten are gathered around the stereo system. One looks up and waves me over. We walk toward him together. I introduce her to the group. I lift my chin in the direction of the sound system.

"What are you doing?"

"He just bought a remastered CD of *The Wall*," he says, pointing to someone I don't know. "We're trying to play it. The system's giving us trouble. Want to look?" It would be a useless effort. I'm terrible with technology.

I turn to Rondesia. "Would you help them out?"

"What?" he interjects.

"Rondesia's great with electronics. And she loves Pink Floyd."

"Really?" He is looking at me, not at her. I'm not sure which of my statements strains his credulity. Her eyes narrow, just a fraction.

"I used to run tech for a television station."

He pauses, then smiles and shakes his head. "Hey. Don't worry about it. We'll figure it out." She shrugs. We wander away, get drinks, and mingle. Fifteen minutes pass. They've made no progress. I turn to her again.

"Please help them."

She curls her lip. "Fine." She steps to the group. There is a negotiation I cannot hear. Eventually, they step back. She begins to work. Conversation stops as the sound of a guitar grinding out power chords fills the room. She steps back. I walk toward her, hopeful. There is a face of triumph she uses sometimes that makes her even more beautiful, but it is absent.

"Come on." She walks away to mingle again. Her face is blank. The rest of the evening is not fun.

13

Rondesia holds my hand. We wait by the podium with my parents, to be seated. The maître d' greets my father.

"Table for three?"

She grips my hand. Hard.

"No, we're four," Dad answers.

"Of course, right this way."

14

I climb the stairs to the stage, walk to the dean of the school, receive the paper with my left hand, and grasp his outstretched palm with my right. I look at the sheet. It is a prize for multicultural ministry. I worked with a Latino congregation for the last two years of my studies. It was difficult for me.

I look out at the audience offering polite applause from their seats. My classmates and several underclassmen are among them. Two are Black, three are Asian. They work in White congregations. I imagine that is difficult for them. They have not received prizes. I have an urge to hand the certificate back. Instead, I look down, leave the stage, and take my seat.

Debriefing Berkeley

Even between the closest people infinite distances exist.
                              —Rainer Maria Rilke, *Letters to a Young Poet*

I was unprepared to fall in love quite so hard and fast. I don't intend any grand romantic overture by this statement, though I do have such sentiments. Rather, I mean that Rondesia took a central place in my life before I could understand what this change would mean. Specifically, with regard to the work you are now reading, I did not understand how this change would bring the question of race into every day of my life that followed.

Of course, race had always guided my life, as it guides every life in this country, but up to this point I was able to ignore its nudging, as I think most White people are able to do. In our nation's racial structure, to be White is taken as default. We don't notice the rails of race that our lives run on because they are built for us. They direct and shape our paths, but they do so gently and comfortably.

There were moments when I had switched tracks and found myself on ill-gauged rails where Whiteness was not assumed. This was the case when I camped out with my Boy Scout troop and during the year I lived in El Salvador. But these were all just sojourns away from my life. They were trips I took to strange-seeming places with the knowledge that I would eventually return to the courses I knew.

Meeting Rondesia was different. I could see early on that our relationship was more than a fling, though I was hesitant to admit that even to myself, much less to her. Our relationship was a part of my life, not some place outside of it. Today, that relationship is very much at the core of things for me. By natural consequence, our love introduced the question of race into my heart, into the places I knew well. It seemed that the world had changed around me. The rails of race never quite fit right again. They were just slightly twisted. I think I still ignore them, most of the time, but there are always twinges of discomfort, jostlings here and there that unbalance me.

I could put it this way. Before I fell in love, I thought of myself as a man who happened to be White. Now I frequently face the fact that I am a White man. Though it is not always on my mind, it is also never far from my thinking. It seems this is not true for all White people who love across lines of color. I find that fact perplexing. Interracial romances are strange, both statistically and by definition. According to the 2010 census, interracial couples accounted for under 7 percent of all marriages.[3] Our relationships unintentionally trouble the racial logic of the country. Conversely, the fundamental injustices of this nation play out within our personal lives. These two facts complicate the already tricky business of maintaining a loving relationship for the long term.

Things have changed somewhat in recent years. When we started dating, interracial couples made up just 2 percent of all marriages.[4] We meet more mixed families than we once did, though still not many. Now and then we see couples like us portrayed in the media. I am grateful for these changes, though they are not unambiguously positive. According to the most recent CDC report, interracial marriages are a third more likely to end in divorce than marriages within race.[5]

Even in fantasy, the outlook is grim. Rondesia and I are both great fans of the cult series *Firefly*. It is unsurprising that a show portraying a complicated, but nonetheless loving, committed, and healthy interracial couple would find itself cancelled after one season, despite rave reviews. We eagerly bought tickets to see its cinematic sequel, *Serenity*. The death of Wash, the husband, during the final act came with the force of inevitability. The pattern is so reliable that when we see an interracial couple in film or on television we play a game, betting how long they will last before betrayal or death tears them apart. We are not meant to live happily ever after.

Because of the strangeness of our relationship, we draw an instant, if sometimes deceptive, sense of kinship with our peers. When we pass a mixed family on the street we share a nod and the hint of a smile.

3. U.S. Census Bureau, *Households and Families: 2010*, 2010 Census Briefs (Washington: U.S. Census Bureau, 2012), 15.

4. U.S. Census Bureau, *America's Family and Living Arrangements: 2000,* 2000 Census Briefs (Washington: U.S. Census Bureau, 2001), 14.

5. National Center for Health Statistics, *Cohabitation, Marriage, Divorce, and Remarriage in the United States* (Washington: National Center for Health Statistics, 2002), 19.

We are drawn to other mixed couples; especially those who have the weight of decades behind them. They give us hope for our own future. And yet, there is often a sense of uncomfortable distance in our experience. We have met a few mixed couples who engage the question of race in ways that seem at least similar, if not identical, to our own negotiations. But, more often, we meet mixed couples who report that race is a non-issue in their relationship. The first person with whom I ever discussed the topic said, "When I look at him, I don't see a Black man, I see my husband."

I have heard many versions of that same statement since. They always unsettle me and leave me with the impression that I am somehow failing at marriage. Every day there comes at least one moment when I am keenly aware that Rondesia is Black and I am White and that there is between us a gulf we cannot bridge. Sometimes an external cue draws attention to the divide. A stranger will treat the two of us as unconnected—as if we just happen to be in the same place, even when all reasonable clues indicate that we are a couple. An acquaintance may take a prurient and crass interest in our sex life. Some institution or authority will grant me deference without merit, while Rondesia is overlooked.

Sometimes the cue comes from within. There are gaps in our experiences. Our childhood reminiscences are fundamentally different, not only in the details, but also in their essence. Artifacts of prejudice rear up in my thinking and assumptions, then land painfully in my actions. Or perhaps, I catch these thoughts before they give rise to action, but still feel their weight. Whatever the case, the divide is laid bare.

I know the contours of the gulf between us better than before. I understand its nature more than I did at first, though in many ways it still confounds me. I walk its edge more nimbly. Early in our relationship, when I glimpsed the divide I was always shocked. I would lunge away, into denial, deflection, or overcompensation. The divide no longer shocks me, though it still surprises me when I trip into it. While I still flail from time to time, in general I manage these missteps with somewhat greater skill.

Rondesia has also grown more skillful, though in truth she came to this canyon already practiced. I have the impression people of color learn to walk the precipice of race at an early age as a matter of necessity and survival. That was certainly true for my wife.

None of our growth has closed the space between us—not even a little. Speaking personally, my ability to carefully tend the question of race has grown exactly in proportion to my awareness of the depth and breadth of that gap. More importantly, it has grown in proportion to the recognition that my side of the chasm was lifted above hers by deliberate human design before either of us was born. This saddens me, but I cannot escape it.

When I meet couples who seem, somehow, to have bridged the divide of race and met at the middle, that sadness grows more acute. I wonder where my wife and I went wrong. I have come to believe that these couples are in denial. Much like Wile E. Coyote, they stand hanging over the chasm, suspended only until one of them looks down and falls. There may be jealousy and bitterness in my assessment, but I think there is truth as well. I have seen some such couples fall apart when the question of race, long ignored, suddenly demands attention.

Rondesia and I have not always faced the question of race well, but I think we have done so honestly, even if that honesty is inconsistent. Much, though not all, of the credit is hers. She is a woman who knows herself and cherishes that knowledge. Pretense may sometimes be an unfortunate necessity of her professional life, but she refuses it at home. Honesty was a precondition of our partnership. I have done my work as well. Together we strive to speak the truth. This is its price: we know we will never bridge the divide between us. And this is its possibility: we may still learn to care for each other until the end.

PART V
Virginia

1

We sit at the table sipping coffee. The mug sits in my left hand. I lay the right one on the table, palm down. I don't know what else to do with it. I'm terrible at coffee hour. I've just graduated and joined Rondesia in Virginia. She's been living and working here for the last year. This is the first time I've visited the congregation where she is volunteering. It is an entirely White church in a very White town. I suppose that works in my favor, but I am, as always, uncomfortable around new people. I remind myself that I came to support her work. I force myself to smile. We all make small talk. Rondesia sees my discomfort. She lays her left hand on top of mine and takes hold. I am grateful. I see the ring I recently placed on her finger.

She checks in with one of her congregants at the table, asking questions about the woman's life. There is a reply, and the woman asks her own question.

"What's new with you?"

"I'm getting married next month." Rondesia smiles as she says it. She has a stunning smile.

"Say, that's right! Congratulations! So, when do we get to meet your fiancé?"

I tense. Rondesia continues smiling, but it is now a fake smile. She lifts the hand with the ring, the hand holding mine, and raises my arm along with hers. "This is him."

I wave, timidly. "I'm the fiancé."

The woman's face flushes. "Oh. I'm sorry. I didn't know."

I am embarrassed. I force a smile. "That's okay. How could you have?" I suppose it's equally likely that I were some random guy holding an engaged woman's hand.

2

I take Rondesia's hand. She kisses me on the cheek. I turn to look at her. She's beautiful. We dressed up, of course. Her parents did too. They sit further down the bench. Across the waiting room is another couple. They did not dress up. And they came alone. They get called first. We wait. Then it is our turn.

We pile into the office. A man is seated at his desk. Under the fluorescent lights, the paleness of his skin takes on a green tone that is not becoming. I look at the underside of my forearm and it is also green. I will suggest that we take pictures outside. He looks at her, and then at me. His mouth tightens.

"Are you the couple?"

"Yes."

He sighs and looks down. I don't know if the sigh is just the monotony of his work, or because we are interracial. Her brother, Ron, who is also in an interracial relationship, once mentioned how this kind of uncertainty is always present—and it's maddening. I hand the man the paper. He scans it, sets it down, and looks up again. I catch a hint of eye roll.

"Dearly beloved . . ."

3

We're heading back to San Francisco for my ordination to the priesthood. We take our seats on the plane. They're too small. The air is stale and funky and they haven't even closed the doors. Rondesia sits by the window. I take the middle. A stranger lays her bag in the aisle seat and walks away. A moment later, she returns.

"Excuse me, I hate to be a bother, but I was wondering if you would trade seats, so I can sit with my boyfriend?" She points to a man sitting several rows ahead.

I look at the man, then back at the stranger. "No."

The woman looks surprised, then angry. "Excuse me?"

I put my hand on top of Rondesia's. "I'm going to be sitting with my wife."

From the corner of my eye, I see Rondesia smile at the stranger; the very sweetest smile you could imagine. Anger turns to embarrassment. The stranger mumbles an apology and walks off to tell her boyfriend.

My wife leans in and whispers, "Queen takes rook." I laugh. She's teaching me to enjoy these moments, when it's possible.

4

We sit down in the bishop's office side by side and wait for him to arrive. We wait for some time. Of course, Rondesia has waited longer. By protocol, he should have seen her more than a year ago, shortly after she arrived in the area as an ordained minister. She called several times but never received an appointment. They said his schedule was full. I called two weeks ago, after we arrived back from my ordination. Two days later, his secretary scheduled a joint appointment.

The bishop enters the office and takes his chair across the desk from us. It is a big chair. We exchange pleasantries. He asks us the standard stuff: who we are, where we are from, what kind of work we would like to do. And then he says, "Do your parents know you're married?"

"Yes?" I am confused, and my answer sounds like a question. He has me off-balance. I look at Rondesia. She is steady—extra steady. It occurs to me that she is bracing herself. The conversation continues.

"And your parents know you're married?" He asks her casually, as if he hadn't asked once already.

"Yes." Her voice is relaxed. I can see she's trying to be casual. I follow her lead. We talk more.

He asks a third time. "So, you've talked with your families about your marriage?"

"Yes." This time her face is blank and her voice is flat.

The conversation continues. We are all polite. At the end, he tells us he is pleased to have us in his diocese. We thank him and leave. We walk to the parking lot. She takes my hand.

"We need to move. There's nothing for us here."

I begin to argue the point. I remind her that she has been called to interview for several positions. "I mean, you've made it to the final round of interviews, like, three times."

She pulls her hand from mine and turns to face me. "And I will keep making it to the final round. I will always make it to the final round. They want me on the slate, because it makes them look good to

105

be considering a Black woman, but they will never hire me. They don't want us here." She pauses. "They don't want me here."

I don't want to believe her. These are good people. Nice people. But all at once, I see that it comes down to a simple choice: do I trust her, or not? I've already made that decision.

"Okay. Let's talk about where else we should start looking."

5

I step into the call center. We've agreed to look for church work out of state. Until that comes through, we need cash. I've taken a customer service job with Cingular Wireless. I scan across the rows of partitions for an open seat. I find one and start to get situated. I have exactly four minutes to get everything in order. I log in first, which gives me time to do the rest while the system loads.

I grabbed three towelettes on the way in. I tear the packets open. They are, technically, moist. They do not smell of alcohol, or soap, or anything that could be considered a cleaning product. I suspect they are just paper towels dipped in water. A woman sits down next to me and pulls a large bottle of hand sanitizer from her bag. She squirts a glob directly onto her keyboard and a second glob onto her headset. That's a new one. I quietly laugh at the absurdity of it. Then I look at my keyboard. There are smudges of something, everywhere. I look at my headset. There is crusted spittle on the mouthpiece. I turn to her.

"Excuse me. Can I get some of that? Please?" She nods and passes the bottle. I thank her. After drowning my own equipment, I wipe it clean with towelettes. Two minutes remaining.

I pull two knitted muffs from my pocket. A coworker makes and sells them. Without the muffs, the bare plastic earpieces of the headset are gross, too loud, and miserably uncomfortable. So, she does good business. My screen is up. I arrange the necessary windows and tool-bars in an efficient configuration, or the one setup that I can remember, anyway. One minute. The supervisor walks down the aisle.

"We're in queue." The whole line sighs. Calls are now coming in back-to-back, with no downtime. I still have thirty seconds. Twenty-five. Twenty-four—forget it. I open the line. A digital sticky note on my screen reminds me, "Greet. Affirm. Empathize. Reassure. Resolve. Evaluate."

The first call beeps in.

I Greet. "Hello, thank you for calling Cingular Customer Service." I give him my name. "May I have your name and telephone number?" He provides it. "How can I help you?"

He's loud. "I'm stranded on the interstate, my friend drives a tow truck, but the call keeps getting dropped. And every time I call, you guys are charging me for a full minute, even though I'm only on the line for five seconds. My balance just went to zero."

I struggle to type a summary of his complaint. I must document everything, but I shouldn't take extra time for notes. I must type, talk, listen, and think at the same time. I am not a good multitasker. As I type, I remind myself to Affirm.

"So, if I understand correctly, you're stranded on the interstate, and trying to call a tow truck. Every time you call, the call gets dropped, and even though you're on the line for a short time, you are being charged for a full minute at each call. Is that correct?"

There is a pause. "Yes! That's what I just said!"

Empathize. "I do understand that this is frustrating."

Reassure. "And I will be able to resolve this issue for you."

Resolve. I suspect there is nothing I can do for him. I check his location on the tower map. It's remote, but he's got good reception.

"I see that you're in a remote area. Were you trying to contact a cell phone number?"

"Yeah. The driver's got a cell phone."

"Well, though we have excellent service in your location, it is a remote area. It's possible the driver is using another carrier with poorer reception." We must imply that other carriers are inferior, but not say so explicitly—that's advertising's job.

"So you're not going to do anything about it?"

"Your phone is working properly, sir."

"Fine, whatever." He breathes out hard. "What about the charges?"

I can credit him; it would be fair. But giving credits without supervisor approval gets checked. You can get points. Enough points and they'll let you go. I believe the supervisors also have to account for the credits they approve.

"Just a moment, sir. Let me put you on hold while I find out what we can do." I raise my hand and wait. A few minutes later, a supervisor approaches.

"What's going on?"

I explain the situation and say, "I'd like to give him a credit."

"The other guy's network is the problem. Cingular's not at fault. You can't give him a credit. Tell him he can add more minutes by card."

"He's gonna want to talk to you."

The supervisor starts to walk away. "If he asks, raise your hand again." I take the customer off hold.

"I'm sorry, sir, but as the other network is at fault, we can't credit you for those calls. I can help you add more funds to your account by debit or credit card, if you'd like."

Silence. "Get me a supervisor."

"Of course. Just a moment while I put you on hold." I raise my hand again. A few minutes later, the same supervisor returns. I take off the headset and hold it out to him. "He wants to talk to you."

He takes the headset. He greets. Affirms. Empathizes. Reassures. He offers, nearly word for word, the same explanation I gave. Then he is silent.

"I'm afraid that's all we can do. Thank you for calling Cingular." He hands the headset back to me and walks away. The customer grudgingly declares that he needs to add funds to his account. I complete the transaction.

Evaluate. "Have we resolved the issue to your satisfaction?"

A long pause. "Are you kidding me? No! You haven't! You know, back when I had a contract phone, I always got good customer service. As soon as I switched to prepaid, it's like you guys don't care anymore." *Of course they don't care*, I think to myself. *They already have your money.*

"I certainly apologize. Cingular works hard to provide first-quality service to all its customers."

"Yeah? Well you suck at it." Click.

A beep informs me the next call has come in. I rush to enter the notes on the previous customer, while simultaneously greeting the new arrival.

"Hello, thank you for calling Cingular Customer Service . . ." I see the words "Hello, thank you for calling Cingular Customer Service" that I've just typed into the log of the previous call. Again, I'm not good at multitasking.

Two hours pass. We're finally out of queue. A supervisor walks by and hits the "log out" button on my phone.

"After this call, head to Feedback." I nod. Twice a week we go to Feedback for work evaluations. I finish my call, and head to a small cubicle in the rear of the room. The man there waves me in. He doesn't speak to me. He brings up my file and retrieves the log of a random call from yesterday. He motions to me to put on one of the two headsets plugged into the computer. A window opens and I see the image of my own desktop on the call line. He's about to play the call, but pauses.

"What's that?" He points to the digital notepad in the corner of the screen. Hyphens, slashes, and Os trace out a crude frowny face:

```
      -    -    -
 /  0  _  0  \
 \  /      \  /
```

I shrug. "We must have been out of queue." He looks at me and blinks. I feel my face flush. "Sometimes I doodle if we've got downtime."

"The notepad is for logging calls."

"Okay."

"And if you have downtime between calls, you should be using the tutorials program to expand your skill set." He says these words entirely in monotone, with his eyes half closed. He hits the play button. The cursor jumps to life on the screen and I hear my own voice in the headset. "Hello, thank you for calling Cingular Customer Service . . ." We listen and watch until the end of the call. He takes off his headset.

"What did you do wrong?"

I stare blankly and shrug slightly.

"You didn't empathize." Not true. That man was being spammed with text message jokes. It burned through his account balance. I felt his pain.

"Right."

"Make sure you look at the prompts."

"Right."

"Other than that, it was okay." He brings up my call stats. "You are taking way too long, though. Remember, par time for a call is one minute fifteen seconds." Greet, Affirm, Empathize, Reassure, Resolve, Evaluate. Document everything. Seventy-five seconds. He taps a number on the screen. "Your average is two minutes thirty-two seconds."

A hundred and fifty-two seconds. How to cut eighty seconds? I imagine a scenario: "Hi. You have a problem? That sucks. I'll fix it. Sorry, can't do anything. Was this good for you?" Eight seconds. Another eight to document. Sixteen seconds. I'd be a rock star. I nod.

"Right."

He marks a couple bubbles on a sheet of paper with my name. He looks down at a clipboard. "You can go back to your station."

Things are slow until lunch. I clock out and head to the break room. It's hot and it's raining hard. I eat lunch. The TV hanging in the corner reports that a storm outside has been upgraded to a tropical depression. Good. With luck it will spend the day slouching on the couch in Cheeto-stained sweatpants. I finish lunch and go back to the line. A customer needs to add funds with American Express. There's a third-party vendor for that. I put him on hold and call the number.

Per policy, I should make a "cold transfer"—I would dial the Amex number, switch him over, and hang up. If the customer is confused about the process, I can make a "warm transfer" and stay on the line until the other agent picks up, then explain the situation, introduce the customer, and hang up. We are trained to do this only once for any given customer. The first time I did a warm transfer I learned the Amex service line plays a continuous loop of Debussy's "Claire de Lune" for customers on hold.

This customer has called in before. He asks to be transferred to the Amex line. He knows the drill. I open the call log: "Customer was confused. Warm transferred to Amex payment." I hear the overly sentimental tones of a piano solo and breathe normally for two minutes. The call ends. I hear the storm outside. A supervisor passes through the aisle.

"There's some flooding on the roads, but it's mild. Be careful driving home at the end of your shift." He emphasizes the word "end."

My wife used to work here. She heard employees talk. Two years ago, a hurricane came through and they wouldn't let anyone go home.

The fire department arrived and forced them to close the call center. I assume one of the employees put in the call.

People at the back corner of the room start coughing. It spreads our direction. I feel my eyes itch. I cough. A supervisor walks down the aisle quickly.

"We're getting fans in to clear the air. Stay calm. Stay on the line. We're still in queue."

After he passes, I ask myself out loud, "What's going on?" My customer is probably confused.

The man next to me shakes his head. "Someone set off pepper spray." The flatness of his tone contrasts with his rainbow sweater, which contrasts in turn with his dark skin. I heard him chatting once in the lunch room. He hates it here, but he's got a conviction for possession on his record. I think he said it happened in high school. He had tried for a while to find another job, but this was the only place that would hire him, so he's stuck. He was wearing a different rainbow sweater when he told that story, which was what caught my attention. He relayed the whole account with the same flat monotone. He is unsurprised by the pepper spray incident. I assume his customer is probably confused too.

A woman runs through the aisle towards the door. Her eyes stream. She hacks. Between coughs, she whispers to no one and everyone, "I'm sorry. I thought they would let us leave."

The man in the rainbow sweater shakes his head. "Another day on the plantation." Now I know his customer is confused.

———

I arrive for another day at the call center. I scan the rows of partitions for an open spot. For the first time ever, I am happy to be here. I find a seat, log in, get myself situated, and begin. The first call comes in.

Greet. "Thank you for calling Cingular Customer Service, may I have your name and telephone number?" The caller provides the information. "And how can I help you today?"

"I want to set it up so my number doesn't show up on caller ID. I also want it so that if someone calls me without caller ID, they can't get through."

It occurs to me that, if universalized, this scheme would render telephones useless. I ignore the thought and Affirm. "So, if I understand correctly, you want to turn on caller ID blocking and screen out callers who are using caller ID blocking?"

"Yes. That's what I want to do."

Empathize. "I can certainly understand your desire to protect your privacy." Reassure. "I'm sure I can take care of it for you." Resolve. I handle the process in a matter of seconds. It's "standard." Evaluate. "Was I able to address you concerns today?"

"Uh. Sure. Thank you."

"Have a good day." Before logging out of the call, I credit her account twenty-five dollars, the maximum the system will allow. The next call comes in. At the end of my shift I log out and walk away. I've given away over seven hundred dollars in credits today. I imagine my supervisor will want to talk with me about it tomorrow. Except I won't be here tomorrow. I've gotten a better job and I don't need this place. The automatic sliding doors open ahead of me. I turn for one last look and see the man in the rainbow sweater. He is on a call. His voice is as flat as ever.

6

I've just completed training at the shipyard. This will be my first day working. I follow the supervisor up the gangplank, carrying my locker. Thankfully, there's nothing in it yet. We pass a name stenciled across the side of the boat: USS *George H.W. Bush*.

I imagine it must be nice to give your father an aircraft carrier as a gift. I follow the green triangle on the supervisor's hard hat as he winds down several twisting corridors. I try to memorize the turns. I almost hit my head as we pass through a porthole. He walks toward a group of men standing together. He jerks his thumb in my direction.

"New guy." They nod and he walks away. I extend my hand in greeting to the oldest-looking man. He ignores it, and points to his head.

"Hat."

"What?"

"Put your hard hat on. You gotta have your hat on before the first bell. Regulation." I put my hat on. When I'm done he extends his hand. I offer my name. He cuts me off. "I know." He points to the other two. "General Frog, Smoothbite." I gather these are nicknames. He taps his chest. "Boone. When Mr. G isn't here, you do what I say."

I nod.

He points to the locker. "What you got in there?"

"Nothing."

"You got a ruler?"

I shake my head.

"Pencil? Pad?"

I nod. He strokes his chin. The bell rings. He gives directions to the other two, then turns his attention to me.

"Drag your locker over there to the corner, then follow me." We descend even further, into the engine room. There are more twists and turns. He stops in front of a mass of small, interconnected pipes. "The crew is working on the secondary air system. That's the next couple weeks right there. You have to remember that. Navy boys come

through sometimes—they may ask you what you're doing. You gotta
have an answer. When they ask, you say, 'I'm working on secondary
air.' Can you remember that?"

I nod. "What does secondary air do?"

"Doesn't matter. They never ask that." He points to the mass of
tubes in front of him. "This is the control system. That's my job today.
You'll be working with me. First thing you need to do is get your tools.
Take out your pad." He lists six items. I know what two of them are.
I write them down. He has me read this list back to him. "Go up to
the tool library. Check out everything on that list. You have to give
them your employee number. And buy yourself a ruler. They take it
out of your paycheck. Drop everything but the ruler in your locker,
then meet me back here when you're done. Got it?"

I shake my head. "Where's the tool library?"

He jerks a thumb toward the stairs. "Main deck. Then ask
somebody."

He gets to work; I head for the stairs. I hit my head at the door.
It only startles me, thanks to the hard hat. I reach the main deck but
I have to stop three times on the way for directions. I find the tool
library, buy a ruler, and then hand over the list. The man at the desk
shakes his head.

"You can't carry all this in one go." He hands me back the list,
along with a grinder and two large pipe cutters. "Take that, then come
back for the rest."

It takes three trips. I stow the tools and head back down to the
engine room.

Boone sees me. "Did you get everything?"

I nod.

"Get your pad." I get it out, along with a pencil. He points to two
small pipes above us. Their ends turn down towards us. "I'm about to
finish up. When I do, we'll connect the control system to the overhead
pipes. I need you to go to the supply shed and pick up the pipe we're
going to run."

"I know where the supply shed is." He looks at me blankly. It is the
look one would give a grownup who declared they had just learned to
tie their own shoes.

"Write this down: Ten feet of three-quarter-inch copper. Get six of them." He cocks his head slightly to indicate I should go. I do. It's a ten-minute walk. The man behind the counter is my age. I give him the order. He brings the pipe.

The six pipes are heavy. But more than that, they're ten feet long, and don't want to stay together, at all. I struggle my way out of the shed. I'm certain I look like something out of a Chaplin movie. At the door, one pipe gets loose. I reach to recover it and the other five fall to the ground. A woman has just entered the shed and looks somewhere between amused and annoyed.

"First day?"

"Yeah."

She points at a tape dispenser on the counter. "It helps if you tape them. Wrap two pipes together at the ends and the middle. Then do the other two. Then the last two. Then wrap the whole thing at the ends and the middle." She walks away without waiting for a reply.

I collect the pipes, haul them back, wrap them, and head out again. There are more Chaplin outtakes as I navigate the ten-foot-long bundle through the narrow corridors of the aircraft carrier. A couple times I almost knock someone over. My arms are shaking from the load by the time I make it back to Boone. I hope he doesn't notice this fact.

He sees me and frowns. "Use the hole next time." He points at a load of hangers being lowered on a cable through a section of unfinished flooring. "It runs all the way to the top deck."

"Right." I set the pipes down. He glances at them and gets back to work.

"That's the wrong pipe."

"I told the guy exactly what you said."

"Six, ten-foot, three-quarter-inch, copper?"

"Yes."

"What did the guy behind the desk look like?"

I describe him as best as I am able. Boone cuts me off.

"New guy. Like you. He didn't know." He points again, without looking. "That brown color? That's copper-nickel. Copper is orange.

Like this." He taps the pipe he's working on with a wrench. "Go back and get the copper."

My shoulders fall. "Sure." I stoop to lift the copper-nickel pipes.

He waves me away. "Leave 'em. We'll need them for something else."

I make the trip again. The lunch bell rings as I deliver the second set. Everyone flees the engine room. I begin to follow. He puts a hand on my shoulder.

"Wait." When everyone's left he speaks again. "We work through lunch."

I'm confused. "So, we don't eat?"

"We take a fifteen-minute break at one thirty. That way we get off work fifteen minutes early."

"It's just fifteen minutes. Why bother?"

"Thousands of people work the yard. At five o'clock they all run to the parking lot. And then every single one of them has to get across the bridge. That's an instant traffic jam. We're only getting out fifteen minutes early, but it saves forty-five minutes on the commute. So you get home an hour earlier for the same pay."

"Okay."

"We'll fit that pipe now."

While I was gone he had finished the control system and welded two L-shaped bends onto the pipes above. He points to the ceiling. "It's about sixteen feet to the overhead. We do it in two parts."

"Eight feet and eight feet?"

He shakes his head. "Ten and six. Always use the longest length of pipe you can. Less weight, less waste, less work."

"Nice alliteration." He looks at me and seems to roll his eyes without actually moving them.

"Give me one of the pipes." I unwrap one, and hand it to him.

"Wait, there's one intake and one output, and two lengths of pipe for each." My arms are still burning and I'm angry. "We only need four lengths. You had me get six."

"I did." I can see there won't be any more explanation. I hand him the pipe. He fits it into a bend at the top of the control system and holds it vertically against the wall. His free hand points to a small copper something on the ground. "Get that fitting off the floor, climb up there, put it on the pipe, and measure the distance from the top of one fitting to the bottom of the other. Then add half an inch for the space in the fittings."

I am relieved. Climbing is something I'm good at. Hanging off a beam with one hand while getting an accurate measurement using a folding ruler with the other, not so much. Eventually, I manage it.

"Five feet, seven and a half." I look down.

He shakes his head. "Try again."

"What?"

"You did it wrong. Try again."

I do. He talks me through it. He is satisfied with my third attempt. Five feet eight and a quarter. I climb down. He's already working when I land on the deck.

"I'll get this in place. You cut another pipe, five feet eight and a quarter. After you cut it, use the file to clean the cut. Then bring it to me."

When I get back, he's welded the first pipe into the system control, attached the fitting to the open end, and welded a pipe hanger in place along the wall. I hand him the pipe.

"That's short."

"I measured it."

"It's short." He sees my disbelief and shrugs. "Go ahead and put it up."

I climb up and fit the cut pipe in place. It's about two inches short. I would be impressed that he eyeballed the difference between five feet six inches and five feet eight inches, except that I'm more embarrassed about messing up.

"Go cut another. If my math is right, we've got two extra pipes." He manages to say this with almost no snark. Almost. I pick up another length of pipe. He stops me. "Measure twice." We finish both the ascending pipes. Folks have filed back into the engine room. He checks his watch. "Break time."

I follow him upstairs. There's a small room the crew has claimed. The same one I dropped my locker in. I have no idea what its purpose will be when the ship is complete. We all get our lunches and sit. I eat.

"Look at that!" General Frog is pointing at the sandwich in my hand. "How much peanut butter you got on that?"

I look at the sandwich. "I don't know. A lot?"

"Smoothbite, look at this man's sandwich: peanut butter three-quarters-inch thick." The statement is oddly specific. I wonder if he's as good as Boone at estimating lengths. I shrug it off. Smoothbite looks and shakes his head, takes out his lunch and eats.

I try to make small talk. "So, why do they call you Smoothbite?"

He sighs, stands up, walks to the far side of the room, sits again, and starts eating his lunch. General Frog rests his chin in his hand and looks at me. He's smiling.

"What was that about?" I whisper.

"He's got no teeth."

"Yes he does. I saw them."

He shakes his head. "Dentures. Top and bottom. He's embarrassed about it. You shouldn't have asked."

"But, you called him Smoothbite."

"That doesn't mean you get to ask about it."

There are too many rules here. We finish. Boone manages to eat his lunch and get in a ten-minute nap before his watch alarm goes off. I imagine this takes practice. We get up, and file out. I start to follow Boone.

General Frog yells out. "Hey Boone, do you need him? I could use some help." Boone looks at me, then back at General Frog and nods. Frog jerks a thumb over his shoulder. "Peanut, you're with me." I'm confused. He points at me. "You, Peanut. Follow me." I've acquired a nickname. I wish it had been something else, but I guess Smoothbite isn't happy about his either. He takes me to another section of the engine room. As we walk, he asks, "So, how bad did you screw up today?"

"Excuse me?"

He turns, and repeats each syllable. Slowly. "How . . . bad . . . did . . . you . . . screw . . . up . . . to . . . day?"

I laugh, then think back. "Pretty bad?"

"Don't sweat it. Everybody screws up their first day."

"I don't know. Boone seemed pretty happy to get rid of me."

"Did you break anything?"

"I cut some pipe the wrong length."

"That's no deal. Did you make the same mistake twice?" I shake my head. "It's fine then. Boone only gets mad if you make a mistake he already told you how to fix." We've reached the back corner of the engine room. He squats down and points to the floor grate. There's a length of pipe running under it. "That's the bottom half of secondary air." He looks up at me. "Secondary air is what we're working on. You gotta remember that."

"Boone told me the Navy officers ask about it sometimes."

He nods. "Anyway, I laid the pipe. I can do that from here. But, the hangers have to attach to the bottom deck. And I'm too big to fit down there." He stands, smiles broadly, and puts a hand on my shoulder. "You're going into the bilge." I take it this is not a good thing. "I already measured and cut the hangers, but I can't get the right angle to weld them in place from the deck. I need someone to do the work from below. That's your job."

"Oh. I'm sorry. I haven't had the welding class yet. I don't know how."

"Good thing I'm going to show you, then."

"What I mean is, I'm not certified. It's not allowed."

He pantomimes looking around. "There's no one here but us. You snitching?"

"No."

"Me neither." He lifts up one of the floor grates, and points down. "Get in the bilge." I step down. I can see what he means. The clearance is really low. He hands me three small rods, a piece of dark glass, and what looks like the end of a jumper cable. "You're gonna have to get on your belly and shimmy over to the pipes. I'll switch on the juice when you get there." I stuff the rods and the glass into my pocket, grasp the jumper cable thing, and start to lower myself onto my stomach. "Oh. And watch out for the crap."

I stand up again. "What crap?"

"Crap? It comes out your rear." He raises an eyebrow. "Or do you need a certification for that too?" I know I will be opening myself up for another joke. But I do require more clarification.

"Why would there be crap down here?"

"Bathrooms are on main deck. That's ten flights of stairs. I don't know if you've noticed but there are some nasty, lazy people in this world."

I pause. "Please tell me you're messing with me."

His face doesn't move. My face scrunches. "Is this some kind of hazing?"

"No." I hear a voice behind me. It's Boone. "You're the smallest man on the crew. By far." I hate that I'm embarrassed by this statement. Regardless, it is true. "We need someone in the bilge. You're the size for the job. That's all. Get to it." As he walks away, he adds, "But make sure you watch out for the crap."

I breathe in. Then get onto my belly and start to shimmy. I find the pipes. General Frog passes me a hanger through the gap between the grate and the wall. He talks me through fixing it in place. He shines a flashlight down, to confirm I've done it properly.

"Now put the stick in the electrode."

"The what?"

He points to the clamp in my hand. "That. Once I turn the power on, strike it against the deck, like a match, then drag it across the gap between the hanger and the deck. Make sure your hand is only touching the rubber part of the grip. Use the glass to see what you're doing. You ready?"

No, I'm terrified. "Yep."

"I'm turning the power on now." It takes several tries to strike the stick. I finally get it and begin welding. I'm far more excited and scared about this than I should be. I finish. I've burned through about two-thirds of the stick. General Frog shines his light down to look. "Wow. That is the ugliest welding job I've ever seen."

I want to protest, but I can see what I've done. It looks like a small metal dog took a dump on the deck. I breathe out.

"Do I need to redo it?"

"Pull on the hanger. Hard as you can."

I do. It doesn't move.

"It'll do. Next time, keep the tip of the stick right in the gap. And don't use so much. You just need enough to fill the space." He hands me another hanger. And another. And another. After the last one is welded in place, I look to my left. There is a row of ten neatly spaced hangers already set up. The welding at their base is tidy.

"Say, Frog?"

"Yeah?"

I point to these other hangers. "Who did those?"

"Me."

"When?"

"Yesterday."

I frown. "I thought you said you couldn't fit down here."

"I can't."

"But you did yesterday."

"Yesterday, you weren't here."

I turn awkwardly and shimmy my way out. My hand lands in something. It seems the General was not messing with me. In the bathrooms on the main deck, I scrub my hand for twenty minutes. When I get back to the engine room, there's a man in a vest addressing the crew. In one very obvious respect I have more in common with him than anyone else here: he and I are White and they are not.

He sees me. "Hi, I'm Frank. I just finished handing out the assignments for tomorrow. You'll be working with Thomas again." I look, and see he's pointing to General Frog. "Martin says you did alright today." He points again. I'm surprised. I had assumed Boone was his real name. He turns to face me. "Have you thought about applying for the supervisor training?"

I glance to the left and right to make sure he's talking to me. "No. Not really."

"You should, I think you'd be a good fit." In three respects this statement makes no sense. First, I've made a fool of myself ten different ways today. Second, I have done nothing that resembles leadership or supervision. Third, Mr. G doesn't know me at all. He smiles and checks his watch. "Anyway, day's over in five minutes. Go ahead and stow your hat." He heads for the main deck. We find our lockers. I wait until Mr. G is out of sight, then turn to Boone.

"So, I guess he says that to everybody on their first day." He doesn't reply, so I clarify. "I mean about applying for the supervisor training."

Boone takes a seat and unties his work boots. He doesn't look up. "No."

I get home and head straight for the shower. The water rolling off my body is black. I finish, dry off, and blow my nose. I look at the tissue. It is black too.

7

Tomorrow we have off for Thanksgiving. I am grateful for the break. General Frog organized an impromptu potluck for today. I can't cook and our household budget is thin, so my contribution is three cans of Glory Greens drained and emptied into a bowl that I covered with tinfoil. I'm banking on folks thinking they're homemade. It is a typical potluck: some dishes are amazing, some require me to choke down mouthfuls and force a smile. Mr. G brought a white potato pie. I can't understand why anyone would do such a thing.

Smoothbite is finishing off a helping of the greens I brought. I've put a lot of work into mending fences with him. He jabs the pile with his fork. "Hey, Peanut. These greens got soul." I smile at the subtext: despite my Whiteness, the greens are good. Though my success came under false pretenses, I appreciate the sense of welcome in the compliment.

"Don't do that." Boone shakes his head. Smoothbite looks up. Boone stares him in the eye. "Don't do that. You know these are canned greens." My smile fades and I look down. As my de facto boss for most of the day, Boone is stern, fair, and not unkind. But he has no patience for pretense. I am pretending, and he is not fooled.

8

Frog kneels down to inspect the section of pipe I just completed.
"Getting better. Slowly."

"What?"

"You're getting better." He smiles. "Very slowly."

I laugh. He winces as he stands up. "So, what do you think?"

I don't understand. He puts his hand against the small of his back and grimaces again. "You've been here a few months. What do you think?"

"I like it. I learn something new every day. It's fun."

He seems to frown and smile at the same time. "Yeah. I remember that." He pats me on the shoulder. "Just wait till your knees are torn up and the coughing starts."

"Coughing?"

"You get black boogers at the end of the day?"

I laugh. "Yeah. It's pretty nasty."

His face goes blank. "You think about what you're breathing in that makes them black?"

My face goes blank too. "No."

"Yeah. I try not to think about it either, but that doesn't keep it from getting in my lungs."

"They say the new stuff is safe."

"They said that about asbestos." He sits and rubs his knees. "This job? It's less fun after the first year." I put on a serious face, like I'm thinking about my future, but I'm pretending again. I got the call I was waiting for this morning—a church job in Maryland. I'll give notice tomorrow. In two weeks I'll be gone. And then, I realize that, for me, this job has been fun precisely because I knew I would be leaving. It's a bizarre, exhausting vacation. For Frog, it is life. "Come on. Someone screwed up one of the valves. I gotta pull it apart and start over. I'll show you how to clean the braising off."

I follow. As always, I'm happy to learn something new.

Debriefing Virginia

No matter where you go, there you are.

—Buckaroo Banzai, *The Adventures of Buckaroo Banzai
Across the 8th Dimension*

Rondesia graduated and was ordained a deacon a year ahead of me. There were no church jobs available in Spokane, her sponsoring diocese. So that she could help support her mother, she moved to the Tidewater area in Virginia. We were engaged at the time and we decided that I would finish my studies and then come out to join her.

Our year apart was difficult but clarifying. It confirmed that we wanted no future except the one we could build together. I missed her every day. She felt the same, though her situation was compounded by the sting of rejection. During a year of submitting resumes, taking interviews, and networking, she made no inroads toward a paying position in the Diocese of Virginia. She took secular employment and volunteered as a minister at a local congregation.

After completing my degree and being ordained a deacon, I joined her in Virginia and also in rejection. The diocese made some initial overtures of interest. I received a couple calls from congregations in the area but nothing came of them. We got an appointment to talk with the bishop, something that had not been given to Rondesia alone. The meeting made it clear that we, as a couple, were the issue. As an individual, I was welcome in the diocese. Together we were not.

Having no immediate prospects for church work, I turned, like my wife, to the secular world, where I faced still more rejection. Unless you were military, jobs were scarce in the area. This had nothing to do with our relationship, but it was new for me. I had never before been turned down when applying for a job. I had never been fired. And it had never before occurred to me that class, as well as race, shielded me from these things.

Now it seemed I had misplaced that shield somewhere. Money was tight. Our future felt uncertain. I had a three-month forbearance on my student loans. I watched those months slipping away. Finally,

Rondesia suggested I take a job at a nearby call center, a place she had once worked. She had initially recommended against it because it was a terrible place to work and the pay wasn't good. But they had high turn-over, and so they were always hiring.

I was hired the day after I interviewed. It was, as Rondesia had warned, a terrible place to work. I searched for something better, but the search was complicated. The call center paid minimum wage. I had to put in lots of overtime to pick up my end of our budget. By the end of my time there I was covering eleven-hour shifts Monday through Saturday. Rondesia once joked that I had traveled across the country just so that we could never see each other. Neither of us laughed. In any case there was little time to find another job. On my one day off, I was usually too tired to look.

A friend of the family suggested I try applying at the shipyard. I had no interest, but I was desperate to find something else. I took a sick day and applied that morning. I set an appointment that afternoon with an employment agency. Both the shipyard and the agency got back to me the next day. The two opportunities held equally little interest for me. So, I flipped a coin. Three weeks later I started at the Newport News Shipyard and Dry Dock Company. Despite my low expectations, I loved it. The pay was better. The labor was physical, and exercise improved my mood. I was always learning. The work environment, if strict, was also fair and consistent—two things the call center lacked. Nonetheless, I had an abiding sense of being out of place.

I thought of this time as a kind of sojourn from my class, much as El Salvador had been a kind of sojourn from my race. It offered similar insights and was bound by similar limitations. It was temporary, for instance. I didn't know how we would exit our current situation, but I had a confidence that it would happen. I knew that, sooner or later, I would return to a trajectory towards a life in the professional class. This moment was passing, and that awareness made it more bearable.

I remember thinking at some point during my time in Virginia that it was class, not race, that divided the communities where we lived. This was by no means an original thought. It is the habit of many Americans, especially White liberal Americans, to explain racial injustice as arising from class inequalities, or else to dismiss it entirely as secondary to considerations of class. I understand the allure of this way of thinking.

We imagine race to be biological. We think it has something to do with genetics and how we trace our ancestry. Serious research into the matter has long since proved such imaginations both fanciful and mythic. Nonetheless, these ideas persist.[6] Accordingly, we assume racial divisions to be immutable "scientific" realities. Personally, I notice this assumption holds at a subconscious level, even as consciously I affirm that race is a social construction. By contrast, we imagine class divisions to be permeable. Indeed, the foundational myth of our nation, the American Dream, depends on the idea that a person can climb from the class of their birth to a higher class.

Faced with the choice between "immovable" race and "shifting" class, it is unsurprising Americans, with our professed love for equality, prefer to think in terms of class. If class can be altered, then it carries the hope that the enduring inequalities of our nation can be remedied. Further, for we who are White, a class-based analysis of society offers the possibility of ancestral absolution. As a nation we are roughly fifteen generations old. This depth of ancestry means a majority of White people, regardless of our current class, can identify at least a few poor ancestors who climbed the social ladder. For those of us born into the middle or upper class, this fact is vital for our ability to claim the myth of the American Dream as our own. It may also provide a counter-narrative to the recognition of class-based oppression in our family tree.

No such possibility exists when we consider our world through the lens of race. The "one drop" rules still apply in America. If you are White, by assumption, all your ancestors are White. Should it come to light that this is not the case, many White people will wonder if they should check a different box in the "race" category of government forms. And I suspect few of us want that. We would prefer to go on claiming a White identity, while simultaneously finding absolution from its oppressive history. A class-based analysis accomplishes this.

---

6. For a succinct summary of the evidence, see Michael Yudell et al., "Taking Race Out of Human Genetics," *Science*, vol. 351 (2016): 564–565.

Unfortunately, class fails to fully explain the world we live in. Race may indeed be an artificial construct, but mere recognition of this fact does not rob its durability or power. Steam-rollers are also artificial constructs. Knowledge of this fact provides no comfort to a man being flattened by one. Indeed, for all their artifice, racial categories appear more durable than those of class. Black children are less likely to ascend beyond their parents' economic level, as compared to White children. And Black children born to parents who have ascended economically are more likely to slip back down the economic ladder than White children in similar circumstances.[7]

Racial inequalities persist at all class levels. I think, if we looked honestly at our own life experience, this fact would not surprise us. I saw it very clearly in Virginia. Working at the call center was certainly the worst job I have ever held. And as far as I could see it was bad from the top to the bottom. The supervisors and trainers were only marginally better paid and afforded only slightly more dignity. But that did not change the very obvious fact that people who looked like me were overrepresented among the supervisorly ranks, and underrepresented among those working the call line. When my coworker declared our call center to be "the plantation," he was speaking hyperbolically but he may have been accurately describing an aspect of the call-center's lineage. The same dynamic was evident at the shipyard. Here there were good jobs, paying a decent wage and affording respect. This was due, in no small part, to the yard's strong and active union. But here as well, the workforce was racialized. Whites were disproportionately represented among supervisors. My own foreman immediately designated me as "supervisor material" despite my lackluster performance and the fact that I had listed my education only as "high school diploma."

Though our situation was uncertain, I could be confident that my skin would open doors before me, somewhere. When money is tight, a vague awareness of this fact has always offered hope. Of course, there is some fantasy in that feeling. Many White Americans live in

---

7. Tom Hertz, "Rags, Riches and Race: The Intergenerational Economic Mobility of Black and White Families in the United States," in *Unequal Chances: Family Background and Economic Success*, ed. Samuel Bowles, Herbert Gintis, and Melissa Osborne Groves (Princeton: Princeton University Press, 2010), 165–91.

abject poverty. But there is also some reality in that hope. My skin is a resource that cannot be taken away, regardless of circumstance. While it offers no certainties, as a matter of probability, its benefits are concrete and measurable. It suggests that, come what may, there is a limit to how far I can fall. This fact is a comfort to me, despite all that is wrong with it. And there is much that is wrong with it. That a foreman who did not know me at all would identify me as supervisor material was dependent on him overlooking more qualified candidates of darker tones. The comfort and security my skin provides is a simple mathematical corollary of the discomfort and insecurity inflicted on the skin of others. The privilege I enjoy is built on the oppression of others. And this holds true regardless of how my financial situation may change.

PART VI

MARYLAND

1

We have settled into our new apartment. Sunday will be my first worship service with the congregation. I want to make a good impression. I should trim my hair; I let it get a bit shaggy the last couple months. The clippers are dirty. I need to clean them.

I bring them to the bathroom and take them apart. I push the plug down on the sink and pour three fingers of rubbing alcohol into the basin. One by one I drop the parts into the liquid and let them soak. I look through the bathroom door at my wife. She sits on the bed talking to her brother on the phone. How long does it take alcohol to disinfect? I'm unsure. Minutes later, I pull the plug and drain the basin. I remove the parts, wipe them down, and lay them on the counter to air dry. The process has left quite a lot of alcohol on my fingers. I can feel the strange thinness of the stuff: a liquid that feels dry.

It sparks a memory of a cold Halloween night when a group of friends and I were about to play with fire in front of a crowd of drunken college students. It was a thing we did every year. There were some marginal safety procedures in play. We had discovered that it was possible to soak tennis balls in alcohol, light them, and juggle them without protection. Alcohol burns relatively cool, so it wasn't dangerous. If the breeze was chilly, the heat was actually pleasant.

I look at the bottle of isopropyl in my hand, and the lighter we use for incense in the corner of the bathroom. I wonder if I can light my hand on fire without suffering injury.

I discover I can. However, I did not consider the fact that while pouring alcohol on my fingers, I was also coating the basin below them. A drop of flaming liquid rolls off my thumb and into the sink, creating a fireball beneath my hands. My wife sighs and rolls her eyes.

"I should go," she says to her brother. "My husband just lit the bathroom on fire. No, we're still on for next Thursday. Okay, I'll see you then."

I turn on the water, rinse the flames away, and smile. I love the way she puts up with my absurdities. My smile fades as I wonder what else she puts up with.

2

Rondesia asks if I want help.

"Don't worry, I've got this." I step out onto the stoop and sink to my calves. I'm cold. And thrilled. This is the first storm of the season, and for me, the first that I have ever had to really deal with.

I tromp down the steps to our cars and begin shoveling. The work and the Saturday morning sun warm me quickly. My neighbor makes his way out and begins shoveling out his Taurus. We greet each other and smile. He makes a terrible joke about shoveling. I laugh anyway, and not just to be polite. More people file out of their homes and begin working. My neighbor and I finish first, and then move on to help the others. Some children are in the mix, running through the drifts as best as they are able. A snowball battle breaks out. Laughter and smiles are everywhere. We all work until every car and stoop is clean.

An hour later, I fall back into the house, exhausted. But it was a beautiful morning. Rondesia sits at the kitchen table in pajamas, sipping cocoa.

I tell her, "Snowstorms aren't half bad. There's a real sense of community. You know? Looking out for each other, helping out, and all that."

She smirks and shakes her head. "Just wait."

I scoff at her cynicism.

———

It is Wednesday. It snowed again. She asks if I want help.

I shake my head. "I've got this."

"You sure?"

"Like I said, it's fun." I step out onto the stoop, shovel in hand, and sink up to my knees. I see my neighbor shoveling.

"Good morning!" He limply waves back, before continuing to shovel. He makes no eye contact. I begin shoveling. It rained at some point. The top layer of snow has frozen into a thick sheet of ice. I chip at it, and shovel. I shovel, and chip. Others appear and do likewise. No one speaks or looks at one another. Their reclusiveness bothers me. Then, slowly, I understand. Half an hour later, I finish. Everything hurts. A man walks up. I see a request forming in his eyes. I adopt a defensive posture that he pretends not to notice.

"Say, would you mind helping me dig my car out? I hate to ask, but I'm late for work."

I want to kick him. My eyes narrow. As I glare at him, I see my wife looking out from the window of our home. She smirks. I can see her eyes forming the phrase "real sense of community." I look back to the man.

"Fine." I wonder if it would still be considered neighborly if I helped him first, and then kicked him. Another fifteen minutes and we are done. I stumble away without a word as soon as we finish. It is possible he thanks me. I don't know and I certainly don't care.

I trudge back to the building. As I reach the door, the man from the last house on the end steps out onto his stoop. He always parks in the corner—the same corner that the plow used as a snow depository. I can only assume his minivan lies somewhere under the icy hill I see. He looks at it for a moment and then turns back into the flat and closes the door behind him. I trudge up our steps. She sits, sipping cocoa.

"Did you have fun?"

I sneer at her sarcastic insight, but she was right. Work that is exciting and new the first time quickly becomes tiresome. Then it's just a matter of continuing to shovel.

3

I realize I'm midway through reading a paragraph describing the echidna's foraging habits and stop myself. Wikipedia sings a terrible siren's song for procrastinators. I close the browser window. "Focus." I hear a clicking noise, and look down. My right hand is sliding two paper clips apart and then back together in quick repetition. "Stop. Focus." I put the paper clips down and look again at the scripture for Sunday. This is also a dodge. I've read it so many times I have it memorized. "Just get it done. It doesn't matter if it's bad. Everyone writes bad sermons sometimes." I open Word, look up at the ceiling, and type. I know this is a mistake. I am a terrible typist. I talk to myself as I write.

"Today we heard a reading from Luke's gospel. It's his version of the Christmas story. When we think about the story of Jesus's birth, we tend to smash all the accounts together. We imagine a manger, shepherds and sheep, and a chorus of angels, three kings, and a star overhead. Of course, all of these elements appear in scripture, but they don't appear together. By combining them, we obscure the unique perspective of each gospel. We lose the message. Luke's gospel has a particular message to share: the Son of God was born into poverty and hardship."

I hear my own words and I hate them. I've been working here two years and already Christmas has become a chore. I hate that, too. I look to see what I have written, and review the expected massacre of letters my touch-typing has produced:

Today we heard a reading from Skywalker's happy book. It's his version of the Capitalist Pay Day story. When we think about the story of Star Baby's birth, we tend to smash all the accounts together. We imagine a manger, shepherds and sheep, and a chorus of flying pigs, three kings, and a star overhead. Of course, all of these elements appear in tabloids, but they don't appear together. By combining them, we obscure the unique perspective of each happy book. We lose the message. Skywalker's happy book has a particular message to share: the Son of Godzilla was born into poverty and hardship.

I have a flash of that one scene from *The Shining*. This does not bode well. I delete the paragraph, and re-type. This time I look at my fingers. I look up after the first sentence.

"Today we heard a reading from Skywalker's happy book."

Not good. I delete the sentence and start again, looking at the screen.

"Today we heard a reading from Luke's gospel."

I watch the words snap and change one by one.

"Today we heard a reading from Skywalker's happy book."

I go back through to correct the words one by one. They snap back again. I delete the sentence and start again.

"Good morning." I wait a moment. No change. "It's good to see you all today." Still no change. I rub my eyes and continue. "During this season, it's almost a cliché for the pastor to bemoan the commercialization of Christmas."

The words snap again.

"During this season, it's almost a cliché for the Head Clown to bemoan the commercialization of Capitalist Pay Day."

I force myself to breathe and think. I defer the question of my sanity, along with that supernatural communication, and focus instead on the mundane.

I call out, "Hey Joe, you got a minute?" Joe started as office administrator a few months back. I like him. He pads in, coffee in his hand.

"What's up?"

"My computer's doing something weird. I think maybe I picked up some kind of, I don't know, snarky virus?"

He looks puzzled. "What do mean?"

"I'll show you." I turn the screen for him to see, and type, "The birth of Jesus in Luke's gospel is a story of the triumph of God's kingdom against the degradations of the world."

And then, "The birth of Star Baby in Skywalker's gospel is a story of the triumph of Godzilla's kingdom against the degradations of the world."

"That's bizarre."

"I don't know what to do about it."

"Search for a fix online." I bring up the browser, and search "snarky Christmas virus." I wait for the results to load. I hear something. Joe is gripping his sides to contain a laugh.

"I'm sorry, I can't. I can't. It was me. I was just messing with you." I stare at him blankly. "Ass."

"You feel better though, right?" He smiles.

"Yeah. A little."

"Merry Christmas. I'll fix it for you." I wonder if all the important friendships in my life will begin with someone poking fun at me.

Debriefing Maryland

We all want to forget something, so we tell stories.

—Commoner, *Rashomon*

Writing this book has been a kind of mental archaeology. I remember the facts of my life with decent accuracy, or at least I think I do. Of course, my flawed recollection of the night I was robbed certainly calls my proposition into question. Still, I feel confident that I remember that history about as well as most people remember theirs, which is to say, I remember an interpretation that roughly corresponds to the events as they transpired. I've worked hard to refine, corroborate, and check those events, to come as close as possible to things as they were.

Where I have struggled most is in recovering my thoughts and feelings at the time of these events. I find I cannot see these memories except with the eyes of "now." I remember the facts—who said what, where I stood, how the space around me looked—but the questions of my inner life at the time stand obscured by the way I understand and feel these memories now. To put it another way, I can only see my ten-year-old self through thirty-seven-year-old eyes. I can no longer see him, or the world around him, the way he saw these things. So I must try to reconstruct my earlier perspectives from half-remembered fragments. Phrases from my inner monologue give clues to my mental state at the time. Sensations from my body—the tightening of my fist, or the coldness of my face—suggest something about the workings of my heart.

These scraps of memory and the parchment I reconstruct from them grow more complete as I approach the present. Of course, this is unsurprising, memories being what they are, but this trend makes the gap representing our first years in Maryland all the more glaring. It was a period of two and a half, nearly three years, and not that far removed from the present. And yet, when I went to uncover my thoughts and feelings concerning race during this time, I found almost nothing. The brevity of the preceding section speaks to that. The gap is, itself, revealing. This was after I had begun considering the question of race with some level of seriousness, and after I had begun examining my own life for race's influence. While we were in Virginia, race was very much on my mind. And then, it seems, I tabled the question entirely for almost three years.

I think I know why. Our arrival in Maryland was a great relief. I had, at last, landed a job in my chosen field. Rondesia found church employment six months afterward. We were still living paycheck to paycheck, but we weren't falling behind, even considering payments on our student loans, which were no longer in deferment. Silver Spring, where we settled, was the most diverse, if not the most integrated, community I have ever known. Though they were still not many, we saw more interracial couples on the street than we had before, or since. A young, charismatic, Black senator from Illinois seemed poised, against all the logic of our nation, to claim its highest office.

From my perspective, our crisis, and specifically the crisis of race, had receded from our lives, and along with it the urgency of its examination. This was not so for my wife. Certainly, she shared in the relief of our new circumstances, but for her, it was only a partial respite. Even a cursory review would have revealed this fact. Her job search lasted, in total, two and a half years. Mine lasted one. The final resolution for her required accepting a two-hour commute every day. My drive to work took ten minutes. The role of race in these differences could have been obvious to me, but it wasn't. I am tempted to consider this time as a simple repetition of my childhood racial amnesia, but I think that analogy is false. After all, when we came to Maryland, I knew better. Or at least, I should have. The reality is race simply didn't seem as important in my life as it once had. This, I think, is among the greatest privileges afforded by my skin: the privilege of ignorance. I can choose when I want to ignore the question of race. Or, more accurately, I can choose when I want to consider it. Absent an active choice to encounter the issue, I default to an agnostic position.

No such option is offered to people of color. In the heady months leading up to Barack Obama's election, I heard many proclaim the advent of a post-racial America, which is to say, an America in which race is not a question. The statement reflected, above all, the hope for a world where we would no longer have to hear or think about race. I do not remember a single person of color repeating that prediction. This is one memory about whose accuracy I am confident.

PART VII
ETHIOPIA

1

My father, my wife, and I wait in the cramped space at the back of the plane. He's organized a group trip to Ethiopia and invited us along. Actually, he invited Rondesia along. I asked if I could come. After Christmas, I needed to get away for a while. She looks out the window, thinking.

I ask, "What's up?"

She looks at me. It's not a look I've seen before. "I'm going home."

Dad smiles, the way he does: his eyes shine. "I'm so glad to hear you say that. I know what you mean. Because it's home for all of us: this is where humanity came from. So, I'm going home too."

Her face changes to a look I have seen before. The bathroom door opens. A passenger steps out. I wave my dad in. The door closes.

She says to me, "You know it's not the same, right?"

"Yeah, I know. He's trying to reach out, to connect with you."

"I know he's trying to reach out. And I appreciate it, I really do, but it's different for me. And I want to just be able to experience this. I don't want to have to accommodate or explain."

I look down. "He's a good person."

She sighs. "I know he's a good person. That's not what this is about. This is special for me. I want to have some space. And I want to know you will help keep it for me."

I breathe in. "Okay. I'll try."

The plane lands and we get off on the tarmac, which always seems more exciting to me than walking up the boarding chute. She takes a picture of her feet. I look at her quizzically. She shows me the photo on the camera's screen.

"I'm standing on the motherland."

There's business to take care of. We meet the other members of our group. Our tour guide greets us. We exchange money. We find our hotel. When all of the little details are taken care of, we gather for dinner. It's the first time the whole group has met. We sing and we pray and share about our hopes for the trip.

One of the trip organizers says, "I know that most of the African Americans in our group are visiting for the first time. And I'm really interested to find out what this experience is like for you; what it means for you."

I remember the conversation by the bathroom on the plane. I try to find my voice. It is a struggle. Why is this so much easier in the pulpit? I clear my throat.

"I won't deny that I'm also curious about that." I'm looking down at my plate as I speak. If I make eye contact, especially with my dad, I think I won't be able to finish. I force my voice to be louder. "But I think it's important that we respect everyone's space." I feel my face flush. "And give people room to let this trip be whatever it is for them, without having to explain." My voice cracks. I feel very much like a child. "I don't think we should be grasping at anyone else's experience."

Dinner ends. I avoid Dad, avoid even looking at him. We go back to our room. My hands are shaking. She takes them.

"Thank you."

"It wasn't a big thing." My voice is still cracking. I hate that I get like this.

"Whether it was big or small, it was hard for you. But you did it anyway. And I'm grateful." She's right. It was hard for me. I don't know why. My dad is a learner. He is always striving to grow. He doesn't run from being challenged, and I have challenged him before about other things. But challenging him about race feels like a betrayal somehow. It has left me shaken. The feeling is clear, though I don't understand it. I will not let it rule me. I remind myself, as I have many times before, that courage is not a talent, it is a skill. We practice it by being afraid.

2

The next day we step into a church, dressed in white. We bought the clothes the night before. They're traditional for Timkat, the Ethiopian Orthodox celebration of Jesus's baptism. The building is packed. A deacon sees our group; moves his way through the crowd to meet us and escorts us to the center, in front of the members of his congregation. I don't believe it was arranged in advance; he saw us and decided this was where we belonged. Four priests emerge from behind the curtained sanctuary at the center of the church. One carries a box on his head. Our guide, Yemi, whispers an explanation. It is a copy of the Ten Commandments, in stone. Apparently, it is an honor. I ask her how they decide which priest gets to carry it.

"The one with the strongest neck."

There are more hymns and prayers. The church doors open and we follow the four priests and the tablet. The deacon clears a path so we can stay at the head of the group, just behind the priests. We spill into the streets. Other churches join the procession, all headed in the same direction. There are people everywhere, dressed in white, singing and praying. The streets are packed. It's only warm out, but with the bright sun and the crowd, I'm sweating.

We converge on a field at the center of the city. There is hardly room to move. We are tens of thousands, at least. The crowd parts for the priests. The deacon motions us to follow. We arrive at a fenced enclosure at the center of the field. A gatekeeper lets us in. The press of the crowd fades away. There is room to breathe, chairs to sit in and shade. They separate us, men from women. I let go of my wife's hand. We sit, grateful to rest our legs. From across the aisle, I catch her eye and smile. She smiles back. Outside the crowd presses in against the fence.

The patriarch of the church stands and addresses the crowd. He introduces the dignitaries. I think one is the mayor, another a Catholic archbishop. He points to us and speaks, and I wish I spoke the language. He preaches and prays. He walks to a large pool in the center of the enclosure and blesses the water. Six priests take up garden hoses that pump from the pool and begin spraying the crowd. The shouts are deafening. Something flies into the air, and lands near my feet. It's an empty water bottle. Another follows.

My wife stands. She takes the closest bottle, walks to the pool, fills it, twists on the lid, and tosses it over the fence. A pair of hands catches it. I follow her example. More bottles sail over the barrier. We work as fast as we can as the rain of bottles continues. We can't possibly keep up. I toss over another bottle, perhaps the tenth I have thrown. A man catches it. His hand is wrinkled. He might be seventy or older. I wonder how long he had to wait to get a place so close to the pool. Yemi said people begin gathering at the field the day before the celebration. Most of them keep vigil all night. Most of them will leave without water in hand. I wonder how many years this man has been coming here. I wonder how many times he has gone home without water. I wonder what the water means to the people gathered, and what they will do with it. I don't know the answer to any of these questions. I arrived yesterday, yet if I chose to, I could jump into that pool and swim a lap. I fill another bottle, cap it, and toss it over the fence.

3

We will leave tomorrow for Axum, in the north. But tonight, our new American president will be inaugurated. One of our group found a bar with a big screen. They are broadcasting the whole thing. A few of us head over together. Yemi goes with us.

We arrive at the bar and Yemi greets the owner and points to us. She says something. Again, I wish I spoke the language. He smiles broadly, and shakes our hands, one by one. He leads us to a table on the balcony, overlooking the big screen. It is clearly the best table in the house. A banner over the television reads "OBAMA!"

The place fills quickly. The crowds are not quite as dense, and not quite as ecstatic, as those from yesterday, but it is close. We watch George and Laura step out of the White House. We cheer, more for their departure than their appearance. The whole bar cheers with us. Then there is a long pause, during which very little happens. Commentators jabber to fill the void. They cut to the stage in front of the Capitol Building. Various ex-presidents file into their seats. We clap for some, and not for others. We cheer especially loud for Carter. Several faces in the bar turn our way.

Yemi frowns. "Why are you cheering for this man?" We explain that he was one of the better presidents we've had, though he wasn't appreciated at the time, and that he's done good things since he left. She frowns again. "We don't like him here."

"Why?"

She explains his history with the country. It is problematic, to say the least. We are all surprised. This was history none of us had learned. She shakes it off.

"Don't worry about it."

The tension passes; we go back to watching. Finally, our new president appears. The bar roars in triumph. Hours later, we walk back to the hotel. Children are setting off firecrackers in the streets. I had no idea this would matter so much outside our home country. The next morning at breakfast, Yemi returns, the national newspaper under her

146

arm. She shows us the front page. President Obama's picture is there, of course. And underneath it, our picture. We're stunned. I ask her what the headline says. She draws her finger across the letters. "American Tourists Watch Presidential Inauguration at Local Bar."

"That's front-page news?"

She nods.

"In a national paper?"

She nods again.

4

We've had a good day in Axum. We saw the building that might hold the Ark of the Covenant. Actually, I saw it. Because she is a woman, Rondesia was not allowed to come within view of it. We walk to the dining room. The others from our group are already gathered. We say grace and eat.

The trip organizer stands after the meal and says, "So, I've got some bad news." There are grumbles around the table. There has been some growing dissatisfaction. "The airline is restricting service throughout the entire country tomorrow. So, we won't be able to fly the next leg of the trip with our bags."

There are roars of outrage. We debate and negotiate until a solution arises. Six of us will stay behind an extra day, along with the luggage. The rest will go ahead to Lalibela with carry-ons. All of us (luggage included) will meet on Thursday. The solution satisfies no one. Those going on will have to make do without their things. Those staying behind have already seen everything there is to see here. The organizer points out that there is an isolated monastery some distance away that sits atop a mesa and is accessible only by rope ladder, and only to men.

Four men agree to stay behind. Both the organizers are among them. Some breathing room will be good for the group. Yemi will go ahead with the rest, and make sure they are taken care of. This is for the best. Everyone likes her. They still need two more volunteers.

"We'll stay behind," Rondesia says.

I look at her. "But you can't go to the monastery." I am wary after the business with the Ark.

"That's okay. I wouldn't mind a day to just chill."

I frown.

"Really," she reassures.

"Okay," I say to the organizer. "I guess we'll stay behind."

We head out early the next day. I'm hesitant about leaving her on her own.

She kisses my forehead. "I'll be fine. I can take care of myself."
I know this is true, but I still worry. "Okay. I love you."
"I love you too."
The drive is hours long, down a very dusty, bumpy, windy road.
The minibus is cramped and sweltering. At one point someone opens
a window, which is a mistake. The van immediately fills with dust.
The window is quickly shut, but we are covered. Finally, we arrive. The
monastery is awe-inspiring. We are there for an hour and then back in
the van. I return to the hotel sore, sweaty, and caked in dirt. I shower,
change my clothes, and go looking for Rondesia. She is sitting at the
hotel bar. She's radiant. I pass the maître d'. He gives me a withering
look. I say hello. He ignores me. I sit down next to her.
"Hey there," she says.
I smile. "I'm so glad to see you."
"Have you had dinner yet?"
"No."
"Me neither." She takes my arm. "I was waiting for you. Come on."
She heads for the dining area, which is on a patio overlooking the city.
I can see the giant and fallen ancient steles of the Axumite civilization
below us. We take our seats and discuss the menu. The waiter greets
her by name. He smiles, takes her order, and begins to walk away.
"Excuse me," I say, but he continues walking.
"Excuse me," she says, and the waiter returns.
"Yes?"
She orders for me.
"Of course," he says. He still hasn't looked at me. I'm confused.
"So," she asks, "what was the monastery like?" I tell her the story.
She works hard to pay attention. It's not her fault. I'm long-winded.
It's my nature.
"What about you?" I ask. "What did you do?"
"I read here for a while, then I walked down to the city center and
strolled around. I got a lot of attention."
"Oh yeah?"
"Yeah. I was invited to two parties."
"Total strangers?"
"Yeah."

I frown. "You didn't go though?"

She smiles. "No. But it was nice to be asked."

The waiter arrives with our dinner. He smiles at her. I finally catch his eye. He glares and walks away. I turn to her.

"Do I smell bad or something?"

"No. I think the staff isn't too happy with you."

"Why?"

"Well, after you guys left this morning, I came down for breakfast. The desk clerk asked me where you all were. I told him that my husband and the other men had gone off to the monastery and I had stayed behind. I think, maybe, they didn't know we were married. Anyway, he asked me what kind of husband would leave behind a beautiful woman like me."

"So what did you tell him?" My voice has gone up in pitch and volume.

"It's okay. I told him you're a good guy, and I didn't mind staying behind. But I guess word got around."

My face is flushed. I talk quickly. "Well, tell them we agreed to this in advance. Tell them it was your idea." She lays her hand on mine, and smiles.

"Babe, it's never like this for me when I go to a new place. I'm never welcomed right away. Just let me enjoy it. And, maybe, try to learn from it."

5

We take our seats. The plane is full. Too full. It will be a long flight. Our trip is over and we are eager to get home. We take off. Two hours pass. She nudges me.

"I need to get up." I stand so she can pass. She heads for the bathroom. Minutes later she returns. She looks bothered.

"What?" I ask.

She turns to face me. "Did you see all those babies up front?"

I had noticed them when I went to the bathroom about half an hour earlier. There were four rows of women holding infants in their arms. The babies were Black, the women White.

"I assumed it's an adoption trip," I said.

"I was walking up, and one of the babies saw me. He smiled and started reaching for me. Then the mom noticed and moved him over to her other arm. She turned him so he couldn't see me anymore. And he cried."

I'm troubled. I suppose it's natural. The baby saw a face that looked like the faces he was used to, so he reached for her. But I'm still troubled. I imagine the children we might have one day and how people will see us when we're together. I wonder how much I will understand those children. I wonder how they will respond to me. I think about the woman turning a child away from a face it connected with. I am angry with the woman, and yet, I think I understand her defensiveness. I think I would share it.

She watches my face. "Are you okay?"

"Yes. Just thinking."

She leans back. "Yeah. Me too."

Debriefing Ethiopia

Those who build walls are their own prisoners.

—Ursula Le Guin, *The Dispossessed*

The city of Adwa sits in Ethiopia's northernmost expanse. It is a dry, rocky country. In 1896, Ethiopian forces, under the command of Emperor Menelik II, routed an invading Italian army just outside the city. The battle ended the First Italo-Abyssinian War and secured Ethiopian sovereignty, leaving it as the only African nation never to fall before European colonization. I knew none of these facts before visiting Ethiopia, but I learned them upon arrival. That is, I was taught. I remember listening to six different accounts of the battle of Adwa, told by six different Ethiopians. I heard the first less than an hour after landing in Addis Ababa. The rest trickled in over the course of the next two weeks. I think there may have been more tellings than the six I recall, but, in my memory, they blend into the background of that trip. Suffice to say, it was a history many Ethiopians felt we should know.

The precise details varied from one account to another, which is the case with all retellings of history. A docent at the old imperial palace informed us it was Emperor Menelik's cunning that carried the day. A local guide at Adwa gave credit to the soldiers of his hometown who knew the terrain. A deacon at the church of St. George proclaimed that his congregation's patron saint had delivered victory to the nation. And a young, disaffected waiter in Lalibela explained the triumph as a simple matter of superior numbers. For all their differences, the accounts ended with remarkable consistency. The teller would finish their story and then declare, "It was a victory, not only for Ethiopia, but for Black people everywhere," or something to that effect. These last words were always directed toward one of the Black members of our tour group.

At first, I admired the pride of this synopsis. That admiration faded quickly. With each telling, I grew more uncomfortable. I would feel my shoulders tense at the last sentence, before relaxing again. It felt wrong and unfair, that this history would embrace the Black members of our group, but not those of us who were White. After all, our Black compatriots were not Ethiopian. This was not their history, their culture, their language, or their people. We were all foreigners here. Surely, we had more in common with one another than we did with the people of this land. By what right could Ethiopians claim fellowship with them?

The sense of exclusion and my defensiveness in response were strange feelings, but not completely new. I had felt them before. In high school, my best friend Travis joined an organization for Students of Color. I remember the day of their first meeting. Travis and I had the last class of the morning together. When it let out for lunch, we walked toward the second floor lounge where we usually ate together. As we passed a classroom, Travis stopped.

"This is me." He pointed at the room behind him with his thumb. A handwritten note hung on the door: "Students of Color." I had forgotten. "I'll see you later, okay?"

I nodded. He turned and walked in. I glanced into the room beyond as he went. Our school was small. I knew all the students in that room. They were Black, Latino, and Asian. I felt the same twinge: exclusion and defensiveness. It felt wrong to me that these students should claim fellowship together. They were as different from one another as I was from them. I remembered when Travis had corrected me once for calling him Japanese. His family is Okinawan, he said, and that is a different thing. I looked on a map. It seemed to me they were part of the same nation. Why would he give weight to so fine a level of distinction, but still accept a designation so broad that it's only definition was "not White"?

I knew their fellowship was not an easy one. Among those called "people of color" there lies not only difference but discord. The history between these groups includes alliance and support, but also hurt, disappointment, and competition. When I heard Ethiopians proclaim Adwa a victory for Black people everywhere, they would stretch out the word "e-v-e-r-y-w-h-e-r-e." But when they declared their country the only African nation to resist conquest, emphasis fell hard on the word "only." If these fellowships could embrace such ambiguities, why couldn't they embrace me?

Both times, in high school and in Ethiopia, I tried to put my hurt away by means of intellect. Travis had spoken about what it meant to be Asian at an overwhelmingly White school. I had heard Black students allude to similar experiences. There was a reason for their fellowship. Likewise, I honored my wife's assertion that, in Africa, she was going home, a truth I could not fully understand, but I knew it mattered to her. I tried to keep space for our Black compatriots to let that time in Ethiopia mean whatever it might for them without having to give explanation, because I knew it was their right.

These understandings all occurred in my head. But heads have precious little influence over hearts. Whatever I might have told myself, when the plane touched down in Addis Ababa, I wanted to claim a homecoming, just as my father had. When our Black compatriots looked thoughtfully across the scenes before us, I wanted to know what they were thinking, just as my White companions did. And when Travis turned to walk into that room, I wanted to follow. That he later told me White students were, in fact, invited to attend the Students of Color meeting made little difference. They had gathered to discuss an experience that I could not know.

There is, I think, a quiet anxiety that most White people share, which is a fear that the history of White Supremacy has somehow separated us from humanity at large. In striving to subjugate the world, our ancestors drew a circle on the ground. Inside that circle we stand, and outside that circle stands everyone else, joined in an uncomfortable, motley fellowship by the single fact that our people declared them, collectively, "other." I believe this anxiety, in part, drives our impulse to abolish history. That circle on the ground is a circle of history. So, we ask people of color why they can't move on and get over the past. We cling to every small sign of progress as proof that the history of race has come to an end. We latch onto theories of race as social construct, believing that, if we imagined race into being, we can just as easily imagine it away. If history can be abolished, so too can our separation.

The problem, of course, is that what we call history is not history at all. It is the reality of today. In 2016, Black men earned, on average, seventy cents on the dollar compared to White men. Black women earned eighty-two cents on the dollar compared to White women.[8] More starkly, as of 2017, the wealth of the average Black family is only 15 percent that of the average White family.[9] And all these numbers have actually fallen in the last two decades. The circle still surrounds us. Knowingly or not, we reinscribe it each day, and its border grows wider. There must be redress. Justice precedes reconciliation, and reconciliation precedes community. Until we reckon with these facts, we will remain, in some fundamental way, apart.

As I watched the inauguration of our forty-fourth president from a table in an Addis Ababa sports bar, I was startled by the celebration of Ethiopians around us. He was not their president, and the country on the screens before us was not their country. I wondered if they imagined, as I did, the beginning of a new era, the start of a new relationship between our nation and the world. I felt, for a moment, that strange warmth of fellowship. And then I recalled something my brother-in-law had said. That the week following Obama's election, he had shared a nod and a smile with every Black man he passed on the street. I wondered if the reason for the celebration around me was something less grandiose and yet, more honest: this inauguration was a victory, not only for our president, but for Black people everywhere. In claiming the highest office of the United States, Obama had struck a blow, if perhaps only a symbolic one, against White Supremacy everywhere. And I felt, once again, apart.

8. Mary C. Daly, Bart Hobijn, and Joseph H. Pedtke, "Disappointing Facts about the Black-White Wage Gap," Federal Reserve Bank of San Francisco, September 5, 2017, *https://www.frbsf.org/economic-research/publications/economic-letter/2017/september/disappointing-facts-about-black-white-wage-gap/*, 2.

9. Lisa J. Dettling et al., "Recent Trends in Wealth-Holding by Race and Ethnicity: Evidence from the Survey of Consumer Finances," Board of Governors of the Federal Reserve System, September 27, 2017, *https://www.federalreserve.gov/econres/notes/feds-notes/recent-trends-in-wealth-holding-by-race-and-ethnicity-evidence-from-the-survey-of-consumer-finances-20170927.htm*.

PART VIII
MARYLAND, AGAIN

1

We have made it through Christmas and Lent and Easter. Things at the church have quieted down, for the moment, but there's a lot to get done. I step into Joe's office. He's typing, working on the bulletins, I assume. I hate to put one more thing on his plate, but I need to add an announcement.

I knock. "Hey. Have you finished the events section yet for this wee—"

"Wait." He raises a hand. "I had this idea."

"Okay."

"Have you seen the thing about Susan Boyle?" The name doesn't register. I shake my head. He tries to help. "Middle-aged British woman. Incredible voice. Came out of nowhere on *Britain's Got Talent.*"

"Oh yeah."

"Okay. Imagine she has a biopic. Who plays the lead?" I shrug. "Just picture it."

An image crystalizes for me immediately. I hate myself for it, but the words come regardless. "Jack Black."

He jumps up with an exclamation that is half laugh, half roar of triumph. "See, that's why you my n****!"

Joe and I have become close. Of course, I know he's Black and he knows I'm White. These facts are obvious, but we have never talked of them. Now my face goes slack. I don't know how to respond. With no other words to offer, I tell him so.

"I have no idea how to respond to that."

He smiles. "Yeah. I was messing with you."

"Oh."

"You're okay though."

"Thanks?" I turn and walk back to my desk. I have forgotten whatever it was I needed to ask him about.

He speaks to my back. "You still don't get to say it, though."

"Right." I pause. "Wait, were you just messing with me, or was that a test?"

"Both."

"Right." I want to ask him if I passed, but I suppose that's beside the point.

2

(Guatemala)

The youth group is tired. It's summer, and we are on a mission trip. They have been working all week and they're ready for a break. I know they will love these ruins. We pile into the microbus headed for the Ciudad de Guatemala airport. I start to tell the story of my last visit here, but I don't even get as far as the travel agent's handwritten note.

Mark interrupts, "You told us this before—like ten times." That's probably true. I tell the same stories over and over. It's a thing.

"Okay, I'm just saying, get ready for the strangest airport ever. It's surreal." I stretch out the word "surreal" as the bus pulls in.

Things have changed in seven years—a lot. We enter a small, state-of-the-art terminal. Its decor is very millennial. We walk up to a bank of ticketing windows. Overhead digital displays direct us to the correct line. I give our documents to an agent behind a computer. She scans them and prints our boarding passes. We put our bags onto a conveyor belt and they are carried out of sight. A high-end P.A. system provides crisp, clear directives, first in Spanish, then in English. We follow placards to the security check. We are metal-detected, x-rayed, and un-shoed. On our way to the gate, we pass by five duty-free stores, a McDonald's, and a Starbucks. We arrive at the gate and wait. The seats are comfortable. A huge flat screen TV is broadcasting a soccer match. Boarding begins. We walk down the gangway onto a brand-new 737. After we are seated, the flight attendants walk us through the plane's full complement of safety features. They bring us each a single-serving package of honey roasted peanuts and a mini bottle of water.

I turn to the kids, embarrassed. "I'm sorry. It was different before. Much crazier."

Mark looks puzzled. "Why are you apologizing? It sounds like it's better now."

Then I remember what I learned on my first trip here. For me, the underdevelopment of this place was exciting and strange, but that was all a matter of my perspective. Mark's right. In many ways, it's better now. I open the packet, empty a small handful of over-salted peanuts into my mouth, and frown. They didn't have to get rid of the fresh-baked shortbread, though.

3

The bailiff escorts us into the deliberation room. We take our seats. Someone clears their throat.

"Well, I guess the first thing we have to do is choose a foreman."

The woman in the Green Shirt speaks up. "I'll do it, unless anyone else wants to." No one does. She thinks a moment. "Well, let's take an initial vote on each of the charges. Just to see where we're at." There are nods all around.

"Assault? Raise your hands for guilty." All hands are up.

"Assault with a deadly weapon?" Four hands go down. Mine is among them.

"Armed robbery?" Two more hands fall.

"Well," she says, "we can deliver a guilty verdict on assault right now."

The woman in the Gray Coat speaks. "No, the judge said that's only thirty days. This is serious." I agree.

Our Forewoman thinks. "Okay, I think we can't say guilty on armed robbery if we don't also say guilty on assault with a deadly weapon; one implies the other. So, let's hear from the four who were against the deadly weapon thing."

The woman in the Red Sweater says, "It was the 911 call."

The Forewoman turns. "What?"

"The victim says he ran away and called 911."

"So?"

Red Sweater raises her eyebrows. "In the call he said, 'This guy was hitting me with his fists.'"

Gray Coat interrupts. "That's not what the translator said."

"Excuse me?"

"That's not what the translator said."

"Look, I know what the victim said. He said, 'This guy was hitting me with his fists.'"

The Forewoman intercedes. "Let's check." She looks through the box of exhibits but the transcripts aren't there. She takes the pad of paper and scribbles something down. She knocks on the door and the bailiff opens it. She hands him the note. We wait. There is a knock on the door. He hands her a binder. She flips through it.

"She's right," the Forewoman says, pointing to Gray Coat. "It doesn't say anything about fists."

Red Sweater insists. "Check the tape."

We dig out the recording of the 911 call. I hear the victim's voice. The dispatcher doesn't speak Spanish. She transfers to an interpreter. There are about five seconds of Muzak while the call is on hold. As before, when I heard this recording in the courtroom, I have to keep myself from laughing. The Forewoman fast-forwards through it in short bursts.

The interpreter comes on the line. "¿Qué tipo de emergencia tienes?"

"Un tipo me pegó con los puños."

"Stop the tape," Red Sweater says. "He says it right there. The guy was hitting him with his fists."

This time I hear it too and nod.

Gray Coat objects. "You can't do that."

"What?"

"The judge said we had to go by the translator's testimony. Not your own understanding of Spanish."

I remember the judge saying that.

Red Sweater rolls her eyes. "That's crazy. I'm a native speaker. I grew up speaking Spanish. I know what he said."

I speak up. "I heard it, too." Several faces look my way. "He said fists." Around the table faces crease in thought. I note that Red Sweater did not provoke this response, which is bothersome. Her Spanish is obviously better than mine. She should receive greater deference as an authority in the matter. I don't have time to reflect further on this fact, though.

"This is against the rules." Gray Coat has crossed her arms.

"You can't expect us to ignore it."

"That's exactly what the judge expects us to do."

There is silence.

Gray Coat continues. "Even if he did say fists, that doesn't mean there wasn't a weapon. It just means he didn't mention it."

The man in the Sports Coat gives a side-eye. He was one of the four who voted against the deadly weapon charge.

"If someone's coming at me with a weapon that would be the first thing out of my mouth." He pauses. "And what about their stories? They don't match, right? The victim says he didn't know the defendant, that the defendant ran up to him with a knife and tried to rob him. The defendant admits trying to punch the victim, but says there was no weapon, and that the whole thing started because the victim owed him money—which means they knew each other."

Gray Coat interrupts. "Of course their stories don't match. He's on trial. He'll say whatever he can to get off."

Sports Coat nods. "Except, the victim did know the defendant." He emphasizes the word "did." There is a pause. I think we had all had that thought. "The victim said so. He said when he saw the defendant running at him, he was scared because the defendant's sister had told him the defendant was dangerous." There is no need to check the transcript. We all remember that detail.

Gray Coat sighs in exasperation. "That doesn't mean they knew each other. He could've known the sister but not the defendant."

Sports Coat seems unconvinced. "If someone says to me, "Watch out, my brother is dangerous,' chances are, I know the brother. Otherwise, why would she bother saying anything? And how would I recognize that it's her brother, if I hadn't met him?"

Gray Coat shakes her head. "The defense attorney didn't say that. She didn't make that argument. The judge said we shouldn't make our own deductions. We have to go by what the attorneys presented."

"I'll tell you what bothered me," says Bald Man, the third of four to vote against, "the officer's testimony. He could hardly remember the details of what happened. I mean, I give him points for being honest about it, but still."

"It was nine months ago. People forget things." Gray Coat points to a paper in front of us. "And we have the arrest report."

Bald Man shrugs. "Yeah, but I have questions. I mean the officer says he saw the defendant threatening the victim with an awl while he was driving the other way across the street. Okay, so he sped to the intersection, pulled a U-ey, stopped, and chased the defendant down.

Then he walked him back to the bus stop where the altercation happened and found the duffle bag, under the bench, with an awl inside." He pauses. We're all waiting for the rest. "That seems weird, right? I mean, he takes off running because he sees a cop coming, but first he stops to put the weapon inside a duffle bag and stashes it under the bench? I know this street," he says, pointing to the diagram the prosecutor used of the intersection. "There are woods all along that sidewalk. Why wouldn't you just start running into the woods and toss it?"

"So what? You're saying the officer lied?"

"No. No. I'm saying, we all tell ourselves stories. So maybe the officer sees a fight, and he goes to stop it. He apprehends the one guy, walks him back, finds the awl, and then suddenly remembers that he saw it before. But maybe he didn't see it. And the fact that now he doesn't seem to remember anything about it doesn't help."

"You're doing it again." Gray Coat shifts uncomfortably. "You're making an argument. A deduction. You're not supposed to do that. The judge specifically said so." She is right. We all remember him saying that.

I speak. I was the last of the four to vote against. "There are just too many questions: the officer not remembering the details, the 911 call, the victim not being straight about knowing the defendant. I'm fine with the assault charge. The defendant basically admitted to it. Assault is thirty days. But once you add the deadly weapon we're talking, what, sixteen years? There's not enough here for that."

Gray Coat looks away from the table. "We're not supposed to consider sentencing." The judge said that too.

"You were the one who brought up sentencing. You said it as soon as we got started," I reply. "Anyway, why would they give us the sentences for the charges if they didn't want us to consider them?"

"I don't know. But we're not supposed to consider them. He said that." She crosses her arms. I intentionally drop the tone of my voice. I relax my face and shoulders. I'm trying to appear reasonable in contrast to her standoffishness.

"I'm sorry, I just don't think I can change my vote."

Something happens in the room. It is subtle. Faces that were watching the proceedings with detached interest are now tensed in thought. And they are nodding. I think I've convinced them, which is a surprise. I'm not used to persuading people. I notice something else in the faces around the table. Our Forewoman, Sports Coat, and Bald Man are Black. Red Sweater is Latina. Gray Coat, the six who quietly held their judgment, and I are all White. I wonder how much race has impacted my ability to win them over. Certainly, their body language changed after I weighed in.

"I'm not changing my vote either," says Red Sweater.

The Forewoman raps her fingers on the table. "Okay, then I guess either we agree to guilty on assault and not guilty on the rest, or we tell the judge we're hung." She stops rapping her fingers. "I'm calling a vote. Guilty on assault, not guilty on the others. Hands up."

Hands raise. Some immediately. Mine is one of those. Some go up tentatively. Eleven hands are up. The woman in the Gray Coat has her hand down.

The Forewoman looks to her. "If we tell them we've got a hung jury, that's a mistrial. From what I understand, they don't usually retry. So, if we can't agree on something, chances are they'll drop all the charges."

Gray Coat presses her palms to her eyes, tilts her head to the ceiling, and answers without looking. "You're trying to negotiate. He said we're not supposed to do that. You keep breaking the rules."

The Forewoman shrugs. "This is how it is."

Gray Coat's hands slowly drop to the table. She's still looking at the ceiling. "Fine. But, I swear, if anyone ever gets me, I hope none of you are there to decide what happens to the one who did it." It is such a strange thing to say. We all feel it, and shift in our seats. The Forewoman takes a scrap of paper and begins writing the verdict. She speaks without raising her eyes.

"I really hope that doesn't come up."

4

I turn up Guns N' Roses on my headphones. I always listen to power ballads when I'm doing our taxes. Somehow it transforms the banal into the heroic. I add the amounts of our several W-2s, check the result twice, and enter it on line 7. The number is about what I expected. There is something else I expected that I try to ignore, but the thought has already registered. The sum of my W-2s is roughly twice that of Rondesia's. This is not a new phenomenon. It has been the case every year I've done our taxes. I'm not overpaid—I don't think so, anyway. We work in the same field. She works as hard and as much as I do. Her gifts are definitely equal to mine, probably greater. Certainly, her credentials are stronger.

Though it makes no sense, it is no surprise. She told me it would be this way. It stings us both, but I know it stings her more.

5

We are on a date. We wait. Rondesia stands in front of me. I watch her shoulders tighten as the hostess looks to her, and then to me and smiles.

"Table for two?"

"Yes. Thank you." Her shoulders relax.

"Of course. Right this way."

She takes my hand and squeezes. I squeeze back. It is astounding how much these little things matter.

6

Under the flicker of fluorescent bulbs, everyone in the room looks slightly
ill. I ask someone to hit the light switch, ostensibly so people can see
the power point presentation. In fact, I just want the lights off. I hate
neon lights. The room gets darker. On the screen behind me, a photo
of an iceberg appears. I look at my hands. I'm worried they may shake.
I've watched this presentation many times before, but this is the
first time I will deliver it myself. It doesn't help that Eric, our boss, is
looking on.

Eric runs an organization called the Kaleidoscope Institute. They
lead diversity trainings, mostly for religious organizations. Rondesia
and I met him a few years back. He invited us to attend an intensive
training. We didn't know it at the time, but he was recruiting us. Since
then, he's hired us now and again as assistants when he's working in
the area. It's our side gig. Plus, we kind of owe him. The insights we
learned at that first training helped us build a marriage. We might not
have stayed together without it.

Today, we're working at a local seminary. If we do well at this
training, we'll be on our way to a promotion within the organization,
which would mean more gigs and better pay, which would be good.
Also, I look up to Eric. I want him to like me. I put my hands in my
pockets and realize immediately that won't work. I need to point at
the photo. So, I do.

"We're going to be talking a lot about culture during the next two
days. Of course, culture is a word we use all the time, but it turns out
it's actually kind of difficult to define." From the corner of my eye, I
see my shadow cross the iceberg slide. I'm pacing. I do that when I'm
nervous. Rondesia says it's distracting. I cross until I'm clear of the
projection, and stand still. "For our purposes, we'll use the analogy
of an iceberg to describe culture. An iceberg has a small piece above
the waterline that we can see." I gesture behind me, without looking. I
wonder if this confused the students. I put my hand back in my pocket.
"And then there's a large piece below the waterline that we can't see.

The size difference between what we can see and what we can't see is what makes navigating Arctic waters so difficult. If you're just going by the part you can see, you'll crash your boat."

I've rushed the last sentence and it came out as one word. I make myself breathe and slow down.

"Culture is the same way. There's a little bit we can see—things like food, language, style of dress, that stuff. This is what we think of when we think about culture. But it's actually just a small part of culture, and it sits on this big bit that we can't see. This is stuff like values, patterns of behavior, patterns of perception, and the stories and narratives that shape the way we look at the world. Most people have some sense of the external elements of their culture—this part up here—but, unless we spend time investigating it, we usually don't know much about what we're carrying down here, the internal elements of our culture. These things are just part of our assumptions of how the world works."

I'm rushing again. I make myself slow down. Again.

"The size difference between what's up here and what's down there is what makes navigating multicultural spaces difficult. If you're trying to navigate cross-cultural spaces based just on external cultures—what you can touch, see, hear, taste, and smell—you're setting yourself up to do a lot of damage. If we want to negotiate intercultural relationships carefully, and with skill, the first thing we need to do—" I stop. A thought has plowed through my mind, throwing me off. I try to push it away and pick up where I left off, "—we need to examine our own internal culture, the part of the iceberg down there, and learn about—" The thought intrudes again, and I stop. I shake it off and continue, "—we have to learn about what we're carrying with us: our own values, patterns of perception, and narratives."

I push through the remainder of the presentation and give the students directions for a small-group exercise. They huddle in clusters and I walk to the back of the room. I glance at the clock. The presentation took a little over ten minutes. It should take fifteen. That's not good. It means I skipped over some elements. I look to Eric. He's walking from group to group, checking in. He has a pensive, discerning look on his face, but that tells me very little. He always looks that way. He has resting analyst face. I take a seat next to Rondesia at the back of the room.

She pats my knee. "Hey, you did good."

"I guess."

"No, it was good. You rushed a little, and you forgot the middle bit, but then you remembered, and closed it out."

She is wrong, but I won't tell her that. I didn't forget the middle bit. The middle bit derailed me. The presentation has always troubled me, but I had never delivered it before. This was the first time it made me feel like a hypocrite. I picture that iceberg. I have no idea what I'm carrying below the water. If pressed as to the values, assumptions, and stories of White culture, I could offer no answer. And this is not for lack of looking.

Debriefing Maryland (Again)

Whitewash on the forehead hardens the brain.

—Charles Dickens, *Great Expectations*

It was unseasonably warm when the vestry of my congregation, Calvary Episcopal Church, interviewed me for the pastor's position. I had walked to the church from Union Station and had gotten lost on the way. I hurried to make up time. I wore the only suit I owned. I am not the sort to wear suits. They always chafe. As I arrived at the door, I felt one bead of sweat slide down the inside of my arm, and land in my palm. The singularity of that drop grabbed my attention and held it as I was welcomed and escorted to the conference room. I was flustered.

My meetings with the search committee had been easy. I imagine because I hadn't expected anything would come of them. The assistant's position at my previous church was coming to an end, and I needed a job. Rondesia initially encouraged me to apply at Calvary. I had misgivings, but my mentor advised me to try for every position that opened up. "Along the way you'll start to get a sense of where you belong." I enjoyed meeting with the search committee. We got along well, but I didn't think we fit together. They valued their legacy as a historically Black church, and specifically, the fact that they had always had a Black pastor. I also could not ignore the fact that I was nearly thirty years younger than the average age of the congregation. So I was startled when they moved me on to the next round.

Now the job was a real possibility and the interview mattered. Now there was pressure. So perhaps it was just nerves talking when the subject of race came up.

I don't remember how we arrived at the topic. Someone asked how I, a White man, thought and felt about Calvary's legacy as a historically Black congregation. I answered quickly.

"I think everyone should be proud of who they are. Of course, you should be proud of being Black. Just like I am proud of being White."

Dianne, one of the vestry members, said, "You know, I think I understand what you're saying, but when I hear the words 'pride' and 'White' together, I can only think of White privilege."

I acknowledged her response, then said that was exactly the problem. If those who celebrate privilege are the only ones who proclaim pride in White identity, then they control the definition of what it is to be White. My anxiety so overwhelmed me throughout the whole interview that I find it difficult to recall anything about my state of mind in that moment. As often happens with my memory, I know what I said to Dianne and the vestry, but not why. I imagine, at the time, I thought it was a savvy and politic response. I would not offer it now. Looking back, I think Dianne's reaction was closer to the truth of the matter.

If I declare that I am proud to be White, then I should know why I am proud. And I didn't know. I still don't. While working on this essay, I found myself stuck. The question of where I could find my pride seemed intractable. Frustrated, I sought distraction, as so many of us do, in social media. Scrolling through inane arguments over pop culture and news stories that confirmed my various indignations, I stumbled onto a blog post by a colleague, the Rev. Enger Allen. She described attending a training at the People's Institute, an anti-racist educational collective. The participants were all asked, "What do you like about being your race?" The people of color in the room responded with elements of their culture: values, behaviors, modes of expression, history, and art. The White people in the room responded with elements of their privilege: access, opportunity, the freedom to live without scrutiny, and a sense of belonging in the authoritative institutions of society.

As I read her account, I remembered attending a similar event. We split into groups by demographic. As all the men at my table were balding, we labeled ourselves "The Rogaine Caucus of White Men." The facilitator asked each group, "What do you like about being part of this demographic?" After fifteen minutes of small-group work, we reported to the large group. The results mirrored Rev. Allen's experience. I was startled by the uncanny similarity. As I continued reading her words, another memory bubbled up of standing before a group of seminarians with the image of an iceberg projected behind me and declaring the importance of knowing one's own culture. And I remembered how the question of White culture had left me dumbstruck.

I saw in each of these moments, and in my current writer's block, a failure to identify the content of White identity apart from the privileges it confers. Even my small group's humorous, self-deprecating designation, "The Rogaine Caucus of White Men," was a kind of evasion—an effort to find some other basis for our affinity beyond our shared Whiteness and masculinity.

As I finished reading Rev. Allen's reflection, I wondered if these were actually failures at all. Perhaps there is nothing to being White except its social and economic power. I knew there was strong evidence for this possibility. Abundant historical research demonstrates that our categories of race are both artificial and recent. W.E.B. Du Bois articulated this idea in his essay "The Souls of White Folk": "The discovery of personal whiteness among the world's peoples is a very modern thing—a nineteenth and twentieth century matter, indeed. The ancient world would have laughed at such a distinction."[10]

While Du Bois may have been the first to name the artifice of Whiteness, my own first encounter with these ideas came by skimming through a copy of Theodore Allen's *The Invention of the White Race*, which some student had returned while I was working the circulation desk at Yale's Sterling Memorial Library. The book is thorough, and commendable for anyone interested in the subject.[11] The critical point of all these sorts of analyses is not so much the assertion that Whiteness is invented, but rather the recognition that there was a purpose in its invention. Whiteness was consciously created to divide, and to establish a hierarchy within that division.

In 1676, almost one hundred years to the day before the founding of our nation, enslaved Africans and European bondservants joined together under the leadership of Nathaniel Bacon, a European landowner, to rebel against the governor of Virginia. The situations of the enslaved Africans and the European bondservants were not identical. The Europeans enjoyed many benefits the Africans did not. Nonetheless there was enough commonality of experience, and sufficient social

10. W. E. B. Du Bois, "The Souls of White Folk," in *Darkwater: Voices from Within the Veil* (New York: Harcourt, Brace & Co, 1920) 29–52.

11. Theodore Allen, *The Invention of the White Race, Volume I: Racial Oppression and Social Control* (New York: Verso, 1994).

ties between the two groups, for them to align more with one another than with the landowners for whom they toiled.

Bacon's own motives in the matter were perverse, and certainly not pure from drives we can identify as proto-racist. He sought license to wage a genocidal campaign against local Native American tribes and so to expand his own territory, despite the fact that these tribes were protected under mutual treaty with the British. Bacon quite opportunistically seized on the division between landowners and uncompensated laborers to advance his own position.[12] Nonetheless, the alliance he galvanized, between dispossessed Africans and dispossessed Europeans, seems both startling and refreshing when compared to our current racial climate.

Certainly, it startled Virginia's House of Burgesses. Bacon's rebellion nearly succeeded in toppling Virginia's colonial government before the rebels were defeated. Following the rebellion's end, the House of Burgesses passed laws to harden lines between Europeans and Africans. The intent was clear: to prevent an alliance like Bacon's from ever rising again. These efforts culminated in the Virginia Slave Codes of 1705,[13] which called Africans "negros," and declared that negros were not only enslaved, but property, to be bought and sold, without substantive legal rights. The Codes called Europeans "whites," and declared that whites were, by definition, free and protected by law. The Codes imposed economic penalties for those who married or bore children across these lines. The Codes used the terms "white" and "christian" almost interchangeably. The Codes made some distinctions between "negros, mulattos, or Indians, although christians, or Jews, Moors, Mahometans, or other infidels," but just as frequently lumped these groups together. In the main, the Codes drew a line between "whites" (or "christians") and everyone else.

In all these ways, the Codes defined the rules of the racial structure we still live under today, notwithstanding some change and evolution

---

12. For an excellent treatment of the rebellion and its consequences, see Anthony S. Parent, Jr., *Foul Means: The Formation of a Slave Society in Virginia, 1660–1740* (Chapel Hill: University of North Carolina Press, 2003).

13. "An act concerning Servants and Slaves, 1705," Encyclopedia Virginia, accessed January 5, 2018, *https://www.encyclopediavirginia.org/_An_act_concerning_Servants_and_Slaves_1705.*

through the years. Bacon's rebellion and the Slave Codes that followed were not the unique genesis of these racial categories. There
were antecedents, contemporary efforts, and later developments. But
the Codes were, perhaps, the most critical moment in the early history of race. They defined the essential nature of race—what Michelle
Alexander calls the "Racial Bribe":[14] those who would be called White
received economic, social, and psychological benefits in exchange for
alliance with all other Whites, and separation from all non-Whites,
irrespective of class relationships or common history. By means of this
bribe, Whites would elevate themselves over non-Whites. This is the
nature and content of Whiteness, a nature that confounds my efforts
to name and claim a cultural identity for myself.

I identify as White. Most Americans of my complexion do. I
know it is an artificial and vacant label. I know it is a label that binds
together a history of oppression. On some level, I would very much
like to be rid of it. But I hesitate. In part, this hesitation is a matter of
principle. So long as White Supremacy persists, we should acknowledge our participation in it, and the benefits we receive from it. To
deny my Whiteness would be to run from that fact.

But I know there is more to my hesitation. When I consider the
possibility of abdicating my Whiteness, I wonder what, if anything, I
could claim in its place. What would I be without it? This hesitation
points, I think, to a hidden price of the racial bribe that demands a
certain erasure of the self. When Du Bois announces that the ancient
world would have laughed at such a label as "White," I think he is
noting that those who eventually gathered under the tent of "Whiteness" did not conceive of themselves as one tribe. The idea would
have been offensive to them. The Germans knew that they were not
English. They did not wish to be English. The English, in turn, prided
themselves on their distinction from the Germans. The same was true
for the French, Dutch, and Swedes. Embracing a shared identity of
Whiteness required filing down the differences between these groups.
For the sake of the racial bribe, English, Germans, French, Dutch, and
Swedes assimilated into a more homogenous White culture.

---

14. Michelle Alexander, *The New Jim Crow: Mass Incarceration in the Age of Colorblindness*
(New York: The New Press, 2010), 25.

This process of cultural rejection was particularly evident as the category of Whiteness slowly expanded to include the Irish, Scottish, Northern Mediterraneans, and Eastern Europeans. Because these groups all broadly looked the part, they received the benefits of Whiteness, but only up to a point. To fully enjoy White privilege, they were expected to assimilate as "Americans," a term that has often been a code for White. Such assimilation held two requirements. The first, as Noel Ignatiev describes in his book *How the Irish Became White*, was active participation in White Supremacy, especially anti-Black racism.[15]

The second requirement was a willingness to abandon, or at a minimum downplay, ethnic identities. We can observe this dynamic today. To whatever extent a White person in America holds onto a connection with a specific European heritage, they are perceived as being "ethnic," which is to say their Whiteness is troubled. Because the social and economic privileges of Whiteness are so seductive, most Americans of European descent accepted the bargain, assimilating and becoming fully White. The process moved in fits and starts and encountered internal resistance along the way, but the results were almost inevitable.

And so it is, three centuries later, that I, like many Whites, have very little sense of connection to the history and culture of my ancestors before their arrival in this country. I know, for instance, that I am of English, Scottish, and German stock, but I don't know what it means to be English, or Scottish, or German. These designations hold little weight for me. When considering the question of heritage, I find myself unmoored. I wonder how that conditions my perspectives around race.

In her article "White Fragility," Robin DiAngelo describes some defensive and disruptive responses of Whites when considering race, and racism. While these responses are diverse in character, their consequence is generally to derail any such discourse. DiAngelo traces these responses to six underlying factors of White upbringing: Segregation, Universalism, and Individualism; Entitlement to Racial Comfort; Racial Arrogance; Racial Belonging; Psychic Freedom; and Constant

---

15. Noel Ignatiev, *How the Irish Became White* (London: Routledge, 2008).

Messages that We Are More Valuable.[16] Her analysis is insightful and
challenging, but I would add an additional factor to her list: Lack of
a Robust Cultural Identity. When we—that is, White people—come
to consider structures of racism, we come to face the reality that we
participate in, and benefit from, oppressive privileges. Conscience
requires us to reject them if possible. But, and often at the very same
moment, we begin to see how cultural identity provides people of
color with resources to address hardship: it is a fountain of strength,
encouragement, and wisdom.

To some extent, we lack these resources. We filed them down in
the process of becoming White. To confront our privilege would be
to reject the wages we received for abandoning these resources. Hence,
we react defensively. I think this cultural cavity also conditions the
proclivity of many Whites, myself included, for cultural appropriation. We look to ourselves, and find, to one extent or another, a defi-
ciency where cultural identity should be. We see how people of color
draw strength from culture and identity and we are envious, so we
attempt to claim what they possess that we do not.

In his essay collection "Toward the Abolition of Whiteness,"
David Roediger argues simply and convincingly that, if the designation, separation, and elevation of "White people" is the foundation of
racism and race, then durable racial justice and equity will emerge only
through the dismantling of White identity.[17] I find it hard to refute
his logic, but such logic begs the question, What next? If we who call
ourselves White abolish the label, what will we claim in its place? We
must have an alternative. Or, perhaps more accurately, we must create
one. Such an endeavor is daunting, but not impossible.

There are precedents. Black culture, which, among other things,
developed to survive, resist, and undermine White Supremacy, did not
arise as a matter of happenstance. There have been, at times, specific,
conscious, and intentional efforts to grow and develop such a culture

---

16. Robin DiAngelo, "White Fragility," in *The International Journal of Critical Pedagogy*,
vol. 3 (2011): 54–70.

17. David R. Roediger, *Towards the Abolition of Whiteness: Essays on Race, Politics, and
Working Class History* (London: Verso, 2000).

of resistance and survival—among them the Harlem Renaissance and the Black Power Movement. These efforts are ongoing.

There is also material for us to work with. The erasure of pre-White ethnic identities is, like all human endeavors, incomplete. Remnants of European ethnic identities exist throughout White culture in music, in stories, in faith, and in a vague feeling of connection to our various nations of origin (though often without an understanding of what these connections mean). Moreover, the institution of Whiteness has never successfully enforced complete homogeneity; regional cultures have emerged within it. Having made the trek across the land myself, I know with certainty that the White people in Northern California and those of New England, for instance, are quite different from one another. And there are people making the attempt to construct something new. I suspect the hipster culture of the last decade and a half has been one such attempt (and I say this acknowledging that not all hipsters are White). Unfortunately, it has all too often participated in familiar patterns of appropriation, displacement, and gentrification.

There are certain religious groups that are attempting something similar. I was recently discussing these issues with Ana Hernández, a trainer for Music That Makes Community (MMC), an organization that helps congregations learn to sing without printed music. Ana told me, "We only have to do these workshops because society spent years teaching folks that you need books to do music." I interpret her statement as an acknowledgment of White pseudo-cultural conditioning: a conditioning that generally values depersonalized—that is, written—knowledge at the expense of interpersonal learning. One way to understand the work of MMC is to realize that they are attempting to help people unlearn this conditioning and reclaim pre-White modes of learning. Again, I say this acknowledging that, like Ana herself, not all MMC participants or trainers are White.

There are also several potential pitfalls. Recent years have seen the rise of neo-Odinism, a particularly modern reimagining of ancient Norse religion, among White Nationalists. This seems to be an attempt to reclaim a kind of pre-American identity but carried out in a way that promotes White Supremacy rather than challenging it. The project I suggest could end up on the same road. Likewise, in her article "Whites Only: SURJ and the Caucasian Invasion of Racial Justice Spaces," DiDi Delgado, a veteran community organizer, notes how the propagation of aspirationally anti-racist White affinity groups (among them SURJ, "Show Up for Racial Justice") has often devolved into re-centering Whiteness in spaces of racial justice.[18] A project of rebuilding non–White Supremacist cultures could very easily fall into the same trap.

Finally, there is the danger that pursuing a project to abolish Whiteness will blind us to how White Supremacy continues to operate in our lives. I have, on more than one occasion, seen White people use the claim that race is a social construct to deflect allegations of racist sentiment. Even as we reach for a future in which no one claims the White mantle, we must always be attentive to the damage Whiteness continues to inflict in this moment. The path towards rebuilding a non-White identity for ourselves is thorny and difficult. I find it daunting. But I suspect it is necessary, both for justice and for our own healing.

The recognition that White identity is vacuous promotes a kind of existential crisis. We see that a whole region of ourselves is built on an absurdity, and a hateful absurdity at that. But, like any existential crisis, the confrontation with absurdity is a journey's beginning, not its end. In it, we see the uncertain possibility of building, and becoming, something new. And that, I think, is something of which I could honestly claim to be proud.

---

18. DiDi Delgado, "Whites Only: SURJ and the Caucasian Invasion of Racial Justice Spaces," *The Establishment*, accessed January 10, 2018, *https://theestablishment.co/whites-only-the-caucasian-invasion-of-racial-justice-spaces-7e2529ec8314.*

PART IX
DC

1

It is still dark when I get to the conference center. I made sure to arrive early. This is my first time to meet with them as their pastor, and I want to make a good impression. I enter the lobby and take a seat. I've brought a book, *A Grief Observed*. I left a copy of *The Church Dogmatics* at home because, even though I think I should read it, I can't get into it. I left a copy of *A Wizard of Earthsea* at home because, even though I want to read it, I think it wouldn't give the right pastorly impression. C.S. Lewis seems like a good middle point. I'm about three chapters in when the retreat facilitator walks into the lobby and greets me.

"The vestry just gathered for morning prayer in the conference room upstairs. Come on."

"How's the retreat gone so far?"

"Fine." She bites her lip before continuing. "Yesterday's session went well. But there are some feelings."

I'm not sure what she means. We arrive at the conference room. Four hours later, we stop for lunch and I'm thankful. The morning session has been good, but exhausting. There are a lot of names to learn, and details to work out for the transition. I need a break. I look for a quiet corner where I can give Rondesia a call. A woman hurries past me. She is one of the vestry members. She has neither spoken to me nor made eye contact all day. I think for a moment to recall her name.

"Sherrill." She stops and turns to face me. "Is everything okay?"

She looks at me and then back towards the door. "This was a mistake," she says.

"What was a mistake?"

"Hiring you." She looks away. "We have always had a Black pastor. Always." She takes a deep breath and holds it. "There aren't many Black Episcopal congregations that can say that. Did you know that?"

I shake my head.

"Yeah, I figured." She pauses. "I have seen Black congregations take on a White pastor, and it never, ever works out." She points to the conference room. "I told them that, and they wouldn't listen." Her eyes tear; her face goes tense. "I'm sure you're a perfectly nice person, but this isn't right. And I can't stay."

I notice my arms are crossed. I make myself uncross them. "At the retreat?"

"At this church. I've been here longer than you've been alive, but I can't stay."

There is silence between us. She stares at me and searches my face. I don't know what to say. I try anyway. It doesn't go well.

2

I move furniture and arrange books on shelves. My old boss, Robert, suggested it's important to immediately rearrange the layout of the pastor's office. It's something about claiming the space. There's a knock. Sherrill stands in the door.

"May I come in?"

"Yes. Of course." I lay down the book I had just picked up.

She sits down in the chair opposite my desk. "My mother is homebound. I call her every day."

"That's good. I'm sure she appreciates it."

"I told her about how I was leaving the church. She said I need to give you a chance, and, well, I respect my mother. So, I will, but I'm not happy about it." She pauses to see how I will respond. She's waiting for me to say something, but I'm still not sure what. I try to think what Rondesia would do. She's good at these things. She usually asks a question.

"You told me it was a mistake to hire a White pastor. What do you think will happen?"

"You'll try and change us. Make us White, or at least acceptable to White people." She puts air quotes around the word "acceptable."

"I wouldn't do that."

"You won't do it on purpose, but you will do it."

I stroke my chin, then notice the pretense of it, and put my hand down. "You told the vestry that? When they were making their decision?"

She nods.

"What did they say?"

"This neighborhood is changing fast. And it's going to change faster. People that look like me are getting forced out. People that look like you are moving in. The vestry wants to get ahead of the change. They figure either we bring these new folks in, or we die out. And they think you can help with that."

The significance of her words hits me. "You're saying they brought me in to gentrify the church."

"That's not how they see it, but that is the idea." I try to sort out what I think and feel. She interrupts my meditation. "You must have realized that. I mean, you're not dumb."

"I guess—I wondered about it. I mean, I wondered why they chose a White priest."

"Why didn't you ask? During the retreat that morning, the facilitator invited you to ask any questions you had for us, but you didn't ask anything." There is a note of anger in the last sentence.

I'm about to offer an excuse. I force myself to think about her question. I try to answer honestly.

"I didn't want to know."

She rolls her eyes, shakes her head, and looks away. "My mother said to give you a chance. I'll give you one." She pulls the scrap pad from my desk, and a pen. She writes down three names and three telephone numbers. "These are three of your members. They haven't attended church since you arrived. You call them and ask them what they think about having a White pastor. When you've made all three calls, we'll talk. You've got one week. If you haven't talked with them by then, I'm gone." She turns and walks out.

I gather the courage to start making calls. The conversations take about an hour and a half. By comparison, my talk with Sherrill went smoothly.

3

I pull up to the baggage claim. At the curb I see Tony, a friend from college, and Alison, his new girlfriend. I get out and we share hugs. He takes shotgun. She sits in the back. He points to the stereo and shakes his head. "Bowtie" is playing.

I raise an eyebrow. "What?"

"You're not fooling anyone."

"What do you mean?"

"Outkast won't get you any street cred. They're very White."

I protest, "I know lots of Black people who listen to Outkast." I am about to call out the absurdity of one White guy—a very White guy—dictating what qualifies as legitimately Black to another, even Whiter guy, but I stop because that's exactly what I was doing. Because he knows me. And he's right. I was posturing. I do listen to the album privately, but I put it on in the car for his benefit, not mine. I was performing for him. I can't imagine putting it on if I were picking up a Black friend at the airport. I would feel absurd. But I played it for him. I reflexively wince. He sees it. I realize that I've been silent for some time now. I say the only thing I can think of.

"So, what do you guys want for lunch?"

4

I have the day off. I've been lounging around. I found a copy of *Hancock* at the local Redbox and watched it for the second time. It seemed different to me this time. I walk to the sink, drop my cereal bowl in, and begin washing it. Rondesia comes home as the soundtrack credits begin to roll. She points to the TV.

"What were you watching?" I tell her. I've been thinking about what I want to say.

"I don't know why I didn't notice it before. That movie is a hot mess. I mean, you've got this super-powerful Black guy, but when he first shows up he's belligerent, ill-mannered, alcoholic, and destructive. Nobody really wants him around. Then this White guy arrives to teach him how to be a valued member of society, which includes basically talking, acting, and dressing like the White guy. Specifically, he has to stop landing in his dramatic two-footed superhero stance, which, while destructive, also marks the fact of his presence—that he's been there. Instead, he should land in such a way as to leave no record of his having been there, like he's assisting in his own erasure. And then, to top it off, the White guy suggests it would be a really good idea for everyone if the Black guy would just go to prison for a while, which is insane.

"Then we find out that the White guy is actually married to a superpowered White woman, who has ignored her superpowers to accept the role of housewife. I think that is supposed to be commendable. Of course, her attraction to the Black guy threatens the stability of the White household, as well as the White guy's fragile ego. And the Black guy has been cut off from his past and family so completely that he doesn't remember who he is or where he came from. The only thing he actually knows about himself is the name he was given, 'Hancock,' which, it just happens, is in fact the name of a White slaveholder. Then we find out that when the Black guy and the White woman are in the same place they both become weak and die, as if to suggest that finding any common cause between Black men and White women would

187

lead to the destruction of both. Predictably, there are no Black women anywhere in the movie. And then we find out that they're both the remnants of a whole race of superheroes who assimilated into mainstream society, forgot who they were, and faded away, which feels like it might be a nod to the whole vanishing-people idea of indigenous people. I don't know.

"Anyway, the final resolution is that the Black guy has to go off into self-imposed exile so the White woman can go back to her role of domestic subservience, thus preserving the White family, but not before he inscribes the moon with the White guy's brand logo, literally using the work of his back to wreak environmental havoc for the glory and enrichment of the White man. And in the context of the movie, this is supposed to be a good thing, because the White guy is benevolent. Oh yeah, and it came out during the last Democratic primary when, for the first time, it was clear that either a White woman or a Black man would be president. It was a little too on the nose. I mean, they could have called it 'Hancock: A White Male Backlash Fulfillment Fantasy.'"

She stares at me blankly. "I told you that."

"What?"

"What you just said. I told you that."

I set the bowl down. "Which part?"

"All of it."

"When?"

"Right after we saw it in the theater."

"Wait—really?"

"Yes."

"What did I say?"

"You told me I was reading too much into it." There is a long pause. I pick the bowl back up and begin drying it.

"Well, I feel like an ass."

"Yep."

5

I wasn't much of a Trekkie before I met Rondesia. My fandom connects with our relationship. The release of a new *Star Trek* movie was an obvious occasion for a date. I check my phone. Thirty-five minutes to showtime. I am grateful it's warm out, though I wonder why they won't let us wait inside. The sky gets dark. Ahead a father waits with his son.

The boy points up. "Look, Dad, that's Venus. We learned about it in school."

The father shakes his head. "That's Alpha Centauri. The first star out is always Alpha Centauri. It's brightest because it's the closest star."

The boy looks up and to the right. "But Venus is closer than Alpha Centauri."

"Right, but Venus is a planet and Alpha Centauri is a star, so it's brighter." I feel myself leaning forward. Rondesia pulls me back slightly.

The boy continues. "Venus doesn't have to be a star; it reflects light, like the moon."

"Right, but even so it wouldn't be as bright as Alpha Centauri because, like I said, Alpha Centauri is a star."

"But the moon is brighter than all the stars."

"Well, that's a special case. Because the moon is so much closer to the earth."

The boy frowns. "But Venus is also much closer to the earth than Alpha Centauri."

The dad shakes his head. "Not on the same scale."

My lips begin to move. She grabs my arm and digs her fingers into my elbow. I close my mouth. The conversation goes on. Eventually the line begins to move and we're inside. The father and son head toward the concession stand.

She smirks at me. "I know you wanted to say something."

"He was misinforming his son." I enunciate every syllable.

"You don't ever embarrass a father in front of his children. Ever."

"But he was wrong."

She shakes her head. "When you're a father you'll understand." She turns and heads for the theater. The implication of her words stops me.

"Wait. Are you planning to have kids?"

"Yes."

"With me?"

She stops and turns again. "Who else?"

Debriefing DC

Try again. Fail again. Fail better.

—Samuel Beckett, *Worstward Ho*

For five years, I have worked as the head pastor of a historically Black church. Calvary was once a destination church for middle-class Black professionals in the city. At its height, more than a thousand souls visited our sanctuary each Sunday. It founded a school and a community center. Its longest-serving pastor, the Rev. James O. West, was instrumental in the integration of several local institutions. Now, we bring in between sixty and seventy on a Sunday. The average age of our membership is over sixty. Most live in the suburbs, outside the District.

Our neighborhood, the H Street Corridor, was once the center of DC's Black economy. The '68 riots crippled the area. For decades, it has struggled to get back on its feet. I am tempted to say that the neighborhood is finally recovering, but that would be false. In fact, a new neighborhood is emerging, with little connection to the past. Slowly, but with gathering speed, it is pushing aside what has come before. A new streetcar, under private management, runs down the length of H Street. There is no charge to ride it. It goes nowhere in particular. Long-term residents, used to commutes on underfunded bus lines, grumble at the streetcar's futility. Capital flows into new enterprises. Long-standing businesses face soaring rents and taxes. Many have closed. When we open the doors of our sanctuary, a gleaming Whole Foods greets us. Inside, a loaf of bread costs almost four dollars. Each week three or four residents, working folk, come to the church for help buying groceries. The family renting a house next door to our church moved away last month. The cost of food had grown too high for them.

These changes are complicated. They involve trends of economics, geography, and culture. Still, and at the risk of being reductionist, one trend stands out: the neighborhood is becoming White. And I am undeniably part of that change. This fact has chased me since my first day in Calvary's pulpit. I have tried, in different ways, to allay this anxiety. I reminded myself that it was my wife, a Black woman, who suggested I apply for the position here. It was my mentor, an Afro-Latino, who encouraged me to follow through. It was Calvary's search committee, entirely Black, who forwarded my name to the vestry. And it was Calvary's vestry, also entirely Black, who chose me as pastor. But this line of thinking began to look uncomfortably reminiscent of that classic White liberal talisman against accusations of racism: a roster of Black friends. When Rondesia and I were engaged, I promised myself I would never use my relationships with Black people in this fashion, and so I abandoned this line of thought.

I then told myself that the changes engulfing Calvary and the neighborhood would continue, with or without me. Of course, this was true. The future of Calvary's neighborhood was drafted decades before, as part of DC's thirty-year development plan. The first of the mixed-use, multistory condominium developments that tower over us had already broken ground some months before my arrival. And, after all, Calvary is a small church and I am a person of little consequence. My own decisions would have very negligible effect on the shape of this place. I knew this argument to be an evasion from the start. Regardless of how large or small our influence, we are responsible for what we participate in. The great trends of history do not absolve us of our choices in this moment. So, I abandoned this line of thought as well.

When my excuses were finally exhausted, I thought I should leave. But leaving and tossing the congregation into another difficult transition in the midst of an already uncertain moment seemed just as irresponsible as staying. I arrived, for myself at least, at an uncomfortable compromise—a compromise of necessity. I am here. They have chosen me, and I have chosen them. Sherrill was correct, in some sense. Calvary's vestry had chosen me, in part, with hopes of attracting some of the new, White residents of the neighborhood. But she had also underestimated Calvary's commitment to its identity. Calvary will either find a way to thrive, while holding its inheritance as a Black congregation, or it will walk on in faithful witness until we close the doors. And I am increasingly confident there is a future for us on this path.

So we do what we can, together, in this place, to protect and claim Calvary's legacy, and the legacy of this neighborhood. I seek and heed the advice of Calvary's layfolk. I stretch myself to support and lift up styles of worship and music that are not my own. I ask, "What can we do to make this place more holy for you?" I listen for issues of concern to our members and call the question, "What can we do about this?" I seek out leaders who will challenge me on questions of race, which they do, and it is always uncomfortable. I clumsily walk a line between lifting the voices of our members and using my own privilege to speak on their behalf. It is very messy. Most days I go home thinking I've stumbled somehow. Many days I do stumble, but don't notice until much later.

I think many White people working towards anti-racist objectives feels this ambivalence. Wherever we go, whatever we do, we participate in structures of White Supremacy. My own participation in the changes of the H Street Corridor is only one example of this phenomenon. We participate in these structures even if and when we work to dismantle them. Our works are all tainted. Faced with this reality, we are tempted to make some kind of evasion. We rationalize this taint away, or ignore it, or cynically withdraw, convinced it would be better to do nothing at all. Each of these strategies aims for a kind of ideological purity that would render us free from the racialized consequences of our lives and actions, but no such freedom exists. We cannot find it, not even in the choice to do nothing at all.

Maurice Mitchell, an organizer in the Movement for Black Lives, and the director of the Working Families Party, once told a White anti-racist collective, "Your individual anxiety about possibly getting things wrong has nothing to do with my liberation."[17] There is a tremendous clarity in his words. Our fear of unintentionally, or inevitably, acting racist leads to disengagement and apathy. In turn, our inaction, by default, supports White Supremacy.

The baptismal covenant of my church contains a line that has been the touchstone of my faith and my model for moving beyond this conundrum. It is a call given to the entire congregation when we receive a new member:

---

17. Gigi, "SURJ Launch Report," Triangle SURJ, March 27, 2018, *http://www.trianglesurj.org/launch-event-follow-up/*.

Celebrant: Will you persevere in resisting evil, and, whenever you fall into sin, repent and return to the Lord?

People: I will, with God's help.[18]

Leaving aside spiritual questions, though such questions are fundamental for me, I think this vow encapsulates the attitude we, as White people, must take in encountering White Supremacy. When I teach this covenant to families preparing for baptism, I highlight the fact that it contains four commitments: to continuously resist evil, to acknowledge the certainty of our failure, to get up and try again, and to recognize we cannot do these things without help. The only choice of integrity for us is a choice for messy and imperfect action. It is a choice to work against racism, wherever and however we are able; to expect that our efforts will be flawed, and sometimes problematic; to know that we cannot move forward without help; to listen for the counsel of our brothers and sisters, especially our brothers and sisters of color; to acknowledge our mistakes, and to learn from them. To get up and try again. If I were to offer a more secular summary, it would be Beckett's famous exhortation: "Ever tried. Ever failed. No matter. Try again. Fail again. Fail better."

PART X

Trayvon 1995–2012, Joshua Ibrahim 2013–?

1

The metal movable type letters rattle in their box as I walk across the lawn. It's Saturday—time to update the church message board. I hate this part of my job. I am ill-suited to it. The message should be short, witty, and relevant. I'm long-winded, slow, and stuck in my head. I pull down the letters from last week's message, which was for Resurrection Sunday:

SILLY RABBIT, EASTER IS FOR JESUS.

I shake my head. It took me two hours to come up with that. I pause as I put the last letter in the box.

They announced the charges against George Zimmerman on Wednesday: second-degree murder. I feel like I should say something about it. I want to say something about it. I'm preaching about it tomorrow, but that's different. In a sermon I have time to clarify, to help people understand what I mean, to answer questions after the fact. The sign is one sentence for strangers walking by. It is all they will know about our church. I want to be relevant, but also diplomatic. I keep turning it over in my head. Half an hour later, I begin putting up letters.

David walks by as I put up the last one. He lives in the neighborhood. Like most of the longtime residents, he is Black. I met him last week around the same time. I guess he goes walking every Saturday. He laughed at the joke about the Easter Bunny. He stops to read:

MAY THE TRIAL OF GEORGE ZIMMERMAN
PROCEED WITH JUSTICE AND TRUTH.

He frowns. "Father?"
I wince; I hate it when people call me Father. "Yes?"
"What do you think about the trial?"
"Excuse me?"
"The trial. Do you think Zimmerman did it?"

"Well, yes. I mean, he admits it, right?"

"And do you think he was justified?"

"No. I guess not."

"So what is this?" He points to the board.

I shrug. "It means the same thing, right? Justice and truth would be Zimmerman getting convicted."

He rolls his eyes. "You're hedging. One person looks at that and says, 'Hey, they're supporting Zimmerman.' Another looks and says, 'Oh, they think he should be convicted.' You're a pastor; you need to say what you mean. You put a murderer's name up on a church. Trayvon is the name people should be saying." My shoulders fall. He shakes his head. "If you were a father, I mean a real father, you would understand."

His words are uncomfortably familiar, and now, prescient.

2

It is sometime around 2 a.m. I am lying in bed next to Rondesia. She huffs and groans and turns, first to one side, then the other. She bumps me both times. She huffs again, louder this time. She whips one of the pillows from under her head. It smacks the side of my face. She puts it between her knees. There are more groans. She yanks all the blankets over her shoulders, leaving me none. There is a moment of quiet, then she kicks all the covers off. There is quiet again. I wait to see if it will take.

She is now in her third trimester. There is no comfort for her, but she is still for the moment. I won't have long before she's tossing and turning again. I try to force myself to go back to sleep.

She speaks, "Hey."

"Yeah?"

"You awake?"

"Yes."

She turns away from me, then elbows me. "Good."

3

An orderly brings breakfast to our room on the maternity ward. There is no tray for me. I must go downstairs. I kiss Rondesia on the cheek and our newborn son on the small patch of forehead that pokes out from the blanket. I see a flash of purple—the security anklet. His foot has come loose. I rearrange the blankets to keep him covered and head downstairs.

Two men sit uncomfortably in waiting room chairs. They are looking at an app on their phones. It's a quiz. The object is to identify a baby's needs based on a recording of its cry. They are keeping score and playing for money. I listen a moment. All the cries are identical to my ears.

The cafeteria is empty. The meal is uninspiring, and forgettable. I doubt I would remember it anyway. I drop off my tray and head upstairs. I arrive at the security door to the ward. The doors are shut and a red light flashes by the intercom. They are on lockdown. I am certain it is because of my son, though this thought does not trouble me. Every time I leave, he kicks off his anklet, triggering a ward-wide security check. I think he's messing with me on purpose. There is nothing to do but wait. I lean against the wall and begin to drift off. Another man walks up. His eyes are heavy like mine. The green bracelet on his wrist matches mine. We nod weakly at one another. He raises his arms to rub his eyes. The cuff of his sweatshirt falls an inch. I see a second bracelet.

"Twins?" I ask.

"Yeah. My third set."

"Wait, you've got four kids at home already?"

He nods.

"And now you've got six?"

Again, a nod.

"How old?"

"Two and two, one and one, and the newborns." He stares at me blankly and adds, "All boys."

His revelation so startles me that I swear loudly, but I'm a priest, so I follow it with "God be with you." Both the profanity and the blessing are among the most sincere words I have ever spoken.

"Thanks. Your first?"

"Yep."

"I saw them bring you guys into the ward yesterday. You and your wife."

There was a slight pause between the first sentence and the second. There is always so much unsaid, so much that is uncertain. He is Black, like my wife, and I hear in that pause an acknowledgment of that distance between her and me. And now, between my son and me as well. The pause carries neither judgment nor affirmation, only recognition. Or maybe I'm reading too much into it.

He puts a hand on my shoulder. "You'll be alright."

It is hard to imagine someone from whom I would give this statement greater credence.

"Thanks."

The light turns green, and the security doors click open. I head for the room. Little Man is nursing. I smile.

"Did he kick off the anklet?"

"Yes."

I roll my eyes.

"He's just angry because you left."

"I think he's trying to let me know who's in charge."

I tell her about the father of six.

She fixes me with a hard stare. "Babe, don't take this the wrong way, but if that were us, I would cut it off." She deadpans well. I can't tell if she's joking or not.

I realize it doesn't matter. "Yeah, I probably wouldn't blame you for that."

4

I scan the menu hanging over the taqueria's assembly line. This is the first time I've taken him out since we brought him home. He's squirming in my arms. The woman behind us in line starts up conversation. The topic is his cuteness, which is considerable. I like people who have nice things to say about him, so the conversation flows smoothly. I feel comfortable, which explains how stunned I am when she asks, "Where did you get him from?"

I know she is asking because she thinks we don't look alike. My brain stops. While I am trying to sort myself out, some neural pathway fires reflexively, delivering the most obvious and honest response. "From my wife's uterus."

She is shocked, then she is embarrassed. I am shocked at what I said, then I am relieved. The conversation ends abruptly. I get food for my family and go home. This is not how I imagined our first public appearance would go.

5

After a month off with my newborn, I'm back to work. The meeting I'm walking to is number one on my to-do list. It's part professional, part personal. The café where we've agreed to meet comes into view. In the window, I see my appointment waiting. He's one of the new arrivals to the church's neighborhood, though he's been here a year longer than me. I met him just before my son was born, while he, his wife, and daughter were walking the dog. His family is like mine: he is White, his wife Black, his daughter bi-racial. We made small talk and he invited me out for coffee.

I'm glad to make a connection in the neighborhood—that's the professional concern. But personally, I'm glad to meet another member of the club. I know a few other mixed couples, but none that match us: White fathers married to Black mothers. I step into the café. He stands to shake my hand.

"Good to see you."

"You too."

"I haven't ordered yet; do you want anything?"

We walk to the counter together and order. He gets a small black coffee, the same as mine. I appreciate that. I don't entirely trust folks whose coffee orders include Italian words and more than three adjectives. We head for the table. He takes his seat first.

"So, how are you enjoying fatherhood?"

"I've never been this tired."

He smiles. "It gets better."

"I hope so."

"Did you see the Avengers movie yet?" The first time we talked, we connected over comic book geekery.

"Yeah. It was kind of amazing." I'm a Marvel guy. He's a DC man. We've discussed this already. I set my mug down. "What did you think of it?"

He shrugs and fakes a sneer. "I guess they did okay with it. You know, given what they had to work with."

I laugh. We talk about superhero movies and other things. He tells me about the neighborhood: what he's concerned about, what he hopes for. He's involved with a couple community groups. One of them does work around affordable housing. He asks me about my faith. He's an atheist. This also came up at our first conversation. Still, he's interested. I get the impression it's an academic matter for him. He's neutral with regard to organized religion.

"They do good things and bad things. So, my question is, 'What do you stand for, and what are you doing?' and if you're doing good, and standing up for it, I can respect you. I won't join up, but I can respect you." I smile. This is actually pretty close to my own perspective.

He asks a question about the doctrine of the Trinity. It seems intellectually incoherent to him. He doesn't say this in accusation. It's just his observation. I can see he's actually curious to hear my response.

"It is intellectually incoherent, but it's not meant to be an intellectual stateme—" I'm cut short by the sound of an argument. A couple walks past the plate glass window, a Black man and a White woman. They are walking fast and talking loud—almost shouting. I follow them with my eyes. When I look back his eyes have narrowed. He lifts his chin toward me.

"Can I ask you something?"

"Sure."

"It seems like all the White guys I know who are with Black women are really solid partners and fathers. But all the Black guys I know who are with White women—well, there's always issues. Why do you think that is?"

Crap. I look down at my hands. Several thoughts careen through my head: I like this guy; I wanted a friend who was like me; I should let it pass, but if I let it pass, I'll feel like crap, and it would be wrong. I wonder if there's a diplomatic way to respond. A joke maybe. I've got nothing. My hands tremble. I hide them under the table. I remind myself to breathe. It comes out like a hiss through my teeth.

I speak, "Confirmation bias."

"What?"

"The reason it seems that way to you—it's confirmation bias." My face feels hot. "Um." I pause again, then force myself to continue. "You assume that White men are better fathers and husbands than Black men." My voice cracks. I hate this part. "So, when you see Black men struggling in their relationships, you record it. You know, you mark it down in your mind as evidence. But when you see White men struggling in their relationships, or when you're struggling yourself, you ignore it, or forget it." I shift my shoulders. "Or maybe you explain it away, tell yourself that's just what everyone goes through. Like it's normal." I notice that I'm pushing sentences together. I can't give him a chance to interrupt. If he speaks, I'll doubt myself and equivocate. I lift my right hand above the table and draw circles on the table with my finger. "So this 'evidence' accumulates in your mind, but really you're just trying to prove what you already believed." I look up. He stares at me blankly for a minute, then laughs, and smiles with half his mouth.

"So what, you're saying I'm racist?"

The fingers of my left hand dig into my palm. "I don't know. I don't know you that well. But the thing you just said, it was—" I pause again, "—problematic." I'm equivocating.

"Look, it's just my observation."

"Yes. It is your observation. It's a biased observation." I'm equivocating again.

He smiles and shakes his head. "Whatever." There is silence. I look out the window at nothing. He checks his cell phone. "I got to get to work."

"Sure."

He gets up and leaves and I wonder if I said too much. I wonder if I said enough. I wonder if I could say anything that would make a difference. I wait until he's out of sight, then leave. A week later, I pass him on the street. He's walking the dog with his wife and daughter again. They're smiling and laughing. It's a sunny day.

I wave. "Hey." He nods without looking and continues on his way. I stop and turn. I want to call out and apologize. And I hate myself for this impulse.

6

I dial the number and wait on hold, ignoring the easy-listening jazz. I wonder what happened to Kenny G's self-respect. The music stops abruptly.

"Hello, thank you for calling Bank of America Customer Service. My name is Susan, how can I help you?"

"Hi Susan, I need to report a missing debit card. And I'd like to check my account for any activity in the last twenty-four hours."

"Okay, so if I understand, you've lost your debit card, you'd like to report it missing, and you want to check your account for any activity in the last day. Is that correct?"

This is familiar. "Yes." Why is this familiar?

"I understand that this must be distressing."

Now I remember: Affirm and Empathize.

She continues, "I'll have it resolved in no time." And Reassure. I imagine Susan sitting in the call center in Virginia. I'm sure her call line looks very different, but Virginia is the only one I know.

"Susan, I am so very sorry."

"Excuse me?"

"Nothing."

7

We walk back from the park. Rondesia talks, I daydream. The sidewalk gets narrow and there isn't enough room for the stroller. We cross into the street. Suddenly, her tone goes serious.

"My thing is, this is exactly what he was doing. Just crossing into the street. People do it all the time. And he gets shot for it?"

"What are you talking about?"

She stops and faces me. "Michael Brown." My face goes blank. The name is familiar. I know I've heard it recently. She reads my face and says, "The guy who was shot in Ferguson."

Now I remember. "Oh yeah. That was awful."

We stop in front of our place. I carry the stroller up the stoop, and my son along with it. She gets her key and unlocks the door. We walk inside. He's asleep. If I move him he will wake. I close the door, leave him where he is, and walk into the kitchen. I get bread, peanut butter, and a banana and start assembling a sandwich. I look up and she is staring at me, hard.

"This is not okay."

I put the peanut butter down. "What's not okay?"

"Young men—no wait, boys—are getting shot in the streets, legally. You cannot be calm about this."

"I'm not. It's tragic. I agree with you."

"No, no you don't. I'm angry. Enraged. And you didn't even know who I was talking about."

"Well, I mean, there's always bad stuff in the news. It's hard to keep track of it all."

"This news has to do with us." I stop. I know what she means when she says it, but I hadn't thought of it before. She continues, "I need you to be angry about this. I need you to be at least a little afraid."

My arms and legs tense. "Look, I'm not arguing the issues with you. I agree with you. But my feelings are my own. You can't tell me how to feel."

Her mouth draws tight and she walks away. She has work to do. I go back to making my sandwich and try to put it out of my mind. I am not successful. I feel like my skin is crawling. When she is angry with me, I can't think of anything else. I will do almost anything to make her anger go away. I begin reading. I am looking for the right words to say. I am trying to learn enough to prove that I have been paying attention, that I am "woke." I search and I read. And I read more. Then I am bothered. And then I am afraid.

He wakes up. I take him out of the stroller and we play together on the floor. She has sermons to write and phone calls to make. I play with him for a couple hours. She finishes her work and sits next to him on the floor. It's my turn now. I've got sermons to write and phone calls to make. I start to walk away and I stop.

"I didn't think it was about him. I didn't think he was in danger." She listens. I continue, "But you were right. He is in danger and I was calm, and that was wrong. It is about him."

"Us. It's about us. He and I both. We are both in danger."

That is another fact that I hadn't thought about.

8

The weather's nice today. I've taken him to the park. He stumbles over to the slide. I'm very proud that he started walking so young, but he's still not one hundred percent and I don't want him to smash his face again. I spring to grab him, but it's not necessary. He lunges, catches himself on the end of the slide with one hand, and smiles at me.

"Yes. I saw you do it." I smile. He laughs. He reaches up toward me with one hand. I walk over and pick him up. He snuggles into my shoulder before turning again and stretching his arms out toward the top of the slide. I point to the ladder.

"Do you want to go down the slide with Daddy?" He laughs. I walk with him toward the ladder. We pass two mothers sitting on a bench. They discuss the shooting. Another child killed by police. I read about it earlier today. It seems like a weekly thing now. It's become difficult to keep the names straight. I climb the stairs holding him. There's a platform at the top. A girl and a boy are playing, pretending it's a castle. I assume they go with the mothers down below. The girl's skin matches mine; the boy's is much darker.

I look down at the mothers again and hear their conversation. Their expressions are similar and yet different. The White woman is concerned. The Black woman is scared and angry. I look at the children again. My son's skin tone is somewhere between the boy's and the girl's, though closer to the girl's, and closer to mine. My wife has said he will likely get darker. I can already see it happening. When he was born, he was lighter than me. As I eavesdrop on the conversation below, I pray that my wife is wrong. I pray that his lightness will be a shield that will keep him safe. I hate myself for thinking this, but the thought remains. He lunges for the slide again. It pulls me out of my head. I turn to the two children.

"Can we go down the slide?"

The girl answers, "The slide is only for knights. You have to be a knight."

"How do you become a knight?" They look to one another. It seems they haven't considered the question before.

The boy says, "You have to promise to be brave."

"Oh. Okay. I promise to be brave." They exchange looks again.

"Okay. You can go."

I sit on the slide and arrange my son on my lap. I count down from three and slide. He laughs. We reach the bottom, and he launches himself out of my grasp. It's more of a flail than a jump, but he hits the ground running, or tries anyway. He makes it four steps before falling—just far enough to put his forehead on a collision course with the edge of the sidewalk.

I lunge to catch him, but I don't make it. His head hits the concrete and he screams. I hold him. There's a gash on his forehead, and a bruise is swelling up. All told, I think he will be fine. I feel the guilt of letting him fall. I know it is absurd. I will not always be able to catch him.

9

It's getting dark. My meeting went late tonight. I look down the track to see if my train is coming. I walk across the platform toward my usual spot. Some teenagers are playing at the far end of the platform. They are boisterous, as teenagers can be. I find a pillar and lean against it. I stick my hands in my pockets. It's getting colder. I hear a ping and look over.

One young man yells to the others, "Hey, watch out! No shots over there!" He points in my direction.

"Thanks," I say. They get back to it. They're playing with pellet guns. Someone must have hit the marquee next to me. I look at the ground to see a yellow plastic pellet. It is familiar. There was a party when I was ten, maybe eleven. The birthday kid had a pair of toy pistols, like the ones these kids are using. We went to the local park and took turns having shoot-outs. I got hit. It stung but didn't leave a mark. I'm not too worried now. That said, I don't particularly want to get tagged. I keep an eye in their direction. I notice that I'm smiling. They're exuberant. It's infectious.

The platform lights glint off one of the pistols. It is metal, and very realistic. I remember a news story about a child who was killed in Cleveland last week. He had a toy gun. I scan the platform. Others are glancing nervously at the group. I imagine some are worried for the children, some for themselves. A Metro cop strolls casually toward them. I am suddenly very aware of the Blackness of the teenagers, the officer's Whiteness, and my own. I imagine what might happen next. I imagine how I will respond. Dad told me once it helps to rehearse things in your head, to make sure you'll do the right thing. I tell myself, "Don't be a bystander. Don't be a bystander. Don't be a bystander." My eyes follow the officer. He stops a short distance from the group. A look passes across his face. I can't tell what it means. I force myself off of the pillar and tell myself, "Say something." I reach for my voice.

He yells across the platform, "Hey, put those things away!" The teenagers pocket their pellet guns, and he walks back the way he came.

I collapse against the pillar in relief. My train arrives. I board and take my hat off. The teenagers board the same car. A minute later I hear a metallic ping. A pellet bounces off a handrail.

"Hey!" says the same young man as before. "Not on the train!" The toy pistols disappear into pockets. We arrive at my stop and I stand. They're clustered around the door.

The young man speaks again, "Make some room." They part for me. I nod his way. "Thanks." The train slows and I look to his face. "Hey, do me a favor. When you get a chance, Google Tamir Rice."

"We know who Tamir is." Everyone is suddenly still and silent. The train stops. The doors open. I put on my hat.

"Just be careful." There is no answer. I step off the train. I wonder at my own arrogance. Of course they know who Tamir is. I wonder what I should have said instead. I wonder if I would have said anything at all if he hadn't been so polite. I think about that birthday party shoot-out years ago. We wondered about none of these things. We didn't have to.

10

I pull up to the hotel. We picked up our niece in South Carolina a few hours after we were pulled over. She and my son both fell asleep in the back seat sometime around when we crossed the Florida state line. Ron waits with them in the car while we get checked in. We walk to the front office. It's empty. Rondesia rings the bell.

We wait. I pull my phone from my pocket.

 Peter Jarrett Schell with **Ronald Jarrett** and **Rondesia Jarrett Schell**
Yesterday · Edited · 🌐

While driving on the first leg of our road trip to Florida, with my wife, my son, and my brother-in-law, I noticed a white Dodge Charger in my rear view, tailgating me.

I scroll to the end and scan the comments. There is some push-back. Someone questions how I could have pulled to the shoulder after changing lanes to the left. This was a typo on my part. I pulled off to the right. Someone else points out that, when traveling south on I-95 from Quantico, one does not pass Norfolk. He therefore declares the story to be a fabrication. His geography is correct. I misspoke to the officer. I was nervous and more familiar with the geography of the Tidewater area. I kick myself, wondering if this error raised the officer's suspicions. Perhaps that's why we were held so long. But then, he had already taken me from the car when I spoke. I Google my name. The story has been shared 22,341 times. Someone illustrated it as a web-comic. I feel the corners of my mouth creep into a smile. I fight it. I know I shouldn't be happy about this. But I am proud.

"Check this out." I show her the screen. She frowns. "What?"

She breathes out. "I wrote something about it too." I know. I read it. It was short, poignant, and powerful. "It got shared like twenty-something times."

"That's actually a lot. I mean, I rarely get more than one or two shares." She crosses her arms and frowns, which is fair. It was a stupid thing to say, and patronizing.

"Why do you think yours was reposted so much?"

I search for an acceptable answer. "I don't know. Chance, maybe? Shaun King picked it up. That was where most of the traffic came from. And that's just a question of the right person happening to see it and pass it along."

"You don't think it might have something to do with who you are?"

No. I didn't think that.

She looks hard at me. "We've been talking about this forever." I know she does mean the two of us. "They don't notice what we say. But when you, or someone like you, talks, they do. They believe you. Because of who you are." She means because I'm White. The smile I had been fighting back withers. She looks off to the left, thinking about whether or not to say more. She decides she will. "And the way you wrote it, I disappear in the middle of it."

"What?"

"When you're in the patrol car. You talk about how you were scared for us." She stops. "No. Check that. You talk about how you were scared for him, but I was the one negotiating with the officer while Little Man was having a tantrum. I was the one giving the officer a play-by-play of what I was about to do, before I did it, so he wouldn't shoot me when I pulled snacks out of the bag for our son. I told you all of that and you included none of it."

"That wasn't my story to tell. I was—" I stop. I'm still looking for an acceptable response. "I was telling it from my perspective."

"Exactly. But you weren't the only person there. Everyone is sending you all these comforting words, but I was the one facing him when his hand was on his gun. And no one cares." There is nothing more to say. We wait in silence. The clerk arrives.

"Good evening. How can I help you?"

I wish I knew.

11

The weather's nice today. Our son is sad about being back home after the trip to Florida. I take him to the park. He takes a lap around the playground, then charges the slide at full speed. His momentum fails halfway up and he slides back down. He giggles.

A woman walks up next to me. "He's adorable!"

"Yeah, he is."

"Where's he from?"

I smile. It is a nice feeling to have an answer ready.

12

He sprints around the parish hall, ducking under tables and hiding behind chairs. I glance at the ugly bruise in the center of his forehead. He took another fall at the park yesterday. I'm self-conscious, but so far, no one has taken it as a comment on my parenting. I sit down to sip weak coffee and eat a Nilla wafer. Gladys, one of the elders of our congregation, sits down next to me, and leans in.

"Reverend, did you do your son's hair this morning?" She emphasizes the word "you."

"Yes." I smile. I am the sort of daddy who deals with hair. I'm proud of this fact.

"I see. And did your wife see his hair before you left the house?" I frown. This is not the response I expected.

"Um, no. We had to leave early."

"That's what I thought." She sits up straight and folds her hands in front of her. I'm reminded of a schoolteacher. Then I remember that she was, in fact, a school teacher before she retired. She clears her throat. "Now, when you did his hair, did you use conditioner?"

"Yes."

"You didn't use enough."

"Oh. Okay."

"And you should wet it with water before you put the conditioner in."

"Um. Sure."

"Our hair isn't like yours. It gets dry. Now, you can start with conditioner, but if that doesn't work, you may need to use oil. And make sure your wife looks him over before he leaves the house."

I can feel my face flush. "Sure. Thanks."

"It is good that you're trying." She pats my hand. She walks away and I find an excuse to leave. I'm embarrassed, of course, but my mind is stuck on her statement, "Our hair isn't like yours." She is family, of a sort, but not blood. Still, there is an "us" that includes her, my wife, and my son. It does not include me.

215

13

The weather report says it will top ninety degrees today, so I get him to the park early, before it heats up. When we arrive there are no kids, just garbage strewn around the playground.

"I guess we should go back home," I say, but he doesn't answer. He picks up a bottle from the ground and walks over to the recycling can.

"Can you help me?" I lift him up so he can drop it in and then put him down. He goes to pick up another one. I follow his example.

There's a couple sitting in the shade. It looks like they've just finished a run together. One of them gets up, grabs a paper bag, and drops it in the garbage. The other joins in. We work quietly until it's done. When we finish, the couple says hello, thanks him, and goes back to the shade. I point to the play set.

"Do you want to play on the swings?"

He shakes his head. "Can you chase me over there?" He points to the tennis courts. I nod. We run. When we get there, we see maybe two dozen big grasshoppers sunning on the court. He points at the closest one. "What's that?"

"That's a grasshopper."

"Can I help?"

"Maybe. How can we help the grasshopper?"

"Leave him alone?"

"Yeah. That's probably best."

"Can I look?"

"Sure." He gets close and squats, looking carefully. A moment later he gets up, walks to another grasshopper, squats, and looks again. We pass about five minutes this way. A coach and his student arrive at the court. I tap Little Man's shoulder.

"Hey, it's time for us to go. They need to practice." He gets up suddenly and runs to the coach, shaking his finger in accusation.

"No, no, no! Leave the grasshoppers alone!"

I'm embarrassed. "Sorry, he's at that bossy phase." The coach doesn't answer me. In fact, he doesn't even look at me. He glances quickly around the court.

"It looks like the grasshoppers are all over on that side." He points for my son to see. He's correct. "Can we play on the other side?" The coach points again.

My son looks carefully. "Okay."

"Thank you." We say goodbye and start to walk away. The coach stops me. "He's not bossy. He's a good kid." I know he's right. I think he knows I know that, but he still corrected me. I don't know why he corrected me, so I make an assumption. My son is Black. The coach is Black. I am not.

I have already watched people make assumptions about my son: that he is aggressive, pushy, or rude. It comes up frequently at the playground. I wonder if this was true for the man in front of me, when he was a boy. Does he know what my son will face? Does he worry I will be part of it? He waits for me to respond. I nod.

14

It's summer again, a season for visiting friends. We're about to get on the plane. It's time for a potty check with the Little Man. We go to the men's room. I take him to the handicap stall, so I have room to help him. He says he doesn't want to potty. I tell him if he doesn't want to potty, he needs to wear a pull-up. He squeals like a stuck pig, and yells with all the angst he can muster:

"No! Stop it! I don't like it!" The whole bathroom falls silent. I struggle through the proceedings as quickly as possible. After his pull-up is on, we exit the stall. A thousand accusatory stares burn at me. We walk back to the gate. I tell his mother. She blinks at me.

"See, this is why I said you have to carry a copy of his birth certificate."

15

I hang up the phone.

She asks, "Who was that?"

"St. John's. They're looking for a new head pastor. They want me to put my name in."

"Are you going to?"

"No."

"Why?"

"They did that thing." She widens her eyes, raises her eyebrows, and draws circles with her hands: an invitation to offer more. I put the phone down. "They were wondering if you would apply too, so we could split the position." She frowns. This has come up before—three times. We've talked about it. It would be a bad idea. There are too many questions of oversight and authority. Questions we don't need in our marriage. And it's always seemed like a hustle. "They're always trying to get the twofer." She looks quizzical. "You know, two priests for the price of one."

"No. They want to pay for you and get me for free." She sighs. "Look. Yes, they're insulting both of us, but you are always the one they call."

"I hadn't thought of that. Thanks."

16

At the heavy bag next to me Jackie throws a three-piece combination. She is a regular at the morning boxing class I've been attending. Her form is textbook. I like watching good form in action, but that is not why I look. I make myself look away and I remind myself, "Throw your own punches, focus on your form, imagine the opponent." I slip and jab. I bring my forearms together in front of my face to block my phantom opponent's cross. He follows with a hook. I should weave under it and return with a shot to the ribs, but I do not. I imagine a fist colliding with my temple.

I am distracted. I am glancing at her again; again, I make myself look away. There are two problems here. First, no one wants to be ogled at the gym. Second, she draws my attention more than I find comfortable—more than I consider appropriate for a married man. Part of the attraction might be that she and my wife are two of a type: tough, beautiful, full-figured, intellectual, justice-minded, geeky.

The instructor calls out a final drill. I pull focus and continue. Three minutes later he declares the class over. I go to grab my things. Jackie is sitting already, zipping up a Star Wars hoodie. She greets me. Like my wife, she has a dazzling smile. I remind myself to tell Rondesia about this. Secrets are unduly entrancing.

I inquire how her studies are going. She has almost completed her master's. I congratulate her, wish her luck, and mention that my wife has considered getting a PhD. This last statement is something of a non sequitur. I know that, but I am inoculating. We say goodbyes and I leave. The receptionist wishes me a good day. I reciprocate. She also catches my attention, though with nowhere near the same traction. I step outside. The cold is cutting. Ordinarily, I would rush to my car, but something has stopped me—something I just noticed.

There is another attribute Jackie and my wife both have in common. One they share with the receptionist as well. I review quickly, considering all the people I can remember who have pulled my attention. There is an unsettling consistency. They are all Black. I try the opposite. Who was the last person of my skin tone that drew me? This takes longer. I go back eight years before finding an answer. Eight years, which is to say, before I met Rondesia.

Is it just that I notice people who bring her to mind, or is there something more troubling at work? Is this a kind of fetish? I know everyone has preferences, but types involving race are charged, and because of who I am, this particular preference connects with distressing patterns. Jackie walks out of the gym, drawing the strings of her hood tight. She sees me and stops.

"You okay?"

"Yeah. I'm fine." Though, of course, I am not.

17

I've just put Little Man to bed. Rondesia is at a meeting tonight. It's quiet in the house and I don't do well with quiet. I dial Joe's number.

He answers the phone with exuberant and graphic profanity. He likes to scandalize me. This time, though, the obscenity sounds forced; I can hear it in his voice. "How you doing?" I ask.

"Keeping on. You?"

"Okay. I guess. It's been a rough week."

"Brother, you're not lying." And I'm not. It has been a rough week. For me, personally. For him. And for almost everyone I know. He coughs. "I'm trying to keep my head up. Stay hopeful."

"That's hard these days."

"Yeah." There is silence. I sit down. "I feel awful for saying this but it's become like routine. You know? Like part of the schedule: which unarmed Black victim's name will we learn this week? Like some kind of normalized nightmare."

His tone goes flat. "It is normal. That's the hell of it."

"I know. I just—I guess I got numb to it."

"You don't get to do that. You can't let that happen. You don't get to feel numb."

"Well, I'm not now. I was before. I guess it was hearing about two shootings in one week. Then that whole thing in Dallas and Baton Rouge. It was just too much."

"One." His voice hardens.

I don't understand. "What?"

"One is too much. One unarmed Black victim is too much."

I pause. "Right." There is a long silence. I try to imagine what is happening on the other end of the line.

He sniffles. "I'm done."

"What do you mean?"

"I am done. I am done with this place. I am done with this god-damn country. Let the motherfucker burn." Each sentence is louder than the last. I'm startled by how quickly his tone has changed

222

from mournful to defiant. It scares me. I feel an urge to hang up the phone. I don't want to continue this conversation, but he goes on. "I am disposable."

"No. That's not true."

"Stop. Stop. Stop it. I am disposable. My sons are disposable. Your son is disposable. You have to know this." He is shouting now. A PA system sounds in the background of the call. A voice announces ongoing delays on the red line. There are always delays on the red line. Then I consider the significance of the voice in the background. "Where are you right now?"

"The Metro station! Why?" He barks the words back at me.`

I finally watched *Fruitvale Station* yesterday. This fact does not help. I see my friend shouting with rage on a platform at night. I imagine the glances of those around him. I imagine what could happen next.

"I need you to calm down."

"I cannot be calm."

"You are outside on a Metro platform. In public. I need you to get home safely."

"I don't care."

"Your sons, my godsons, need you to get home safely." There is a long silence, which I expected. I knew these last words would give him pause, though I do not know if I spoke them out of concern for Joe, or out of my discomfort with this conversation. I hear a rumbling in the background.

"My train is here. I gotta go." He hangs up before the last word is complete.

18

My son and I ride the elevator to the apartment. He strikes superhero poses as we rise. I check my phone. Joe messaged me last night. He got home safe. We're okay. I think. I can't stop thinking about what he said—that my son is disposable. He's wrong. I know he's wrong. The doors ding and we step off the elevator.

"Daddy, here comes the lava!" he shouts.

We take off running together. He bounds down the hallway from one dark-colored patch of carpet to another, carefully avoiding all the bright-colored bits. I hear him singing, "DUM-DUM-DUM, dum-dum-dum, DUM-DUM-DUM, dum-dum-dum," because, of course, he has his own action hero theme song. He takes a running leap across a stretch of lava, just as our neighbor steps out of her apartment. They collide. Fortunately, her feet were planted and she had a good stance. He bounces off her knee, barrels on forward.

"DUM-DUM-DUM."

I turn to her as I run after him. "I'm so sorry."

She smiles. "Don't worry about it. He's adorable."

I smile back. He is adorable. My smile fades. It won't last. His cuteness makes him valuable, in a certain way. What happens when it's gone? Will Joe be right? Will he be disposable? How will it be when, instead of three, he is thirteen, and trips into a stranger? I catch up to him and hug him.

"Daddy! Let me go!" He pushes away and takes off running. "DUM-DUM-DUM, dum-dum-dum."

Debriefing Fatherhood

[E]ach child represented just that–a parent's heart bared,
beating forever outside its chest.

–Debra Ginsberg, *Raising Blaze*

I first felt my son move the evening of March 7, 2012. The moment was typical of its sort. We were lying down at the end of the day. Rondesia suddenly stiffened. She took my hand and placed it on her belly. Beneath skin, fat, and muscle, something shifted, and then shifted again. I was unnerved. The tactile experience of something alive within her conjured scenes from the movie *Alien*. I imagine the feeling was even stranger for her. My squeamishness faded, and the new experience unmoored me. The fact of my son's existence landed with almost physical weight. We had seen sonograms and heard a heartbeat, but now I felt him, for the first time. I suspect this awareness arrived much earlier for Rondesia: he had been reshaping her body for months.

I know the question of life's beginning is deeply politically fraught. I lack the scientific, philosophical, or theological acumen to offer an informed opinion, but I suspect the lines are far blurrier than those who claim conception, or viability, or birth will admit. I know this: on the evening of March 7, 2012, my son's life became real for me. Touch has that power. I remember the moment with vivid clarity, because I knew my life had changed. I remember the date with precision because the next morning I first read the name Trayvon Martin. I learned that he had been murdered February 26 and counted. It had happened ten days ago.

The fact that I counted suggests I somehow understood the relationship between the two events. I glimpsed the implications of having a Black son in this country. The fact that I resolved, with some success, to put it out of my mind suggests the extent of my denial. Still, something had changed for me, just as it had changed once before, when I bound my future to Rondesia's, because racism lands in the flesh. As Ta-Nehisi Coates pointedly declares to his son:

All our phrasing—race relations, racial chasm, racial justice, racial pro-
filing, white privilege, even white supremacy—serves to obscure that
racism is a visceral experience, that it dislodges brains, blocks airways,
rips muscle, extracts organs, cracks bones, breaks teeth . . . the
sociology, the history, the economics, the graphs, the charts, the
regressions all land, with great violence, upon the body.[19]

Coates's words speak explicitly of catastrophic racism, but their implication goes further. Chronic racism is also embodied and violent.

The Black community experiences higher rates of hypertension,
heart disease, diabetes, and cancer than the population at large. On
average, Blacks receive inferior care when interacting with medical
institutions. In nearly every measurable health index, save that of
skin cancer, Blacks face greater risk than Whites. Wealth inequalities, environmental policies concentrating industrial pollutants in
minority neighborhoods, the stress of living in a racist society, and
the implicit bias of health care professionals all contribute to these
disparities.[20]

Racism is and has always been an offense against the flesh. I
learned that some years before, in an academic fashion, but I felt it with
a newness when my son moved under my hand, because he is biracial,
which, in this country, means he is Black. Whether catastrophically or
chronically, racism will land on his flesh. It is not a question of if, only
one of when and how.

Last week he was running at the park and fell. It happened in
a blur, but I saw one detail in vivid clarity. His knee hit first. He
skinned it. Without thinking, I grabbed my own knee and then
walked over to comfort him. I don't how I would respond if he
endured more serious harm. And I cannot avoid the question forever.
He is endangered. In that surreal way that parents do, I experience
his flesh as an extension of my own, which is, of course, a kind of
illusion, a trick of the imagination, a neurological and evolutionary

19. Ta-Nehisi Coates, *Between the World and Me* (New York: Spiegel and Grau, 2015), 10.

20. Bijou Hunt and Steve Whitman, "Black-White Health Disparities in the United States
and Chicago: 1990–2010," *Journal of Racial and Ethnic Health Disparities* 2, no. 1 (March
2015): 93–100.

sleight of hand that drives me to protect him. His flesh is his flesh, not mine. His mind is his mind, not mine. And the distance between them is very great.

Once, perhaps a year ago, we were sitting together on the floor. I think we were playing, though I don't remember exactly. He gently pinched the skin on the inside of my forearm, where I am lightest. "Daddy, you're White." It was the first time he had described me that way. He usually calls me yellow. In literal terms, he is correct. I am more sallow than ruddy. But he called me White and I didn't know how to respond. I wondered if I should accept the designation and begin a dialogue. The realities of race will shape his life and he cannot safely remain ignorant of them. I wondered if I should challenge his statement. I know my Whiteness to be an artifice, and a violent one. I don't want him to accept these categories uncritically. I was still stuck in my deliberation when he pulled me back into the moment. "White's nice." He smiled. He pinched his own skin and frowned. "I'm brown. Brown is icky." I felt sadness and anger in a flash. And something else, too. I shook my head.

"No. You're brown and beautiful." The words were less confident and more defensive than I intended. That something else I felt had unnerved me. I felt, almost saw, the distance between us stretch out. His flesh was his flesh and not my own.

Nowhere is this distance greater than in the question of consistency. From time to time, racism has landed, and will land, on his body, with greater or lesser force. Sometimes I will feel it. Sometimes I will not. He does not receive the luxury of that inconsistent choice. And it is a choice. There is instinct, and then there is the decision to embrace that instinct or not. When Trayvon was murdered, I felt the danger around my son's unborn body. I panicked, and so I chose to ignore that danger. I made this choice so cleanly that I felt nothing when I heard Michael Brown was killed. Intellectually, I denounced the injustice of it, but my body was numb.

Rondesia challenged me. I could not remain numb and be a good father. I had to choose between ignorance and my son's body. I chose his body, though I still must remind myself of my choice from time to time. Then she challenged me again. I could not remain numb and be a good husband. This required a new choice, and one for which I had no precedent.

The connection I imagine with my son's body is intuitive, and instinctual. My wife's flesh is dear to me, but I had never felt the same kind of tether to her. I recognized, but did not imagine, her pain. There was a legitimate reason for this. Until recently, my son could not verbalize his experience. Rondesia has always spoken her reality with clarity and precision, so I was always aware of how different the world seems to us. I could not help but recognize the distance between us. The recognition is important, but it can also be a kind of dodge. It serves to separate us and protect me.

So, I have tried to imagine how life lands on her body. It seemed a strange thing to do at first, but I have grown more practiced at it, slowly. My imaginings bring no greater insight into her experience. I must listen for that. But they have developed the response of my own body. When she hurts, I reflexively imagine the pain. That pain brings urgency.

There is no magic in this. In fact, there is nothing unusual about it at all. Recent years have brought the phenomenon of mirror-neurons to the public consciousness. There are synapses in brains that fire when an individual carries out a particular activity, and also fire when an individual sees another perform the same action. In essence, brains mirror the activity of those around them. This response may be the basis for imitative learning, and the ability to imagine another's experience.[21] It may be that regions of our brains have evolved to reflexively recreate the experience of those we see. We may be hard-wired for this kind of empathy from birth. Racism is embodied, but our own human flesh may just carry the seeds of anti-racist agitation. We require only practice to cultivate them. We need only the will to do the work.

---

21. Christian Keysers, "Mirror Neurons," *Current Biology* 19, no. 21 (2009).

PART XI

AN ELECTION AND AFTERWARDS

1

I put on my shoes to go to work.

"Check this out." Rondesia holds up her phone and I read the news.

"You should check in with your sister."

"Yeah, I was thinking the same thing."

I text, "Just saw the results of the Brexit vote. You're both in our thoughts and prayers." They are in Scotland. I hope they'll be okay. I'm worried they won't.

My phone chirps. "Thanks. We're devastated. The economic consequences are terrifying but the political and social more so."

I check the news to find that Brits are Googling "What is the EU?" in droves. I shake my head at the absurdity of it. There are reports of anti-immigrant and White Supremacist harassment and violence. I'm thankful that my sister and her husband can blend in. I comfort myself with the knowledge that it couldn't happen here.

2

It's already late when I pull up to his house. Joe opens the passenger door and gets in; we hug. He takes out his phone.

"Have you seen the returns?"

"No. I told you, I'm not looking tonight."

"Oh. Okay."

I try to resist the urge, but fail. "Fine, tell me."

"Hillary's coming back, I think. Trump started strong, but it was all places we knew he would win."

"Yeah," I say to reassure myself, and him.

"This is just how it was in 2008. Remember?" I do. I take some comfort in the memory.

"When we get to the apartment, we're not talking about it."

Rondesia and I decided that we've done all we can do. We voted, we donated, we phone banked, we talked to family and friends. While we've both approached the work with urgency, I've noticed a difference in how we think about this election. Given the crassness of the debates and campaigning, I see it fundamentally as a referendum on common decency. The Americans I have known are complicated and diverse, but, on the whole, a decent lot. Therefore, I regard the possibility of his election as highly improbable.

For Rondesia, the question of decency remains primary, but she identifies the central question of the election as one of White Supremacy and the choice of the American people to tolerate or reject it. Therefore, given her knowledge of our nation's history, she regards his election as both possible, and indeed likely. For both of us, as always, this election is less about the candidates themselves than the ideas they represent in our heads. Regardless, there's no point in checking every five minutes. We will find out in the morning. Tonight, we watch cartoons. We invited Joe because he understands. When we get to the apartment, my son sees him and lights up.

"Uncle Joe!" he says like a battle cry, the *j* sounding more like a *ch*. The Little Man charges him and hugs his knees. Joe picks him up.

"We made tacos. Do you want some?" I ask.

"Who you talking to?" he answers and smiles. Rondesia is frowning though. I'm worried.

"What's up?"

"I got an email from the university. They want me to come in for an interview."

"That's great."

"They want me to come in tomorrow morning."

"So you couldn't come with us then. Can you reschedule?"

"I shouldn't. This is important."

"Right. Okay. Yeah. That's smart." I frown. I hope she doesn't notice. We make our plates and sit down to eat. We turn on cartoons and talk about inanities. We finish dinner, clean up, and gather on the couch. My son curls up next to his godfather and begins to nod off. My hand clasps the phone in my pocket. One of the cartoon characters has a familiar voice.

"Who is that?"

"I'll check," I answer too quickly. I pull out my phone and find the answer, and then succumb and check the returns. She sees the map on my screen. I put my phone away. "Sorry, sorry, I didn't mean to check," which is a ludicrous statement. She shakes her head.

She waits a moment and asks, "Well?"

"It's not great." We go back to cartoons. She is the next to submit.

I raise an eyebrow. "So?" She shows me her screen. The math isn't good.

Joe says, "Give it a minute. That blue wave is coming." I try to believe him. Our show finishes. The Little Man has fallen asleep and I carry him to his bed and lay him down. I flick off the light.

"We should go to bed. We've got an early morning."

"I'm gonna stay up," he says.

"Sure. Just crash on the couch whenever."

Rondesia and I head to our room, turn out the lights, and lie down. I try to put it out of my mind. I need to get some sleep. I roll on my side and see the glow of her phone's screen against the far wall. She's checking. I will not ask. I will not think about it. It cannot turn out this way. She groans.

I give in. "More bad news?"

"It's worse."

I wait, then clear my throat. "I want you to come with us tomorrow. With all this—you should come with us." There is another pause. "No. The interview is important. I should go." She's right. I know that.

"I just want to be with you tomorrow."

"I know." I roll over again and go back to not thinking about it, or trying not to, anyway. I suppose I go to sleep at some point, but it's hard to tell.

The alarm goes off. It's four. It will be over by now. I pull myself out of bed. A thought flies into my mind—a fantasy: I will check my phone, and Clinton will have won. I will wake my son and his godfather and we'll head out on our trip. I'll let my wife sleep, but I will leave her a note declaring what has happened. Something clever about dodging a bullet. I don't know. I check my phone. Of course, it is not so.

I get ready, pack my son's clothes, grab snacks for the road and two thermoses of coffee. As I walk into the living room, I see that at some point during the night, my son got up and crawled in bed next to his godfather. He does that with family.

"Hey," I put my hand on Joe's arm, "it's time to go."

He rubs his eyes. "I'm ready."

I lift my son onto my shoulder. He wakes up immediately, smiling. Both things surprise me. He's not a morning person. I kiss my wife goodbye, we load into the car, and leave. The drive is about two hours.

Joe speaks first. "Did you see the final returns?"

"Yes." We talk about consequences, possibilities, and the illness of our nation. We try to offer one another hope, levity, rage, and distraction. All our efforts fail in different degrees. My son's nonstop and occasionally nonsensical narration of the drive brings the only laughter. The sky lightens as we approach the city.

"You ever notice that Philly looks like someone took Baltimore and just stretched it?" Joe asks. I hadn't. He's right.

"Weird."

My son chimes in. "That's a big city. We need to paint it for more colors. Daddy, you get the purple paint." We laugh. I turn off the freeway, and wind our way through the narrow streets. I park next to a squat brick building wedged between a tattoo parlor and a nondescript concrete storefront. I'm not sure it's the right place. We get out to check. Each pane of glass in the window has a sheet of printer paper taped inside. Each sheet bears a single letter. They read, "Amalgam Comics & Coffee House." It's the right place, but it is still closed.

I turn to Joe. "Breakfast?" We drive in search of somewhere to eat. He points to a diner whose only sign reads, "Breakfast." Perfect. We park. I get my son out of his pajamas and dressed. We walk into what is every greasy spoon ever. We all order pancakes in various combinations. I try not to look at the commentators on the TV over the cash register. They won't tell me anything I don't know already. My son gets syrup everywhere. We finish and clean up. I go to pay at the register. A man at the counter speaks with the owner. I gather they were talking about sports. Both smile easy smiles.

He asks, "So, who did you vote for?"

Her eyes narrow as though she's reading something. "That's private."

His face hardens and he looks down at his coffee. I have my guesses about how each voted. I think the man shares my assessment. His face softens and he turns to ask the waitress as she goes by.

"What about you?"

"I didn't vote. Every time I do I get called for jury duty. I don't need that hassle."

I hear her words and feel something in my hand. I look down. It is balled into a fist. My knuckles are white. I force my hands to relax. I make myself smile.

"Good morning," I hear myself say. I pay and we leave. As we walk along the street, I see tension in everyone's faces. Maybe I'm imagining it. We pile back in the car and return to the store.

I had expected a line, but the place is almost empty. Posters of jubilant superheroes and brooding protagonists paper the walls. Apart from us, there is a reporter, a cameraman, and the owner. She is the one we hoped to meet. I let go of my son's hand and he takes off running.

I apologize immediately, "Sorry, I'll get him."

"He's fine, don't worry." She looks like a superhero—not like someone dressed as a superhero, but like a superhero. Joe introduces himself.

"I'm Ariell." She extends her hand.

We knew that. Among that particular circle of those interested in comic book geekery, she's become rather famous in a short time; not only because she's the first Black woman to own a comic book store on the East Coast, but also for the kind of store, and the kind of place, she has created. It is as much an artistic hub for the community as it is a store. Joe mentions the lack of a crowd with some concern. She shakes her head.

"The official event isn't until noon. That's when we're doing the signing and the filming."

I frown. "Oh. I was really hoping to get an autographed copy. My wife wanted to come with us, but she couldn't. I kind of promised her."

"So, come back at noon," she offers with a smile.

I motion toward Joe. "I gotta get this guy to work."

"So, come back after you drop him off."

"We came from DC."

"Wow. Is it on fire yet?"

Joe smirks. "Not yet, but give it a minute."

"Wait, you came all the way up from DC for this?"

"It's a big deal. And it seems more important now." She looks at me a moment, and then points to a makeshift desk in the corner.

"Buy a copy and bring it back here." I grab a book and purchase it. My son collides with my knees. I pick him up.

"Let me show you something," I say to him as we walk back to the desk. I hold up the comic book. "What do you see?" He looks between Ariell and the comic. On the cover, her comic book doppelganger shares a cup of coffee with Riri Williams, a teenage Black girl who has taken on the mantle of Iron Man in the Marvel Universe. Little Man's brow furrows in confusion and then opens in surprise. He points to Ariell and then to the cover.

"That's you!" She smiles. He smiles back. I hand her the book. She takes a marker in her hand and then bites her lip.

"Are you alright?" I ask.

"Yeah, just concentrating." She looks up. "Mom says my handwriting is awful."

I laugh. "You should see mine. Anyway, we came to get your signature." I emphasize the word "your." "We want the real deal." She signs and hands it back to me. It looks fine. I glance up. "So, I'm curious." She nods cautiously, waiting to see what's coming next. "What's it like to have your face on the cover of a major comic book?"

She laughs. "You know, I don't think it's really set in yet. I'm a tactile person; I have to touch things for them to feel real." I get that. She pauses and makes her face serious. "Plus, I'm trying to play it cool for the event. But I bought my copy already, and tonight, when this is all done, I'm going home to read it." She looks away at nothing in particular and smiles. "Yeah, that will be pretty great."

I smile, too. My son takes off running. I follow, shepherding him as best as I am able, minimizing damage. He finds a comic he likes. We buy a few more books and some snacks and then take a seat. I lay a granola bar and his comic book before him. For a moment, he's still as he sits, eats, and looks at the pictures.

The reporter comes over to interview us. I'm flattered until I look around the empty store. At the moment, his options are limited. He asks why we drove so far. I think we manage to sound articulate— something about hope in the midst of uncertainty and fear. My son gets restless again. It's time to make the journey back.

As we leave, Joe catches Ariell's attention. "Say, I just wanted to tell you. I know it may not seem that important, but with what happened last night, to see what you've built here, and with Marvel releasing this new character, and at the same time honoring you, and this place you've built . . ." He gestures across the room to the comic books lining the walls. "To see us in these dreams—" He uses a specific intonation on the word "us." I've heard it before. It doesn't include me. Though, as Nina Simone might note, it doesn't put me down, either. It simply ignores me. He takes a breath. "It's inspiring. And I needed inspiration today."

There's the beginning of a tear in the corner of her eye. She wipes it away. "Thanks."

Our conversation on the way back is brighter. We talk about art and perseverance in times of difficulty. My phone rings. I hand it to Joe and he puts it on speaker.

I hear Rondesia say, "They rescheduled."

"What?"

"They decided they needed to host special services at the school. A lot of the students were upset, so they called and asked to reschedule the interview."

"I told you, you should've come with us." That was the wrong thing to say, and I know it. "I'm sorry, that was thoughtless."

"No, you're right. I should have come with you."

I smile. "Yeah, you should have. I got you the comic book."

"She signed it?"

"Yeah, she signed it."

I drop Joe off and drive back to the apartment. My son is asleep seconds after we arrive. I hold out at least two minutes longer.

3

My phone chirps. Rondesia sends me an article about a Jewish family that survived the Holocaust. The father wanted to stay in Germany. He was a doctor, with his own practice. He was convinced everything would be fine. The mother pushed him to make preparations in spite of his objections. Eventually they made it to Britain on a physician exchange program. She sends it to me without comment. I remind myself to ask her about it.

Then I forget.

4

My phone chirps. I read Robert's post on Facebook. While he was getting groceries, he saw two young men corner an elderly Latina woman. They called her a spic and told her the new president would get rid of her. He got out his phone and threatened to call the police. They took off.

Three days later, I walk to my church to prepare for Sunday services. My phone chirps again. He's posted again. His church, across the street from the grocery store, and the church where I used to work, was vandalized during the night. Someone scrawled "TRUMP NATION WHITES ONLY" across the banner announcing the congregation's Spanish-language mass. The same message was written over the church's memorial garden, where they bury the ashes of their dead—where I once buried a friend. She was not White. I look up from my phone. I've arrived at my church.

Our neighbor waves from his stoop. "Good morning, Pastor!"

"Good morning." It is not.

5

I'm making breakfast. Rondesia is working at her computer.

"What's going on with the passports?" she asks.

"I've got the info together. We just need to set an appointment."

"So . . ."

"So, I can make the appointment anytime you like."

"You told me you would take care of this."

"And I will. Like I said, we can make the appointment anytime."

"So make it."

"Fine." I call and set the appointment. "Next Monday is the earliest they've got, at 10 a.m. Little Man has to come with us. We can take him to daycare late. They said the turnaround time may be longer than normal because of the volume." She looks away and purses her lips. I've seen this before. She is deciding whether or not to share what's on her mind. I press, "Go ahead and say it."

"What?"

"Whatever it is."

She's trying to stay calm. "I asked you to get this done before the election. You said you would."

"I'm sorry. Things kept coming up. It was hard to find time. We're both busy."

"You make time for the things that matter to you." I try to think of an answer that will satisfy. Then I try to think of an answer that is true, which is harder to manage than I expected.

"I didn't think he would win."

Her shoulders fall. "I needed us to be ready."

"It still might not get that bad."

"Please stop." She puts her hand up between us. "Yes. You're right. It might not get that bad, but we need to have a plan if it does. For Little Man. He already has a target on his back and he won't be cute forever. You know that."

My fingers fidget. I don't know what to do with them.

240

6

The smell of Peruvian rotisserie always enchants me. Still, I am cautious. I've never been to this restaurant before. Pollo a la Brasa always smells good; taste, however, is less consistent. There was a place near our old apartment. When they were roasting, the whole neighborhood smelled fantastic. Dinner there was an almost spiritual experience. Then they lost their chef. We went back the next week and it was like eating cardboard. It still smelled amazing though. So I reserve judgment.

The line is long, but it moves quickly. As I wait, I eavesdrop on the couple in front of me. Since they're almost yelling, I have to assume they don't mind. They speak in Spanish. I'm embarrassed how rusty my ear for the language has gotten. I pick up about half of what they say, but the rest is guesswork. They're arguing about a friend's new girlfriend. He is in favor; she is against. They step to the register. The gentleman orders for them both.

"Buenas. ¿Nos traes dos cuartos?"

"¿Con papas, o yuca?"

"Yuca."

"¿De tomar?"

"Dos jamaica."

The couple pays and finds a table. Another patron steps up to the register.

"Excuse me. Can I have a couple more sauces?"

"The green ones or the white ones?"

"Um . . ." The patron stops to think.

"Do you like spicy?"

"Yeah."

"The green sauce is better," the cashier volunteers, and pulls a couple containers of green sauce from under the register.

I watch these interactions and plan how I will order. The cashier grew up speaking Spanish. It shows in his accent, though his English grammar and vocabulary are impeccable. I think about the expectation that Spanish speakers should learn English when there is no such expectation for English speakers to learn Spanish, even at a Peruvian restaurant in a predominantly Spanish-speaking neighborhood. So, it would be equitable for me to order in Spanish.

However, the cashier's English is definitely better than my Spanish. I think about the assumption that Latinos don't speak English, regardless of their work spent learning the language, or the mastery they achieve. So, it would be respectful to order in English.

I weigh these options as the patron picks up his sauces and the cashier waves me forward. I still haven't decided how I will engage him. I'm stuck in my head. I hate my anxiety over trying to get it right. It paralyzes and draws me inward—the opposite of what it pretends to achieve. Rather than reaching out across lines of difference, I am trapped in the anxiety of "correctness" and have lost sight of the cashier. I step to the register.

"Buenas. Regálame un pollo mediano."

"Do you want fries or yucca?"

"Yucca." I should have gone with English. I finish my order and find a table. A TV hangs over the dining area. I watch a report on the recent rash of racist graffiti and harassment, listening more out of obligation than interest. The reporter says something about how, though the vandalism is deplorable, it points toward the fact that many White Americans have a real and legitimate fear of finding themselves in the minority. I roll my eyes. But then I remember my discomfort moments before trying to place a simple order: the fear of being out of place, or saying the wrong thing. Like so many of my folk, I am used to being the standard of what is "normal." From that position, the daily negotiations of equality feel claustrophobic. I don't doubt that many would go to great lengths to avoid them. I know what that feels like, but honestly, I really think we just need to get over it. Most of the people in the room where I stand spend their whole lives in the midst of such negotiations. The cashier calls the number on my receipt. I walk to the register to claim my order. He hands me my tray.

"Que le vaya bien."

"You too." I reply.

7

We step outside the house. It's cold. We walk back to the car. I'm relieved. Dinner parties are always exhausting for me. She puts her hands in her pockets.

"How do you think that went?" she asks.

"It was weird."

She looks at me. "Weird how?"

"Well, it's that whole thing about which communities are considered important and which ones aren't. Those decisions always fall along lines of money and color."

"Was there anything else?"

"What?"

"Was there anything else that seemed weird to you?" She has something in particular in mind and I don't know what it is. I shrug. She continues, "They asked about what you were doing to revitalize your congregation: what ideas you had, what challenges you were facing. We talked about it for forty-five minutes."

"So?"

"We didn't talk about my work. They weren't interested in it."

"But they asked you about it."

"Right. And then they changed the subject two minutes later. They were being polite. They weren't interested." My eyes dart around, looking for something in the dark. She continues to look straight at me. "And then they shut me down."

I don't remember that. "When?"

"When we were talking about the new administration. Things got heavy and they said I should stick to telling stories about our son." I do remember that. There was laughter.

I smile weakly. "It was a joke. They were just trying to lighten the mood."

"No. They were putting me in my place. Because I am a woman. Because I am Black. And you didn't notice, did you?" I feel myself preparing an excuse and I stop myself.

2442

"No. I didn't."

We drive home in silence. I run through the evening again. Explanations and rationalizations fly through my mind. Maybe I was more engaged than she was. Maybe I offered more follow-up to their questions. Maybe that's why we talked more about my work. Maybe they were just making light. Things had gotten very heavy. I hear all these thoughts and grimace. I want to trust, to believe her without reservation, but my explanations keep intruding. I make myself put them away, one by one, but they keep returning.

We pick up our son. He's asleep. I carry him to the apartment and lay him in his bed. I close the door behind me, and come back into the living room where she is waiting for me.

"I love you. And you are a good man." This means I'm about to hear something I don't want to. I brace myself. She braces herself, too. "But honestly, this is like living with an addict. You do fine, most of the time. When we're around people of color, you're good, but in White spaces, I never know what I'm going to get. I guess you're just glad to be back around your people. I get that. It's important for you to be around your people. But I need to know that you'll be there for me too. And right now . . . right now, I don't trust that you will be. I don't trust that you will see me."

"I do see you."

"Tonight, your wife was publicly demeaned and you didn't even notice."

Silence.

"You're right. That's not who I want to be." I have more work to do.

8

It finally snowed and I'm taking him outside to play. He's having trouble with his boots. I point to his feet.

"You've got them backwards." He sits down, takes off his boots, and turns them around, so the toes are facing towards his heels. He looks at me with suspicion. I shake my head. "No. I meant they were on the wrong feet." He looks down and then back at me. "Switch them." My index finger traces a circle. He takes the shoes, rearranges them, and puts them on. "See, doesn't that feel better?" He shrugs. "Okay. What else do you need to go outside?"

"A jacket."

"Go get it." He does. He puts it on and looks up at me.

"And Daddy puts on his jacket."

"Okay. Let's go." He starts to walk out the door, then stops suddenly.

"Oh, no. Mommy needs kisses and hugs."

I shout, "Hey, beautiful! He wants to say goodbye."

She steps around the corner, smiling. "Goodbye to my Little Man? Of course." She leans down and he kisses her cheek.

"And Mommy kisses me." She kisses his cheek. "And ugga mugga." They share a nose rub. "And high five." She holds her left hand up. He taps it with his right. "Harder," he shouts gleefully. He grabs her wrist with his free hand and slaps her palm several times. "I love you, Mommy."

"I love you too."

We start to leave and he stops again. "Daddy needs hugs and kisses from Mommy." We kiss. "And hugs." We do. "And ugga mugga." We do. "And high five."

"No," she says firmly, "that's enough." Through ten years of marriage, I have never, ever, received a high five from my wife.

I sigh. "Sorry. I know this is kind of a pain."

She smiles. "Don't pretend like you don't love it." She's right. I do. "I love you."

9

I walk Mom and Dad to their room and say good night. They are visiting for the holidays. They had planned to stay up and watch the ball drop with Rondesia and our son, but everyone was too tired for that. I close the door behind them and walk to the kitchen and pour myself a glass of water. She walks up next to me and lifts her phone with the DMV website.

"The due date for the emissions test was December 21." She holds up a red marked letter. "And the violation date on the citation is December 28. They don't match. It's not the same thing." This was a point of contention earlier tonight. We received an ominous-looking notice of violation from the DMV in the mail, but it didn't specify the nature of the offense. I felt certain it was about our emissions test; we are past due, but we were going to take care of it this week. She wasn't certain. She thought it might be a moving violation. She wanted me to call in and check. I refused. I insisted that I was right. We debated. The conflicting dates would suggest they are for different violations. I think. Monday everything is closed for New Year's.

"Okay. We'll call them Tuesday." I check the clock. The church has a New Year's Eve service tonight. I'll need to get going soon.

"So that's it? You're done with it now?"

"Wait, do you want to argue about it? I'm agreeing that you were right."

She raises the index and middle fingers of her left hand together. "You know what? Just go to work." She turns and walks away.

"Wait. I'm sorry." I don't actually know why I'm apologizing.

She turns and says, "I don't accept because you'll do it again. I just need to be angry now. Go to work." She steps into our son's room and sits down on the floor next to him. I shake my head and begin to get dressed. I know I shouldn't have apologized. I wasn't sorry. I didn't even know what to be sorry for. I don't know why she's angry. We were both arguing. Yes, I dug in my heels, but then I conceded. Why would she hold that against me? I'm not sorry. If she asks again, I will tell her. I finish dressing and walk to the front door.

"I'm going," I call out.

I hear her voice. "Daddy's going to work. Go say goodbye." He runs around the corner in Spider-Man pajamas, rubbing his eyes. He hugs me. I kiss him. "I love you."

"Okay, Daddy, go to work." He runs back to his bedroom. I stand up to leave. She stands looking at me. I say goodbye.

She crosses her arms. "So that's it? You don't want to hug or anything? I don't want to start off the New Year angry."

"We are angry. We shouldn't pretend otherwise."

"Fine." She walks away. She always calls my bluff.

"Stop." She does. "I am angry, but I do want a hug." She walks to me. We embrace. "I love you."

"I love you too."

"I want this to change."

"Me too." We hold each other. She rests her head against my chest.

"It's just—when we disagree, you get so committed to winning. To being right."

I feel my face tighten. "You do too."

"What?"

"You dig in your heels too; you get entrenched. Don't act like I'm the only one who does it." She steps back. Her arms slide from my back and she takes my hands as she pauses to choose her words.

"I offered a concession. I said we should just call in and check."

"Which I agreed to. Just now. I also conceded."

"After they left. After your parents left, you conceded. You want to win with an audience. When we're alone it doesn't matter anymore, so you concede."

I hate it when she's right. I'm really tired of it. It just makes me want to argue more.

10

I sit at the counter, eating breakfast. My phone chirps. The email I was waiting for has arrived. I skip the introduction and look at the spread of numbers beneath it.

"Great Britain 66%, Ireland 20%, Europe (West) 9%, Finland/ Northwest Russia 2%, Scandinavia 2%, Melanesia <1%." This is basically what I expected, except the last one. The percentage is so small that I'm guessing it's a testing error.

I take a pen, and scribble on the back of an envelope, "2 parents, 4 grandparents, 8 great-grandparents, 16, 32, 64, 128 great, great, great, great, great grandparents. 1/128 < 1% of me. Eight generations (including me). 25 years/generation x 8 generations = 200 years. 2017 − 200 = 1717." I put the pen down.

So there was, perhaps, a man or woman of Melanesia born sometime around 1717, a man or woman who had a child around 1742, roughly the high point of European adventurism and colonial conquest. That child was part of my family line. There was an ancestor with whom I have no meaningful connection, apart from a few stray strands of nucleic acid swimming in my cells. Or, alternatively, there was just a bit of statistical noise in my testing. Rondesia walks behind me and glances over my shoulder.

"Anything surprising?"

"No. Not really."

"So what are you going to do with it now?"

"Do with what?"

"Your ancestry results."

I shrug. "I don't know."

She thinks for some time before continuing. "You know he's going to ask someday, right?"

"I'm sorry, what?"

"Our son. He's going to ask about your people. Your culture."

"Oh. Yeah, I guess so."

"What are you going to tell him?"

"I don't know."

"You talk about being Scottish sometimes."

"Yeah. That's important to Dad. And Grandma, I think."

"You can tell him that."

"Yeah. Except, what do I really know about that? Whisky, kilts, and bagpipes. That's not a culture, that's a cartoon character."

"You like shortbread."

"That's cute. But you're proving my point. I'm not Scottish in any way that means anything."

"Sooner or later he will want to know about your people. And you can't just talk about White Supremacy."

"But that's a big part of the story."

She nods. "It is. And we will teach him. But if all you can tell him is a story of oppressors, then he'll have no choice but to hate half of himself. He's going to have enough to deal with in his life. He doesn't need that on top. You must have more for him."

My mind is blank. "I don't think I do."

She lays a hand on my shoulder. "Figure it out. You probably still have a couple years before he starts asking."

11

We've just dropped our son off at daycare. Amazingly, we both have a morning off, together. We walk to coffee. I tell her about the book again. It's almost finished. If I'm honest, I can't wait to be done with it. She asks questions; I answer, and she listens. I walk her through the outline of the thing, the vignettes I've included.

She stops me midway. "Why did you include the story about being on the plane coming back from Ethiopia, when there were all the women who had adopted babies?"

"Oh. I guess . . . the stories all have to do with Whiteness. And, it seemed like an important example. You know, this White lady took in a Black baby, but then tries to keep him from connecting to a grown Black person."

"No, I get that. What I meant was, why did you include it." She emphasizes the word "you." "It didn't happen to you."

"Well, I mean, I know it happened to you, but I was there, I saw it." She shakes her head. "No, you weren't."

"Of course I was; we were on the same flight."

"Right. And when you went to the bathroom, you saw them sitting there. But when I went to the bathroom alone, that was when the woman turned the baby's face away from me. Then I came back to our seats and told you about it."

"Wait. Really?"

"Yes."

I can picture it. I can remember it. "Are you sure?"

"Very." Her eyes are certain.

"Oh. Okay. I'll fix it." My shoulders fall. I was really enjoying being almost done with it.

She sees it. "Tell me about the rest." She's trying to cheer me up. I don't mind. I tell her the rest. She listens. Then she stops walking. I stop next to her. She's framing a difficult question.

"In the book, am I your magical negro?" I lose my breath for a moment, but only a moment.

I pull air in through my teeth. "I don't think so."

"You don't sound too confident."

"I have thought about it. Our relationship is central to the story. That's kind of inevitable. It's a memoir and what we have is the center of my life. And this," I gesture to the space between us, "is where I have learned the most about myself. About what it is to be White." I pause to collect my thoughts. "But, when you show up, it's mostly about how you express your wants and needs. I mean, the whole thing with the magical negro is that they have no ambitions or desires of their own, right?"

"There's more to it than that." There is silence. A lot of it. She points at the space between us. "You should write this."

"I was thinking that, too."

12

I am completing the final proofreading of this book. I hate proofreading. My mind wanders. I give in to distraction and check my various social media feeds. A friend has posted a video from a website called youngcons.com. The video is titled, "The Absolute Best Take Down of White Privilege Myth on the Entire Internet." I shouldn't watch it. It will only make me angry. I watch it anyway.

A reporter wanders a college campus, asking White students and professors if they believe White privilege is a thing. They do. He asks them to give examples from their own lives. They have none. He offers this fact as evidence that White privilege is a myth. As I expected, I am angry, though more at the students and professors than at the reporter. I scorn them for not looking closer, for giving him ammunition. I turn off my phone and continue proofreading.

Ten minutes into my work I can see that, like the people in the video, I have fallen short. My examples are trite and superficial. There are details I have missed. There are stories I did not tell because I was protecting family and friends, or because I was ashamed. I wonder if I've told too much about the people of color around me and too little about the Whiteness of my life. Or maybe it's the opposite. Out of some anxiety over playing into "White Savior" tropes, I have largely omitted accounts of how my reflection became action. Now I worry that choice plays into narratives of passivity. It occurs to me that the title I've chosen, "Seeing My Skin," is also an accurate description of navel-gazing. I fear that's all I've done.

I have an urge to delete the whole thing. This is not the first time I have had that thought. I want the book to be sharp, powerful, completely honest, brave, and thought-provoking. Above all, I want it to be beyond reproach. It is none of these things.

It took me time to understand that my longing to stand above criticism belongs to, and protects, my Whiteness. I know that and I see the irony of it. Whiteness has never perfected anything. Whiteness itself is fallen. My Whiteness is fallen. And it protects itself. The fear of making any misstep will keep me from ever confronting it. My longing to speak flawlessly will keep me from ever testifying to what I have seen.

13

I set my phone to airplane mode. I don't want the world intruding right now. The world always intrudes. The apartment feels strange without Little Man running around. He is small, but he fills the space. His grandmother, Melody, took him half an hour ago. Melody loves our son. She is trustworthy and resourceful. He will be safe with her. I know these facts. I remind myself of these facts. But still, I turn airplane mode off. Rondesia puts a hand on my shoulder as I fumble through the settings screen.

"What are you up to?"

"I'm trying to get it so I can turn notifications off, but still get messages from Momi."

"Here." She takes my phone, does something, and hands it back to me.

"Thanks." I look up. She steps in front of the mirror. Her blouse shimmers as she moves. She is stunning. I stand and button the cuffs of my sleeves. We don't often dress up.

She fixes her collar. "So, you going to tell me where we're going?"

"No."

She turns sideways to see herself in profile. "Fine. You ready?"

"Yep."

She grabs earrings as we walk to the door. "We are going to dinner though, right?"

"Maybe." I flip off the lights and we leave the apartment. We get to the car and I open the passenger side door for her. She looks back at me as she steps in.

"You're not sneaky. I know we're going to dinner." As I drive, she marks each turn, working out our destination. I take the exit toward the water. "So we're going to the Mexican place?" There is, as far as we know, only one good Mexican restaurant in the area. Two years ago, I organized an anniversary party there.

One year before that, I said something stupid to her. I was depressed and confused at the time. A thought had been chasing me:

it seemed like every major decision I had made was made to please someone else.

When I told her, she said, "What about getting married?"

I shrugged. "I don't know." Again, it was stupid. We worked through it. It took time, but I realized there were at least two decisions I had made out of my own longing. Our relationship was one of them. I was certain of it. I still am.

Unfortunately, my moment of self-pity and doubt tainted what is one of the most romantic proposal stories ever. We were lying on the ground, looking up, while a blue whale coasted above us. Cetacean songs serenaded us in dim lighting. We decided to spend our lives together. And yes, this actually happened. The fact that it took place at the American Museum of Natural History and that the whale in question was a fiberglass replica in no way diminishes the magic of that moment. It was epic. But the memory had lost its shine for her. I had tarnished it.

So, I tried for a do-over. I secretly got her a new ring. One day, when we were walking by the water, I kneeled and proposed again. She smiled. Her smile is more beautiful than any blue whale hanging in space.

Down the shore a bit was a Mexican restaurant. I booked it for the date of our anniversary and invited family and friends from all over. We were going to renew our vows. Then things went sideways. Two weeks before the day of the party, police pulled us over and separated us. A week after that, her dad died. I called the restaurant to cancel.

I hung up the phone and she said, "I'm sorry. I wanted to go, but I just can't right now."

Two years have passed. Today is our anniversary, again. So, I expected her to figure out where we were going. From her tone, I gather that she is pleased, but considers tonight something of a consolation prize. I am not discouraged. The restaurant isn't the surprise.

We park the car and she takes my arm. At the restaurant, I give my name and the maître d' asks us to follow. I scan across the room and glimpse my brother-in-law's face. Then I see my parents, her mom, our goddaughter and her family, friends, cousins, aunts. I do a quick head count. Everyone is here. I look at Rondesia. She hasn't seen them yet.

That's not surprising. This place is big, and crowded, and she didn't know to look for them.

Then our son crashes into her and hugs her legs, "Mommy!" She startles, sees everyone, then looks to me.

"Happy anniversary." I kiss her cheek.

The night is amazing. Everyone looks great. The food is incredible. The kids laugh. I made her a photo collage with hundreds of friends surrounding our wedding picture. It's cheesy. She loves it. As we wait for dessert to arrive, I stand and tap my glass. The moment is a contradiction: it is hers, but it matters that I offer it to everyone. I take her hand.

"I love you. I love the life we have together, and I want to keep it. A while back I got confused and I said something that hurt you. It damaged the trust between us. And it was dumb. And it was a mistake. I want that trust back. I want you to know that I choose you, and I choose our life together. I am asking you now, in front of all our family and friends, will you have me again?"

I had practiced these words. I think they were better in my head. There are some bits I forgot. I hear myself think these thoughts and hate them. I can never seem to stop my brain.

She stands and smiles. "Yes." She kisses me. Sometimes she stops my brain for me.

I found the vows we exchanged on our wedding day and printed them on little cards. We trade promises. Our friend Dominic blesses us the way only charismatic pastors can. Episcopalians don't pray like that. People clap. Dessert arrives and we sit again. Between bites, I look down the long table. We are White, Black, Indian, and blends of all these things. Someone has propped the photo collage up on a chair. Faces of a dozen hues smile back at us from inside its frame. My wife's hand rests on mine, and I see the new ring. I feel some kind of fragile hope. Maybe we can overcome the past, end the offense, pay the price, heal the wounds. Perhaps we can find a way forward together. On a night like tonight, it almost seems possible. A waiter comes to clear our plates.

It's pouring as folks begin to leave. We say our goodbyes. Our son leaves with my parents, which was a bit of a negotiation. Melody got to see him the last two days, so he will stay with them tonight. Rondesia suggests we meet up tomorrow to see the monuments. "We've lived here ten years and I've never seen them."

After they are gone, I ask Rondesia to change the setting on my phone again, so I can receive messages from my mother.

"You know, you could just turn notifications back on."

I shake my head. "Nope. Don't want to know what's going on today." I kiss her cheek and then run through the rain to get our car. I'm soaked. I don't care. At the curb of the restaurant, she gets in. "Where to now?"

"I got us a hotel room."

"Where?"

"The Cromwell—wait, that's not right. It is a British prime minister, though." I think. "The Churchill. I got us a room at the Churchill."

She does a terrible impression of Queen Elizabeth. "Ooh. Fancy." She's not wrong. Between the restaurant and the hotel, I've saved for six months for tonight. I do not regret the expense, which is unusual for me. The hotel is strange and charming, as if Tim Burton had designed a Hilton. We have a drink at the bar before going up to our room. The world retreats, and there is nothing between us.

In the morning, we get ready. She brushes her teeth in the next room. I turn my phone notifications back on, because the world cannot be kept out forever. She steps out of the bathroom and looks at me.

"What's wrong?"

"White Supremacists beat some protestors at UVA last night. They had torches."

"How did it start?"

"The city voted to remove a statue of Robert E. Lee. The alt-righters have been planning a protest. I guess they turned out."

I have a college friend who lives near UVA. She's been posting updates about the statue the last couple weeks. I check to see if she's okay. She's traveling, but her husband is at home. She hasn't been able to get in touch with him. He is a photographer, brave, and Black. The combination is risky at the moment. She's asked friends in Charlottesville to contact her if they see him.

I look up at Rondesia. "What do you want to do?"

"I want to see my son." I agree. We check out, call my parents and her mother, and meet up. We discuss the news. Evidently the White terrorists have reconvened. Many are armed. More counterprotestors have arrived.

Little Man is as bright and cheery as ever. I wonder when we will have to start explaining these things to him. I wonder if we have waited too long already. We decide to keep our plans. We take two Lyfts down to the Mall. Parking is impossible there. I check again. Someone saw my friend's husband. A stranger punched him, but he's okay. He's still taking photos.

Our rides drop us off at the King memorial. It is packed. The crowd is mostly Black. The few other faces, sprinkled in, are of all sorts. I catch snippets of conversation. People are talking about what's going on in Virginia. There's energy around their talk, urgency. I wonder if they came here today because of it. The grandparents and my wife stroll around the edge, reading chiseled quotes from King's life. My son will have none of it. There are paths to run, stones to climb, and ducks to chase. I stick with him to minimize damage both to him and to the park.

The monument is strange and conflicted. There was controversy around its construction. I remember reading about it. King stands, his arms crossed and his face grave. His pose is confrontational and, indeed, unnerving. I imagine this King would scoff at the fanciful, inoffensive Rev. King whom politicians now conjure up to chastise young activists. He gazes across the water at Jefferson's memorial with fixed eyes. I wonder if the sculptor intended this subtle challenge. King rebuked White moderates who professed the injury of race, but did nothing to redress it. Jefferson was surely such a one, acknowledging the evil of slavery, but never acting to end it, not even within his own house. The span between their two statues covers half a mile, one hundred forty-two years, and precious little progress. Between King and today, another forty-nine years, and we have lost ground.

Dad shouts to get my attention. He wants a picture in front of the monument with the whole family. This turns out to be tricky. Everyone wants a picture in front of the monument, and there's only one good angle to take it from. There's no particular line or order. People flow past from all directions, stop as camera phones flash, and then keep moving. It's like matchbox cars zipping around tracks, avoiding collisions by hair's breadths and sheer luck. We make four or five attempts to gather when the traffic opens for a moment. Each time we miss our window, Rondesia calls out. It always startles me how big her voice is when she wants it to be.

"Excuse me! My beautiful interracial family would like to take a photo." She emphasizes the word "beautiful." She holds up her phone. "I need someone to get a picture." There is laughter and the crowd pulls back. A man steps forward and accepts her phone. We form up quickly, he snaps a photo, and we move. The traffic closes in again immediately.

"Let's go see Lincoln," Melody points. We navigate crosswalks and park paths crammed with strollers to arrive at the monument's base. Little Man refuses my offer to carry him. He is determined to climb all the stairs himself. He very nearly makes it to the top without stopping.

This memorial is packed too, though the crowd here is much more diverse. We walk through the wide opening between columns. My son stops, startled, at the sight of the enormous sculpture. It doesn't last; he takes off running, darting through gaps between tourists' legs. With his size, he's actually faster than me in a crowd, which is terrifying. I call out several times. He ignores me. I can catch glimpses of him through the crowd. Finally, I catch up with him at the foot of the statue. He is busy climbing over a chain that reads "Do Not Cross" and doesn't see me coming. I pull him back.

"No, Daddy! I want to climb the big man."

"I can see that, but it's not allowed. Come on." I take his hand, and we begin to walk away. He stomps his feet several times in protest. Curiosity steals his anger as we cross between the columns into the south chamber and he sees a wall covered in words.

"What's that say?"

I read to him from the Gettysburg Address. I've read it before, but for the first time it strikes me as strange that such stirring words should be so vacant and generic. I imagine, had the Confederates won the day, Davis would have voiced much the same sentiment, though perhaps not so eloquently. I finish and wait for Little Man to ask a question. He doesn't. The gift store has pulled his attention back to the north chamber. The shop is small. After a quick lap and a near collision with a tourist, he decides there is nothing of interest here. He runs back out to the north chamber, stops, and points again.

"Daddy, what's that say?"

Now, I read from Lincoln's second inaugural address. I have not read it before. The difference between these words and those he spoke at Gettysburg arrests me. Here, as there, he spoke in his odd blend of the grandiose and the humble, the forthright and the coy. But here, there was substance. Here he put his finger on the issue:

> These slaves constituted a peculiar and powerful interest. All knew that this interest was somehow the cause of the war.

Here he saw, if only in passing, a whole nation's complicity:

> If we shall suppose that American slavery is one of those offenses which, in the providence of God, must needs come, but which, having continued through His appointed time, He now wills to remove, and that He gives to both North and South this terrible war as the woe due to those by whom the offense came, shall we discern therein any departure from those divine attributes which believers in a living God always ascribe to Him?

Here he perceived the cost of justice:

> Fondly do we hope, fervently do we pray, that this mighty scourge of war may speedily pass away. Yet, if God wills that it continue until all the wealth piled by the bondsman's two hundred and fifty years of unrequited toil shall be sunk, and until every drop of blood drawn with the lash shall be paid by another drawn with the sword, as was said three thousand years ago, so still it must be said "the judgments of the Lord are true and righteous altogether."

These last lines give me pause. In school, I learned how Lincoln put aside his distaste for slavery in hopes of evading secession. I learned how he raised the threat of abolition as a tactic to end the conflict. I learned how he put abolition at the forefront of his rhetoric to win

Black recruits for the war effort. I think of him as a man who com-
promised principle to preserve the Union and took moral action only
when it served that purpose. But these last words do not compromise.

My son is off again. He finds an open corner and starts running
in circles. I don't always understand his games. But he has, for the
moment, contained himself. I take a moment to look up the history
of the second inaugural address and that of the Civil War. When Abe
ascended the steps of the Capitol Building for a second time, Atlanta
had already fallen. Sherman had made it to the sea and was advanc-
ing north. Grant was on the offensive in Virginia. Lee's forces were
pressed from both sides. Victory was in sight. So perhaps Lincoln
spoke hyperbolically. Perhaps he knew the judgment he proclaimed
was moot and would never come to pass.

The limits of his vision are clear: the obvious and creative destination for "all the wealth piled by the bondsman's two hundred and fifty
years of unrequited toil" evades him. It never occurs to him that, by
rights, it belongs to those whose toil was unrequited. Instead he favors
a tragic nihilism of casting it all into the sea. Did he picture Northern factories, built with slave-driven capital, as he imagined all those
drowned riches, or did his vision include only Southern plantations?
How far did he perceive the sin's taint?

He had many shortcomings, but for all that, he saw the cost of
justice. He announced it. And he was shot one month later. I wonder
if these events were connected. I start to type "John Wilkes Booth"
into the search bar, when my phone dings. There's an alert on my news
feed. A White terrorist plowed his car into the crowd in Charlottesville. He killed one protestor and crippled another. I scroll through
pictures of rally-goers and counterprotestors. There are the militia
men in their not-quite-matching army surplus gear. They hold assault
rifles. This I expected. But the bulk of these White Nationalists look
quite unremarkable. I could not pick them out in a crowd. That bothers me. I would prefer they be immediately recognizable. But more
than that, I want them to be freakish, aberrant. They are not. This is
the problem.

Richard Spencer and his band of would-be-Nazi thugs are not
outliers. Rather, they simply carry the underlying logic of our nation

to its conclusion—a battle to establish uncontested White Supremacy. They believe they have license and justification to enact violence. We have done little or nothing to prove them wrong. I remember, again, King's rebuke of White moderates, those who offer shallow understanding and lukewarm acceptance. I wonder if I am one. I know I have some shallow level of understanding.

Black unemployment is double that of Whites.[22] Blacks earn seventy-six cents on the dollar compared to Whites.[23] Black families have, on average, one-tenth the wealth of Whites.[24] I imagine most White Americans know these things, or at least suspect them to be true. If these facts do not outrage us, then it follows that we have accepted the idea that Black people are worth less than Whites. We incarcerate Black folk at more than five times the rate of White folk.[25] Young Black men are nine times more likely to be shot when interacting with police.[26] If these facts do not disgust us, then it follows that we have accepted the idea that Black people are an inherent threat.

The "redevelopment" of our cities displaces Black families, businesses, and institutions as a matter of course. We whitewash our own history. The work of Black artists is pushed to the margins of mainstream culture. If these facts do not unsettle us, then it follows that we have accepted the idea that Black people have no place in our society. And, if we have accepted, even reluctantly, that a people are worthless, dangerous, and alien, can we claim surprise or innocence when the mob cries for blood? So long as the underlying facts remain

22. U.S. Department of Labor, Bureau of Labor Statistics, *E-16: Unemployment Rates by Age, Sex, Race, and Hispanic or Latino Ethnicity* (Washington: U.S. Government Printing Office, 2019).

23. U.S. Department of Labor, Bureau of Labor Statistics, *E-16: Usual Weekly Earnings of Wage and Salary Workers, Fourth Quarter, 2018* (Washington: U.S. Government Printing Office, 2019), 1.

24. Lisa J. Dettling, Joanne W. Hsu, Lindsay Jacobs, Kevin B. Moore, and Jeffrey P. Thompson, "Recent Trends in Wealth-Holding by Race and Ethnicity: Evidence from the Survey of Consumer Finances," FEDS Notes 2017, no. 2083 (2017): doi:10.17016/2380-7172.2083.

25. U.S. Department of Justice, Bureau of Justice Statistics, *Prisoners in 2016* (Washington: U.S. Government Printing Office, 2018), 8.

26. Jon Swaine and Ciara McCarthy, "Young Black Men Again Faced Highest Rate of US Police Killings in 2016," *The Guardian*, January 8, 2017.

unchanged, I know these events will continue, and they will, from time to time and with increasing frequency, erupt in violence.

I glance up at the immense seated statue that dominates the room. It's been one hundred and fifty years since he named the cost of freedom. We have not yet paid it. Instead, we passed the bill on to the very ones to whom it is owed. And the debt grows.

"What are you doing?"

"Nothing." I look up at my wife.

"Are you okay?"

"I'm fine."

She knows I'm lying. She takes my hand. My son sees it, runs up, and grabs my little finger. He doesn't like to be left out. I am struck, as I have been before, by the contrast in our skin and the dangerous meaning of that difference. I do not want it for them. I do not want it for me either because I can hardly see my own skin, hidden, as it is, under the lie it proclaims.

Their skin is beautiful. I think, perhaps, mine is too. But it is difficult to see in this light.

Conclusion

In 2018, Dr. Robin DiAngelo published *White Fragility*, an expansion of an earlier essay she had written describing the sabotaging, unconscious defenses White people raise when discussing racism and race.[27] I organized a reading group for the book at my church.

As the neighborhood changed, Calvary attracted a small cohort of new White members. I appreciated their willingness to enter, as guests, a space that was not their own and also their intention to meet Calvary on its own terms. At the same time, I began to notice certain disruptive and defensive patterns from these new members. More troubling, I began to recognize these same patterns in myself.

I knew these new members to be good people. I believed myself to be the same. But we had all learned habits that undermined our commitments to be the kind of people we wanted to be and also undermined the church community that had welcomed us. I wasn't sure what to do about the dynamic, or how to address it effectively. My wife directed me toward her longtime colleague and friend Dr. Tee Williams. This problem was very much in his wheelhouse. He pointed me toward DiAngelo's work. In her writing, I found language to describe what I and the other White members were up to: unconsciously and covertly disrupting the difficult discussion of race to protect our own comfort.

I hoped the reading group would provide a way to take collective responsibility for our issues, and work through them together. It was not lost on me that the group might also offer a kind of backdoor, self-selecting evangelistic opportunity. By advertising it to the neighborhood, I hoped to attract people willing to wrestle with their Whiteness—an unstated prerequisite for White folks wanting to join Calvary.

But the group was inherently awkward. We are a historically and predominantly Black congregation with a White pastor inviting our

---

27. Robin DiAngelo, *White Fragility: Why It's So Hard for White People to Talk About Racism* (Boston: Beacon Press, 2018).

White neighbors to discuss White people's defensive responses when discussing race. When I pitched the idea to our vestry, one member asked, "So . . . is Calvary hosting a 'Whites Only' group?"

I didn't quite know how to answer. The purpose of the reading group was for me and, I hoped, my people to take responsibility for our issues and work through them together. With that intention in mind, "Whites Only" is precisely what was needed. But that, of course, would be anathema to the church's identity. More than that, I didn't quite trust myself and my White compatriots to really dig deep without some outside accountability. We opened the group to our membership at large.

The first meeting revealed the awkwardness of the arrangement. The White members of the group, myself included, largely kept quiet, while the Black members discussed how DiAngelo's observations resonated with their experiences. When the White members spoke, at last, we focused, predictably, on the racism "out there" in the world and our distaste for it. I noticed the trend fairly quickly. This was not the work I had come to do. I wanted us to be working on ourselves, not bemoaning some banner-waving White Supremacists we had never met. I tried to lead by example, describing how I saw DiAngelo's patterns play out in my own behavior, and the practices I would take on to make a change. The group did not take the bait.

Then, my associate, the Rev. Dr. Gayle Fisher-Stewart, spoke. In my experience, Gayle has little patience for pretense. Her mind drives straight for the heart of things. So, I wasn't surprised by the question she asked.

"What I want to know is," she said, looking from one White member to another, "why are you doing this? Why are you here? The system, White fragility, whatever you want to call it, benefits White people. You've got nothing to gain, and a lot to lose, by taking it apart. So, what do you get out of it?" I'm always struck by how Gayle manages to ask such pointed questions without reproach. She inquires from a place of genuine, though often stern, curiosity.

There was silence in the room. A pattern was taking hold, one with which I think everyone is familiar. Someone poses a vitally important question to which no one has a clear answer, and the question hangs in uncomfortable ambiguity until, in our anxiety, we change the topic and move on. The question is never answered, only forgotten. This pattern reveals itself from time to time in every aspect of human interaction. But when White people gather to talk race, it lands with metronomic reliability. Certainly, we live in a messy world, and some level of tolerance for ambiguity is necessary, lest we push complicated problems toward simple solutions, with violent results. And yet, I suspect, all too often, we claim "respecting ambiguity" as a way to evade uncomfortable engagement. I had grown tired of this pattern. So, I answered, though even I myself was deeply unsatisfied with the response.

"Honestly, Gayle, I don't know. I don't know why any White person would do this work the way it should be done." As the words escaped my mouth, I was left with the deep feeling that until we could answer Gayle's question our gathering would be inherently untrustworthy.

"What do you get out of it?" The question is vitally important.

In what may be one of the single most comprehensive historical treatments of American racism, *Stamped from the Beginning*, Dr. Ibram X. Kendi argues that our accepted narrative for explaining racism (that ignorance begets hate, which begets racist institutions) is entirely backwards. Examining carefully the chronological sequence of racist policies and racist rhetoric, he argues that self-interest propels the creation of racist policies. Racist policies, in turn, require moral justification so Whites can find them palatable. Then, racist propaganda fills this need, and over time engenders racist hate and ignorance.[28]

Gayle has been researching a pointed example of this paradigm that, for me, hits close to home. In the early British colonial history of Virginia, parishes in the Church of England (the ancestors of my own denomination) found it difficult to find clergy. There were no locally ordained ministers, so employing a pastor required attracting one from England. Educated British clergy had little interest in moving to

---

28. Ibram X. Kendi, *Stamped from the Beginning: The Definitive History of Racist Ideas in America* (London: Bodley Head, 2017).

what they then considered a poor colonial backwater. The self-interest of the congregations was to have full-time pastors. The self-interest of the pastors was for financial advancement. Racist policies followed to satisfy both interests. After Bacon's Rebellion and the declaration of Africans to be property, parishes of the Church of England in Virginia parceled off church lands, purchased African slaves, and attached them to these parcels. These newly created plantations were offered as incentives to lure educated British clergy. For the congregations and their pastors to engage in such a self-evidently inhumane policy required some kind of moral excuse, so they declared Africans to be subhuman, a lower order of God's creation, and therefore not worthy of humane consideration.[29] Pastors preached the idea from the pulpit, catechists taught it in Sunday school, and theologians published it in books. Over generations, White Christians came to believe the idea as God-given truth, forgetting that their ancestors had conjured it up. Self-interest begat racist policy, which begat racist propaganda, which begat racist belief.

Given this order of explanation, Kendi believes that efforts to address racism via education, acquaintance, and personal interaction are doomed to failure, as they address only the symptom and not the cause of the issue, which is self-interest. Therefore, if Whites are to be effective conspirators in dismantling White Supremacy, we must identify and understand our self-interest for doing so. This would allow us to properly diagnose and address the racism in which we participate. Beyond properly diagnosing the causes of racism, Gayle's question, "What do you get out of it?" speaks to the matter of endurance. Dismantling White Supremacy is a labor measured in decades, if not generations. If we are serious about it, we must be committed for the long haul. And long-haul commitments come only by way of self-interest.

Some years ago, I attended a three-day training in community organizing hosted by the Industrial Areas Foundation (IAF). Like most community organizations following in the tradition of Saul

---

29. Rev. Dr. Gayle Fisher-Stewart, "Christian Response to the Violence of Racism" (speech, Harrisburg, PA, November 5, 2018).

Alinsky, the IAF identifies self-interest as crucial to their work. Their reasoning is more pragmatic than philosophical. As one of the organizers at the training put it, "I might be able to get you to show up for a cause once or twice out of guilt, or moral obligation, but if you understand that your self-interest is at stake, you will show up again, and again, and again, until the job is done." Which is to say, unless aspiring White anti-racists can identify what's at stake for us, we will be not only ineffective, but also unreliable.

In recent years, a whole chorus of anti-racist activists have critiqued the trend toward performative White allyship. In brief, this is the pattern among many liberal Whites of calling out White Supremacy with the intention of garnering accolades from other White liberals, but especially from people of color. The self-interest in performative White allyship is clear. It offers the promise of absolution, affirmation, and social prestige. I know its allure very well. Jason Kessler, the organizer of the first Unite the Right rally in Charlottesville, planned an anniversary rally for the following year, to take place in Washington, DC, where I live. It happened on a Sunday. A delegation of Calvary's members, myself included, planned to attend the counter-demonstration, providing water and snacks to our fellow counterprotestors. The Charlottesville rally had ended in violence and death. We knew it might happen again.

Rondesia chose to stay home to protect the safety of our son. As I got dressed that morning, she stopped me. "Do you have bail money?"

I nodded. As I did so, I felt the corners of my mouth bend up. Her eyes flashed with anger. "Wait. You want to get arrested."

I shook my head. "No." This was a lie. I did want to get arrested. I wanted the bragging rights for it. Her face was stern.

"This is not a game. These people are dangerous. They want to hurt us, hurt me and my child, and everyone that looks like us. If you really care about us, your first responsibility is to come home safe to your wife and son."

In the end, the conversation was moot. Unite the Right II was not even a fizzle. A dozen or so White Supremacists arrived and were confronted by thousands of counterprotestors. The event was charged and passionate, but there was no violence. I arrived home without incident. Still, even if only in theory rather than in practice, the self-interested allure of performative White allyship had seduced me away from genuine commitment to the Black people in my life.

That may be a somewhat unusual example, but most examples will follow the same trajectory, even if the details differ. As a rule, performative allyship pulls two critical resources, attention and money, away from the very people it pretends to support. Thus, it reaffirms existing racial hierarchies. And, it becomes an evasion of the real work of dismantling those mundane systems of White Supremacy in which we participate every day.

This is why the current eruption of overt White Supremacy has been a kind of double-whammy. On the one hand, White Supremacists promulgate ideas of hate and violence that are dangerous on their own and also serve to make covert expression of White Supremacy more palatable by contrast. On the other hand, they provide an inexhaustible source of misdirection for White Liberals. That is, we can always tell ourselves that we are not like those alt-righters over there and we can receive accolades for denouncing them. We never have to look at ourselves. We become not only unreliable, but also duplicitous conspirators.

All this comes from turning a blind eye to "what we get out of it." Noting this willful and destructive obliviousness, anti-trafficking activist Laura LeMoon asserts, "An ally should be personally gaining NOTHING through their activism. In fact, if you are an ally, you should be losing things through your activism; space, voice, recognition, validation, identity and ego."[30]

From a moral perspective, I find her argument irrefutable. Viewed pragmatically, I cannot help but think she is offering a deal no one would ever take. And I don't mean that as a critique.

It may be that, because we have nothing to gain and so much to lose, White people are, by definition, incapable of sustained, honest, anti-racist engagement. Based on just such an analysis, many anti-racist

---

30. Laura LeMoon, "Why Ashton Kutcher's Tears Are Everything That's Wrong with the Anti-trafficking Movement," *Wear Your Voice*, March 7, 2017, *https://wearyourvoicemag.com/body-politics/ashton-kutcher-tears-anti-trafficking*.

activists have rejected White collaboration, or else received it only with great suspicion. I cannot fault them for such a decision. Personally, I must reject such an analysis. Accepting it would mean total moral abnegation. For reasons I cannot explain, I refuse to do that, but my refusal requires wading through very muddy waters.

In the author's note to her book, DiAngelo describes the paradox of centering the White experience as a means toward confronting White Supremacy. She notes she has found no way to resolve it.[31] No aspiring White anti-racist can evade this conundrum. Indeed, the book you are now reading is deeply entangled with it. We cannot avoid this contradiction, but we may be able to do better—and that begins by honestly identifying our stake in the matter. Is there anything White people can gain from anti-racist struggle that does not come at the expense of people of color?

"What do you get out of it?" Kendi argues that because racism intersects with and supports other systems of oppression (classism, sexism, homophobia, religious hegemony, ableism, and others), and because most White people are subject to one or more of these systems, dismantling racism is in the rational, material self-interest of a majority of White people. He is certainly right. However, material concerns are not the only self-interests that drive us. We also seek meaning, prestige, and a sense of self. Whiteness provides these things. On account of Whiteness, White people will act, sometimes, against their material self-interest and in favor of an emotional or psychological self-interest. For those of us who are White, sustained, honest, anti-racist engagement requires finding our emotional, psychological, or spiritual self-interest in the dismantling of racism. And this self-interest must not come at the expense of people of color. This is what I am seeking.

"What do you get out of it?" The first answer I could give is deeply personal: the two people who matter most to me in the world are targets for anti-Black racism. I have witnessed it. They cannot be safe and they cannot be free while White Supremacy thrives. This is honest. This is real.

---

31. DiAngelo, xiv.

Unfortunately, my answer is not one that is widely shared. A majority of White folk in this nation count few or no people of color among their close friends. The idea of aspiring White anti-racists seeking out relationships with people of color so as to have skin in the game is a profoundly problematic one. The cultivation of genuine caring relationships across lines of race is a positive good, but such relationships must be ends unto themselves, and they cannot be forced.

My answer also produces unreliable results. I know many White people in close relationships across lines of race who have no apparent anti-racist commitments. Some readers will question the closeness or legitimacy of such relationships. I know I do. Regardless, they give me reason to doubt the power of interracial relationships as an impetus for anti-racist agitation.

My answer is also incomplete. Even the deep love I have for my wife and son has not entirely flooded out my self-interest in upholding the racial status quo. I do find the more I grow in relationship with them, the more I notice the ways I participate in White Supremacy, and the more I deem it too costly by far. But, if I am honest, it is very much a two-steps-forward, one-step-back affair. Alone, my first answer will not serve. Something else is required.

"What do you get out of it?" There is, I think, a genuine stake all White people have in the abolishment of Whiteness. It is a simple matter of integrity. I don't mean some moral condition. I mean simple wholeness. A great part of our identity is built on a fiction—an abusive and hateful fiction and a powerful fiction, but a fiction nonetheless. We are, in some sense, lost in a delusion. We imagine the superiority of our Whiteness. We all do this, though we may tell ourselves otherwise. But we are only imagining. And our fantasy obscures a more profound truth: the dignity and goodness of our humanity. We will never see it, not fully, through our White veil of illusion. If we wish to know ourselves, we must see the illusion for what it is. We must understand its workings and pull it apart bit by bit. Of course, even as we do so, the world will be at work, slathering on new coats of fiction. In fact, none of us will truly know ourselves until Whiteness is wholly abolished and all the people of the world are free from this edifice of falseness we have built, which is the work of many generations. I suspect none of us alive now will see its completion. But the work itself carries the promise that, in flits and glimpses, we may catch sight of ourselves along the way, and truly see our skin, not some false facade of Whiteness (as any three-year-old will tell you, we are not really that color) but rather, the fearfully and wonderfully made flesh of our shared humanity.

"What do you get out of it?" Just that, and nothing else. And I think it might be worth it.

Acknowledgments

I have written and rewritten this section several times. More people have contributed to this book than I can recall. I know I will forget some. If I leave you out, you have my apologies in advance.

This book is about race and Whiteness. There are many who challenged and helped me to wrestle with these issues. My best friend in high school, Travis Lee, first explicitly confronted me with the question of race. The Episcopal Diocese of El Salvador, the members of Iglesia San Mateo (Lourdes, Colón), and the Rev. Ramiro Chavez welcomed and stood by me as I stumbled through culture shock. The Rev. Dr. Tito Cruz taught me the complexity and necessity of engaging these questions. The Rev. Dr. Jeffrey Kuan showed me how different the experience of race is for different people and how much that experience shapes the way we understand the world. The Rev. Roland Stringfellow revealed what it takes to love across lines of race, and very likely saved my marriage. Dr. Jason Crawford helped me parse the many intersections of race, class, gender, and sexual orientation, and the ways this nexus has afforded me extraordinary privilege. The Rev. Anna Lange-Soto pushed herself, and me, to frankly express the experience of race. The Rev. Dr. Eric Law impressed upon me the importance of first examining and exploring my own culture before considering someone else's. Dr. Sherrill Gaye was brutally honest, asked profoundly uncomfortable questions, and stuck around until I answered. The Rev. Dr. Gayle Fisher-Stewart drew my attention to the urgency of the current moment, and posed the central question of this book: "What do you get out of it?" She was one of the first to read this manuscript, provided essential feedback, and generously shared her research regarding the Church of England parishes in Virginia. More friends, family, and colleagues than I can count have stood by me as I fumbled my way through all the thorny questions race presents. I am grateful.

I find the act of writing unnatural and uncomfortable. There are a number of people who helped, and continue to help, me through it.

Mr. Dan Murphy taught me everything I know about crafting a sentence. Ms. Joana Bryar-Matons would not allow me to be a lazy writer. The congregations of Our Saviour Episcopal Church (Silver Spring, MD) and Calvary Episcopal Church (Washington, DC) sat through ten years of my preaching, and offered continual, unsolicited, and invaluable feedback. They provided my principal training arena for the use of language.

There are those who directly assisted me in the writing of this book. Shaun King, whom I have never met, once used his considerable and hard-won platform to share a piece I had written. The response convinced me there might be an audience for a work like this one. While there are many, many writers who have influenced this work, four deserve particular mention. Toni Morrison's *Playing in the Dark* focused my attention on literary expressions of the White imagination, and started me wondering how these imaginations played out, even in my own memories. Debby Irving's book *Waking Up White* and Tim Wise's book *White Like Me* provided the direct template and inspiration for the one you now hold. Pastor Dominique Young, a remarkable writer and personal friend, offered this offhand comment that propelled me to make the attempt: "I like the way you write. You should write a book."

I am grateful for all those I contacted who agreed to let me tell stories about them. Their trust humbles me.

A number of writers, all better than I am, consented to read a first draft of this work. Their feedback and criticism were essential to what it has become. Giovanni Kavota advised me on getting the reader to connect with my perspective, and on the importance of humor to maintain that connection. Anthony Weiss called me out on some unfortunate, self-involved, and pretentious habits that plagued the early version. Jacob Slichter helped me consider and keep focus on the reader's experience. He also provided the single most practical, and helpful, piece of writing advice I have ever heard. I would certainly have given up partway through without it. Dr. Tee Williams challenged me to wrestle with the purpose and intent of this project, and to speak far more explicitly and clearly than I was initially comfortable doing. Ronald Jarrett offered crucial insights into the process of publishing and marketing. Alan and Gail Venable became early advocates for the memoir and opened doors I would not even have known to look for. David Finnegan-Hosey provided the connection that ultimately led me to a publisher. My copyeditor, Jennifer Hackett, caught several important oversights, and, more impressively, made proofreading fun. Roberto Carlos Pérez, one of the best writers I've met, in either Spanish or English, was kind enough to proofread all the Spanish dialogue I included, and provided vital editorial notes for the section detailing my time in El Salvador. Paul Soupiset designed a cover that outshines my prose. I'm not mad. My editor, Milton Brasher-Cunningham, guided me through a smooth and productive revision process. This book is stronger because of his careful and attentive eye. He also convinced the good folk at Church Publishing to take a chance on an unknown author. Without their support you would not be reading these words right now. Their production manager and managing editor, Ryan Masteller, carried this manuscript across the finish line.

This work is a personal one, and I have some personal thanks to give. My parents, Ellen and Donald Schell, are profoundly good people. I know I would not have survived anything at all without their love. They strive to be better, continually, and in spite of their faults. They taught me to do the same. On occasion, they nudged me into uncomfortable situations, situations I would not have chosen for myself, which helped me grow. They were among my first readers and have provided critical feedback throughout the process. Like all good parents they hoped for me to be wiser, more compassionate, and braver than they are themselves. I pass these hopes on to my son. Melody Leak has been a second mother to me and has blessed me in too many ways to count. My siblings, Sasha, Maria, and Josh, have suffered their way through decades of my pretentious nonsense and stuck with me nonetheless. My several brothers-in-law have welcomed me as one of their own. In particular, I am grateful for the love and friendship of Gio and Ron. Joal Bennett-Stenzel has worked with me patiently through years of psychotherapy. Without her guidance, I would not have found the ambition to attempt this.

For ten years, Joe Holliman has offered me daily sacred words, and lifted my eyes to higher things. Just as often he slaps me back down with something profane to keep me honest. He has been there for me in my best and my worst moments. I have never had a friend quite like him.

The Rev. Rondesia Jarrett-Schell remains the most insightful, challenging, intriguing, and fun human being I have ever met. Our conversations have sharpened my wit, broadened my thinking, stretched my compassion, and comforted me. Once I told her I was working on this book, she held me to completing it. She would not let me give up on it or myself. Her insights, questions, challenges, and networking were essential to this work. I would be lost without her, entirely. I'm not sure why she has stuck with me through all my foibles, but I am grateful. I strive each day to be for her what she has been for me. Our relationship is the greatest treasure of my life.

My son, Joshua Ibrahim Jarrett-Schell, brings joy and hope wherever he goes. He fascinates and confounds me. Many days his presence is the only thing that gets me out of bed. I fear we may never definitively crush this thing of White Supremacy. But for his sake, I consider it worth trying.

The Ancient of Days gives the gifts of life and time. I do my best to make good use of them, and I am grateful.

31192021804735